The Intext Series in **ECONOMICS**

Principles
of
Econometrics

Principles

of

Econometrics

Second Edition

KONG CHU

College of Industrial Management
Georgia Institute of Technology

INTEXT EDUCATIONAL PUBLISHERS
College Division of Intext
Scranton   San Francisco   Toronto   London

To Yolanda

Foreword

Econometrics is clearly established as a subject with which any modern economist should have at least a general familiarity. However, quantitatively oriented management, business, and engineering students are increasingly being exposed to econometrics, especially in interdisciplinary "systems" programs. Therefore, Professor Chu's book is a most welcome addition to the literature for it is designed as an introduction to the study of econometrics for college students majoring in economics, business, engineering, and management.

Serious students of economics who are interested in empirical economic studies will also find this book to be of value in their research efforts, for the author has made excellent usage of examples and illustrations.

SHERMAN DALLAS
Dean of the College of Industrial Management
Georgia Institute of Technology

Preface

Economists today are becoming more interested in the applications of economic theories to real life. Numerous empirical researches are being conducted all over the world whose main purpose is to determine the real causes and effects of economic events that are so important to our daily lives, and to seek ways of controlling their outcomes. Mathematics, statistics, and computers are being utilized to assist in the discovery of the true relationships existing among economic variables such as price, quantity, income, employment, and rate of interest. The goal, needless to say, is a very important one. However, the methods of achieving it are slow in developing and are far from perfect. For the average college student or researcher whose formal training is not in statistics these methods may seem difficult to understand.

This book is written to introduce "Econometrics," a field of study that encompasses the combined knowledge of economics, statistics, and mathematics. The reader is assumed to have basic knowledge of calculus. Linear algebra and statistics are briefly reviewed at the beginning. The introduction of econometric methods starts at Chapter 3, Linear Models, and extends to nonlinear models and computer simulation models. The latter portion of the book deals with the problems of model specification, parameter estimation, verification, and prediction.

My intention in writing this book is to encourage students and researchers to undertake more empirical economic studies and to develop better econometric methods so that there will be more efficient ways to improve our economic wellbeing.

I wish to thank Dr. Sherman F. Dallas and Dr. Robert E. Green, Dean and Associate Dean, respectively, of the College of Industrial Management, Georgia Institute of Technology, for their encouragement and assistance, and Mrs. Marion Gwostz and Mrs. Betty Sims for typing the manuscript. Also, I am indebted to J. Johnston, whose book *Econometric Methods* launched my own interest in econometrics. Of course, the responsibility for the errors in this text is wholly mine.

KONG CHU

Atlanta, Georgia
November, 1971

Contents

Principles
of
Econometrics

Introduction

Economic theories attempt to define the relationships existing among economic variables. Their purpose is to help us better understand the economic world we live in—including how production of economic goods and services is organized, and how products are distributed. With this understanding we may design economic policies that will enhance or accelerate our economic welfare, thereby increasing our gross national product and per capita income.

However, theories have to be checked against data obtained from the real world. If empirical data verify the relationship proposed by the theory, we may accept the theory. Otherwise we must reject it. Also, in order to provide guidance for economic policy making, we need to measure the quantitative relationships between economic variables; for example, if investment is increased by 10 percent, we want to know by how much the national income will be increased. These quantitative measurements can be obtained only from data taken from the real world.

Econometrics, utilizing mathematics and statistics, aims to provide methods to accomplish these purposes. Broadly speaking, it should encompass the following steps:

1. Use a mathematical equation or equations to specify the relationship between economic variables as proposed by some economic theories (model building).
2. Design of methods and procedures in obtaining representative samples from the real world, based on statistical theories.
3. Development of methods of testing the validity of the theory with the sample data; for example, verifying whether the sales volume of a commodity is inversely proportional to its price within a specified price range.
4. Development of methods of estimating the parameters or coefficients of the specified relationship, once the theory is accepted as valid.

1

5. Development of methods of making economic forecasts or policy implications based on the estimated parameters and equations.

In Chapter 1 we first give a brief review of the theories of probability and statistics. Because we will be using models to provide answers to the real world, these answers cannot be exact but will be based on probability in order to give us the desired degree of confidence. Also, since we will be dealing with a large amount of data, it is more convenient to use matrix algebra for their arrangement and manipulation. Thus we present in Chapter 2 a review of the elements of matrix algebra.

Next we start with linear models. In the models, the relationship among the economic variables is specified by linear equations. The variables on the right-hand side of the equality sign in each equation are considered as *explanatory variables*; they explain or determine the values of the variables on the left-hand side of the sign. The variables on the left-hand side of the equality sign are called *explained variables*; their values are explained or determined by the explanatory variables. We use differential calculus to derive formulas for the estimation of the parameters of the equations from sample observations. In the process, the sum of the squares of the differences between the sample values of the explained variable and the estimated values of the same variable specified by the line or plane is minimized. Thus the estimator is called the *least-squares estimator*, and the line or plane, the *regression line* or *plane*. Also, during the derivation of the formulas, we make these assumptions:

1. The distributions of the error terms of the explained variable along the regression line or plane are the same (of zero mean and constant variance) and independent (pairwise uncorrelated).
2. There is no correlation between the explanatory variables and the error term in each equation. And if there is more than one explanatory variable in the equation, there is no significant correlation among the explanatory variables.

In Chapter 3 we explore both the two-variable case and three-variable case, and also introduce matrix notations for cases of *m* variables. We also recognize that in the real world the explained variable in one relationship may also be the explanatory variable in another relationship. Thus there are times when we cannot take a single equation and consider it independently; the estimation of the parameters in the equations may have to be done simultaneously in the complete model. A discussion of the simultaneous equations models is therefore included. Also included is a section on generalized least squares which extends the least-squares method to cases when the distributions of the error terms are not the same.

In Chapter 4 we extend the linear models to nonlinear models. The possibility of transforming variables of nonlinear forms into linear form and the formulas for estimating the parameters of polynomial equations are discussed.

When the forms of the equations become too complex, and especially when several equations must be considered simultaneously, the currently available analytical methods may not be able to provide us with solutions of the model. We therefore include in Chapter 5 a discussion of computer-simulation models. Computer simulation also has the following advantages:

1. It will supply pseudo-sample values when actual observations are scarce and difficult to obtain.
2. It will show the step-by-step change of the variables over time.

In the final chapter we first discuss the problems of specification, the effect of leaving out important variables from the relationship, the possibility of having unidentifiable equations in a simultaneous equations model, and the like. We also introduce factor analysis as a method of identifying significant explanatory factors. As for the discussion on the estimation of the parameters of the equations, we relax the assumptions made in Chapter 3 and discuss the possible problems that may arise when the assumptions are no longer valid, together with the methods of overcoming the difficulties. A section on spectral and cross-spectral analysis is also added to introduce another method for analyzing time-series data. We then discuss the problems of verification. We point out some feasible ways of checking the validity of the model as a representation of the real system. And in the concluding section we discuss the use of the model as a tool for prediction.

SELECTED BIBLIOGRAPHY

1. C. F. Christ, Econometric Models and Methods. New York: Wiley, 1966.
2. A. S. Goldberger, *Econometric Theory*. New York: Wiley, 1964.
3. W. C. Hood and T. C. Koopmans (eds.), *Studies in Econometric Method*. Cowles Commission Monograph 14. New York: Wiley, 1953.
4. J. Johnston, *Econometric Methods*. New York: McGraw-Hill, 1963.
5. L. R. Klein, *Introduction to Econometrics*. Englewood Cliffs, N.J.: Prentice-Hall, 1962.
6. L. R. Klein, *Textbook of Econometrics*. Evanston, Ill.: Row, Peterson, 1953.
7. G. Tintner, *Econometrics*. New York: Wiley, 1952.
8. S. Valvanis, *Econometrics*. New York: McGraw-Hill, 1959.

chapter 1

A Review of Probability and Statistics

Whether it is to estimate the characteristics of a population from sample observations or to predict the occurrence or nonoccurrence of some future events from the observations of past and current events, we are unable to make any statement with complete certainty. A statement of uncertainty is of no value unless the degree of uncertainty is specified. Thus we need to have probability as a measure of the degree of uncertainty. A simple illustration is to say that there is a 60 percent probability that it will rain tomorrow. In this chapter, only basic concept of probability theories and statistical theories is stated.

1-1. PROBABILITY

Probability may be defined as the ratio of the number of outcomes that correspond to the occurrence of a predefined experience to the total number of possible outcomes in a random experiment. The concept of probability distribution may be evolved through the following step-by-step derivation.

1. *Sample space.* A sample space consists of all the possible outcomes of an experiment.
2. *Sample-space probabilities.* The probabilities assigned to each of the outcomes of a sample space are the sample-space probabilities. They must be all nonnegative and their sum is equal to one.
3. *Events.* An event may include one or more outcomes of a sample space. For example, an event may be defined as getting a head in tossing a coin or getting an odd number in rolling a die. In the latter case, 1, 3, and 5 are considered odd numbers.

4. *Probability of the occurrence of an event.* The probability that an event will occur is the sum of the probability of all the outcomes associated with the event. In the above example the probability of getting a head in tossing a perfect coin is $\frac{1}{2}$, and the probability of getting an odd number in rolling an honest die is

$$\tfrac{1}{6} + \tfrac{1}{6} + \tfrac{1}{6} = \tfrac{3}{6} = \tfrac{1}{2}$$

5. *Joint events.* In conducting an experiment, sometimes two events will occur together. In other words, they both contain the same outcome. For example, in drawing one card from a deck of 52, we define the event of getting a spade as A and the event of getting an ace as B. Now if we draw an ace of spades from the deck, we have a *joint event*.

6. *Joint probability.* The probability of the occurrence of this joint event will be written as $P(AB)$, which is called the *joint probability*.

7. *Mutually exclusive events.* If when one of the events occurs during an experiment the other cannot occur, they are *mutually exclusive events*. For example, if we draw a spade from a deck of cards, the card we have drawn cannot be a diamond. Thus getting a spade and getting a diamond are mutually exclusive events.

8. *Addition theorem.*

$$P(A + B) = P(A) + P(B) - P(AB)$$

The theorem states that the probability that either event A occurs or event B occurs is equal to the sum of the probability of event A and B minus their joint probability. For example, the probability of getting either a spade or an ace in drawing one card from a deck of 52 is

$$\tfrac{13}{52} + \tfrac{4}{52} - \tfrac{1}{52} = \tfrac{16}{52} = \tfrac{4}{13}$$

If A and B are mutually exclusive events, then $P(AB) = 0$ and the addition theorem becomes

$$P(A + B) = P(A) + P(B)$$

For example, the probability of getting either a spade or a diamond is

$$\tfrac{13}{52} + \tfrac{13}{52} = \tfrac{26}{52} = \tfrac{1}{2}$$

9. *Independent event.* Two events, A and B, are said to be independent if $P(AB) = P(A) \cdot P(B)$. For example, in tossing two coins, the event of getting a head of one coin (event A) is independent of getting a head of the other coin (event B), so they are independent events. If $P(A) = \frac{1}{2}$ and $P(B) = \frac{1}{2}$, then $P(AB) = \frac{1}{2} \times \frac{1}{2} = \frac{1}{4}$, which we may verify intuitively from the sample space ($\underline{HH}$, HT, TH, TT).

10. *Conditional probability.* When the occurrence of one event is dependent on the occurrence of another event, then the probability of the occurrence of this event is a conditional probability. For example, two cards are drawn from a deck of 52 cards. What is the probability

that both cards will be spades? The probability of the first card being a spade, Event A, is of course $13/52$. However, once a spade is drawn from the deck and is not replaced, there will be only 12 spades left in the remaining deck of 51 cards. Therefore, the probability of the second card drawn also being a spade, Event B, is $12/51$. $12/51$ is the conditional probability of Event B which is dependent on Event A, and is denoted by $P(B/A)$.

11. *Multiplication theorem.*

$$P(AB) = P(A) \times P(B/A)$$

In the previous example the probability of both cards being spades is

$$13/52 \times 12/51 = 1/17$$

When A and B are independent events $P(B/A) = P(B)$, the theorem therefore becomes

$$P(AB) = P(A) \cdot P(B)$$

The equation for dependent events can also be written as

$$P(B/A) = \frac{P(AB)}{P(A)}$$

extended to become Bayes' formula,

$$P(H_i/A) = \frac{P(H_i) P(A/H_i)}{\sum_{i=1}^{k} P(H_i) P(A/H_i)}$$

where H_i are mutually exclusive events of the sample space of the experiments.

EXAMPLE:

An urn contains 120 balls of same shape and size. Thirty balls are black, among them 20 with yellow dots. The other 90 balls are white, among them 30 with yellow dots. A boy picks up one ball from the urn in random. If the boy passes out information that the ball has yellow dots on it, what is the probability that the ball is a white ball?

Answer. According to Bayes' formula,

$$P(\text{white} \mid \text{dot}) = \frac{P(\text{white}) P(\text{dot} \mid \text{white})}{P(\text{white}) P(\text{dot} \mid \text{white}) + P(\text{black}) P(\text{dot} \mid \text{black})}$$

$$P(\text{white}) = 90/120, \qquad P(\text{dot} \mid \text{white}) = 30/90,$$

$$P(\text{black}) = 30/120, \qquad P(\text{dot} \mid \text{black}) = 20/30$$

Thus

$$P(\text{white} \mid \text{dot}) = \frac{(3/4)(1/3)}{(3/4)(1/3) + (1/4)(2/3)} = 3/5$$

EXAMPLE:

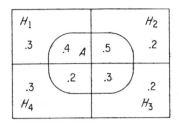

Let H_1, H_2, H_3, H_4, be mutually exclusive events and event A may jointly occur with either H_1, H_2, H_3, or H_4. The numbers in the diagram are the respective probabilities: $P(H_1) = .3$, $P(H_2) = .2$, $P(H_3) = .2$, $P(H_4) = .3$, $P(A \mid H_1) = .4$, $P(A \mid H_2) = .5$, $P(A \mid H_3) = .3$ and $P(A \mid H_4) = .2$. Find $P(H_1 \mid A)$, $P(H_2 \mid A)$, $P(H_3 \mid A)$ and $P(H_4 \mid A)$.

Answer.

$$P(A) = P(H_1) P(A \mid H_1) + P(H_2) P(A \mid H_2)$$
$$+ P(H_3) P(A \mid H_3) + P(H_4) P(A \mid H_4)$$
$$= (.3)(.4) + (.2)(.5) + (.2)(.3) + (.3)(.2) = .34$$

$$P(H_1 \mid A) = \frac{P(H_1) P(A \mid H_1)}{P(A)} = \frac{(.3)(.4)}{.34} = \frac{6}{17}$$

$$P(H_2 \mid A) = \frac{P(H_2) P(A \mid H_2)}{P(A)} = \frac{(.2)(.5)}{.34} = \frac{5}{17}$$

$$P(H_3 \mid A) = \frac{P(H_3) P(A \mid H_3)}{P(A)} + \frac{(.2)(.3)}{.34} = \frac{3}{17}$$

$$P(H_4 \mid A) = \frac{P(H_4) P(A \mid H_4)}{P(A)} = \frac{(.3)(.2)}{.34} = \frac{3}{17}$$

EXAMPLE: Application of Bayes' formula in a sampling problem.

Suppose the purchasing manager of a company buys machine parts from a manufacturer and knows that half the time the manufacturer sends him shipments with 40 percent defective parts, and the other half of the time sends him shipments with 10 percent defective parts. The company may use sampling techniques to assist him in determining whether a particular shipment is of better quality (10 percent defective parts). The accompanying table shows his assessment after taking one or two samples from each shipment.

ONE-SAMPLE CASE

Original Probability	Conditional Probability of One Sample being Defective	Joint Probability	Revised Probability
.50	.40	.20	.80
.50	.10	.05	.20
		$\overline{.25}$	$\overline{1.00}$

TWO-SAMPLE CASE

Original Probability	Conditional Probability of Two Samples both being Defective	Joint Probability	Revised Probability
.50	.16	.080	.94
.50	.01	.005	.06
		.085	1.00

The above information indicates that if one sample is taken and it happens to be a defective part, then the probability of the shipment's being a better-quality shipment is reduced from .5 to .2, or the probability of the shipment's being a poor-quality shipment is increased from .5 to .8. If two samples are taken and both are defective, then the probability of the shipment's being a better quality shipment is further reduced to only .06, or the probability of the shipment's being a poor-quality shipment is further increased to .94.

EXAMPLE: Application of Bayes' formula in a statistical decision problem.

Decision on whether to introduce a new product right away or to postpone the decision until a market test is conducted.

Possible States (Market Share of New Product)	Estimated Profit or Loss (Millions)	A Priori Probability (Prejudgment) $P(\theta_i)$
θ_1 (10%)	10	.4
θ_2 (5%)	2	.4
θ_3 (0%)	-5	.2
		1.0

Possible outcomes of market test:

Z_1 (sales exceeds 10% of test market total)
Z_2 (sales between 5 and 10% of test market total)
Z_3 (sales below 5% of test market total)

Conditional probability: $P(Z_j \mid \theta_i)$ (assume known from past experience):

	Z_1	Z_2	Z_3	
θ_1	.6	.3	.1	(each row probabilities
θ_2	.3	.5	.2	add up to one)
θ_3	.1	.2	.7	

Joint probability: $P(\theta_i Z_j) = P(\theta_i) \cdot P(Z_j \mid \theta_i)$

	Z_1	Z_2	Z_3	$P(\theta_i)$
θ_1	.24	.12	.04	.4
θ_2	.12	.20	.08	.4
θ_3	.02	.04	.14	.2
$P(Z_j)$	.38	.36	.26	

Posterior conditional probability: $P(\theta_i \mid Z_j) = \dfrac{P(\theta_i) \cdot P(Z_j \mid \theta_i)}{P(Z_j)}$

	Z_1	Z_2	Z_3
θ_1	$\dfrac{.24}{.38}$	$\dfrac{.12}{.36}$	$\dfrac{.04}{.26}$
θ_2	$\dfrac{.12}{.38}$	$\dfrac{.20}{.36}$	$\dfrac{.08}{.26}$
θ_3	$\dfrac{.02}{.38}$	$\dfrac{.04}{.36}$	$\dfrac{.14}{.26}$

Possible actions:

> a_1—introduce the new product
> a_2—do not introduce the new product

Decision analysis (by decision tree):

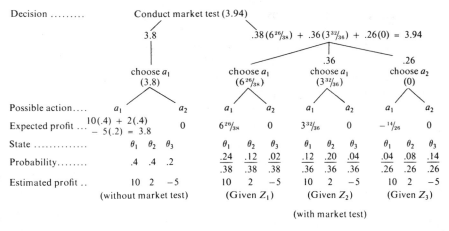

12. *Random variables.*   A random variable is a numerical-valued variable defined on a sample space. The sample space can be either finite or infinite. For example, in rolling a die let X be a random variable whose numerical value is specified by the outcome. Thus X can take on values 1, 2, 3, 4, 5, or 6.

13. *Frequency functions.*   The probability that X will assume specified values in its range of possible outcomes constitutes a frequency function. In the previous example, we get

Random variable	X	1	2	3	4	5	6
Frequency function	$f(X)$	$\tfrac{1}{6}$	$\tfrac{1}{6}$	$\tfrac{1}{6}$	$\tfrac{1}{6}$	$\tfrac{1}{6}$	$\tfrac{1}{6}$

A frequency function is discrete when the random variable can only be integers, and is continuous when the random variable can also assume any fractional values between integers.

14. *Cumulative distribution functions.* A cumulative distribution function gives the probability that the random variable X will assume a value less than or equal to a specified X.

For discrete probability distribution,

$$F(X) = \sum_{t \leq X} f(t)$$

For continuous probability distribution,

$$F(X) = \int_{-\infty}^{X} f(t)\, dt$$

From the previous example,

Random variable	X	1	2	3	4	5	6
Cumulative distribution function	$F(X)$	$\frac{1}{6}$	$\frac{2}{6}$	$\frac{3}{6}$	$\frac{4}{6}$	$\frac{5}{6}$	1

15. *Parameters of a frequency function.* The distribution of the values of a random variable, besides being represented by its functional form, is also described by the parameters of the function. The more often used parameters are those indicating central location and dispersion.

(a) *Central tendency or location.* The arithmetic mean of the variable is most frequently used to measure the location of a frequency function. (The other measures are: mode—the value of X with the greatest of the probabilities; median—the value of X which divides the total probability into two equal parts.)

$$E(X) = \mu$$

If the number of observations can be counted and n is the number of observations, then

$$\mu = \frac{\sum_{i=1}^{n} X_i}{n}$$

When n does not include all possible observations but only a random sample, the computed mean is a sample arithmetic mean, which is denoted as $\overline{X}$.

(b) *Dispersion or variation.* The variance and standard deviation of the variable are often used to measure the variation of the individual values of the variable from the mean.

Variance:

$$\text{var}(X) = \sigma^2$$

Standard deviation:

$$\text{S.D.} = \sigma$$

Again, if the number of observations can be counted,

$$\sigma^2 = \frac{\sum_{i=1}^{n} (X_i - \mu)^2}{n}$$

and

$$\sigma = \sqrt{\frac{\sum_{i=1}^{n} (X_i - \mu)^2}{n}}$$

For sample observations, $\bar{X}$ is substituted for μ. In the case of continuous variables, the summation signs in the equations for computing μ and σ are changed to integral signs.

1-2. SOME THEORETICAL PROBABILITY DISTRIBUTIONS

Frequency functions are often referred to in mathematical statistics as *probability distributions*. The probability distribution of a variable may be discrete or continuous, depending on whether the variable takes on only integer values or continuous values. Since the probability distribution is generally defined by its function, mean, and variance, we list some of the well-known theoretical distributions below.

1. Discrete Distributions

(a) *Uniform distribution.*

$$f(X) = \frac{1}{n+1} \qquad X = 0, 1, 2, \dots, n$$

Mean:

$$\mu = \sum_{X=0}^{n} Xf(X)$$

$$= \sum_{X=0}^{n} X \frac{1}{n+1}$$

$$= \frac{1}{n+1} (0 + 1 + 2 + \cdots + n)$$

$$= \frac{1}{n+1} \cdot \frac{n(n+1)\dagger}{2} = \frac{n}{2}$$

$\dagger S = 1 + 2 + \cdots + n$
$ S = n + (n-1) + \cdots + 1$
_____
$2S = n(n+1), \quad S = \dfrac{n(n+1)}{2}$

Variance:

$$\sigma^2 = \sum_{X=0}^{n} (X - \mu)^2 f(X) = \sum_{X=0}^{n} X^2 f(X) - 2\mu \sum_{X=0}^{n} Xf(X) + \mu^2 \sum_{X=0}^{n} f(X)$$

$$= \sum_{X=0}^{n} X^2 f(X) - \mu^2 = \frac{1}{n+1}(1^2 + 2^2 + \cdots + n^2) - \left(\frac{n}{2}\right)^2$$

$$= \frac{1}{n+1} \cdot \frac{n(n+1)(2n+1)\dagger}{6} - \frac{n^2}{4} = \frac{n^2}{12} + \frac{n}{6}$$

(b) *Binomial distribution.*

$$f(X) = \binom{n}{X} p^X (1 - p)^{n-X}$$

$$X = 0, 1, 2, \ldots, n; \quad 0 \le p \le 1; \quad (p \text{ is a probability})$$

$$\binom{n}{X} = \frac{n(n-1),\ldots,(n-X+1)}{X!} \quad \text{or} \quad \frac{n!}{X!(n-X)!}$$

Mean:

$$\mu = \sum_{X=0}^{n} X \frac{n!}{X!(n-X)!} p^X (1-p)^{n-X}$$

$$= \sum_{X=1}^{n} \frac{n(n-1)!}{(X-1)!(n-X)!} p \cdot p^{X-1}(1-p)^{n-X}$$

$$= np \sum_{X=1}^{n} \frac{(n-1)!}{(X-1)!(n-X)!} p^{X-1}(1-p)^{n-X}$$

$$= np$$

$$\dagger k^3 - (k-1)^3 = 3k^2 - 3k + 1$$
$$1^3 - 0^3 = 3 \cdot 1^2 - 3 \cdot 1 + 1$$
$$2^3 - 1^3 = 3 \cdot 2^2 - 3 \cdot 2 + 1$$
$$\vdots$$
$$\underline{n^3 - (n-1)^3 = 3 \cdot n^2 - 3 \cdot n + 1}$$
$$n^3 = 3(1^2 + 2^2 + \cdots + n^2) - 3(1 + 2 + \cdots + n) + n$$

$$\sum_{X=0}^{n} X^2 = \frac{n^3 + 3\dfrac{n(n+1)}{2} - n}{3}$$

$$= \frac{2n^3 + 3n^2 + n}{6}$$

$$= \frac{n(n+1)(2n+1)}{6}$$

Variance:

$$\sigma^2 = \sum_{X=0}^{n} (X - \mu)^2 f(X)$$

$$= \sum_{X=0}^{n} X^2 \frac{n!}{X!(n-X)!} p^X(1-p)^{n-X} - \mu^2$$

$$= np \sum_{X=1}^{n} X \frac{(n-1)!}{(X-1)!(n-X)!} p^{X-1}(1-p)^{n-X} - n^2p^2$$

Let $Y = X - 1$,

$$\sigma^2 = np \left[\sum_{Y=0}^{n-1} (Y+1) \frac{(n-1)!}{Y!(n-1-Y)!} p^Y(1-p)^{n-1-Y} \right] - n^2p^2$$

$$= np \left[\sum_{Y=0}^{n-1} Y \frac{(n-1)!}{Y![(n-1)-Y]!} p^Y(1-p)^{(n-1)-Y} + 1 \right] - n^2p^2$$

$$= np[(n-1)p + 1] - n^2p^2 = np(1-p)$$

(c) *Poisson distribution.*

$$f(X) = \frac{\lambda^X e^{-\lambda}}{X!} \qquad X = 0, 1, 2, \ldots, \infty; \quad \lambda > 0$$
$$(\lambda \text{ is a positive parameter})$$

Mean:

$$\mu = \sum_{X=0}^{\infty} X \frac{\lambda^X e^{-\lambda}}{X!}$$

$$= \lambda \sum_{X=1}^{\infty} \frac{\lambda^{X-1} e^{-\lambda}}{(X-1)!}$$

Let $Y = X - 1$,

$$\mu - \lambda \sum_{Y=0}^{\infty} \frac{\lambda^Y e^{-\lambda}}{Y!} - \lambda$$

Variance:

$$\sigma^2 = \sum_{X=0}^{\infty} (X - \mu)^2 f(X)$$

$$= \sum_{X=0}^{\infty} X^2 \frac{\lambda^X e^{-\lambda}}{X!} - \mu^2$$

$$= \lambda \sum_{X=1}^{\infty} X \frac{\lambda^{X-1} e^{-\lambda}}{(X-1)!} - \lambda^2$$

Let $Y = X - 1$,

$$\sigma^2 = \lambda \sum_{Y=0}^{\infty} (Y + 1) \frac{\lambda^Y e^{-\lambda}}{Y!} - \lambda^2$$

$$= \lambda \left(\sum_{Y=0}^{\infty} Y \frac{\lambda^Y e^{-\lambda}}{Y!} + \sum_{Y=0}^{\infty} \frac{\lambda^Y e^{-\lambda}}{Y!} \right) - \lambda^2$$

$$= \lambda(\lambda + 1) - \lambda^2$$

$$= \lambda$$

When n is very large and p is small, binomial distribution approaches Poisson distribution.

2. Continuous Distributions

(a) *Rectangular distribution.*

$$f(X) = \frac{1}{a} \qquad \text{range of } X: \text{ from 0 to } a$$

Mean:

$$\mu = \int_0^a X f(X)\, dX = \int_0^a X \frac{1}{a}\, dX$$

$$= \frac{1}{a} \left[\frac{X^2}{2} \right]_0^a = \frac{1}{a} \cdot \frac{a^2}{2} = \frac{a}{2}$$

Variance:

$$\sigma^2 = \int_0^a (X - \mu)^2 f(X)\, dX$$

$$= \int_0^a X^2 f(X)\, dX - 2\mu \int_0^a X f(X)\, dX + \mu^2 \int_0^a f(X)\, dX$$

$$= \int_0^a X^2 f(X)\, dX - \mu^2$$

$$= \frac{1}{a} \int_0^a X^2\, dX - \mu^2 = \frac{1}{a} \left[\frac{X^3}{3} \right]_0^a - \frac{a^2}{4} = \frac{a^2}{12}$$

(b) *Exponential distribution.*

$$f(X) = ae^{-aX} \qquad \text{range of } X: \text{ from 0 to } \infty; \quad a > 0$$

$$(a \text{ is a positive parameter})$$

Mean:

$$\mu = \int_0^{\infty} X f(X)\, dX$$

$$= a \int_0^{\infty} X e^{-aX}\, dX$$

Let $u = X$, $dv = e^{-aX} dX$. Then

$$du = dX, \qquad v = -\frac{e^{-aX}}{a}$$

Substituting

$$\mu = a \int_0^\infty u\,dv = a \left([uv]_0^\infty - \int_0^\infty v\,du \right)$$

$$\mu = a \left(\left[-X \frac{e^{-aX}}{a} \right]_0^\infty + \int_0^\infty \frac{e^{-aX}}{a} dX \right)$$

$$= a \left(0 + \frac{1}{a} \left[-\frac{e^{-aX}}{a} \right]_0^\infty \right)$$

$$= a \cdot \frac{1}{a^2} = \frac{1}{a}$$

Variance:

$$\sigma^2 = \int_0^\infty (X - \mu)^2 f(X)\,dX$$

$$= \int_0^\infty X^2 f(X)\,dX - \mu^2$$

$$= \int_0^\infty X^2 a e^{-aX}\,dX - \frac{1}{a^2}$$

$$= a \int_0^\infty X^2 e^{-aX}\,dX - \frac{1}{a^2}$$

Let $u = X^2$, $dv = e^{-aX} dX$. Then

$$du = 2X\,dX, \qquad v = -\frac{e^{-aX}}{a}$$

Substituting

$$\sigma^2 = a \left(\left[-X^2 \frac{e^{-aX}}{a} \right]_0^\infty + \frac{2}{a} \int_0^\infty Xe^{-aX}\,dX \right) - \frac{1}{a^2}$$

$$= a \left(0 + \frac{2}{a} \int_0^\infty Xe^{-aX}\,dX \right) - \frac{1}{a^2}$$

$$= a \left(0 + \frac{2}{a} \cdot \frac{\mu}{a} \right) - \frac{1}{a^2}$$

$$= a \cdot \frac{2}{a} \cdot \frac{1}{a^2} - \frac{1}{a^2}$$

$$= \frac{1}{a^2}$$

(c) *Normal distribution.†*

$$f(X) = \frac{1}{\sigma\sqrt{2\pi}} \exp \frac{-(X-\mu)^2}{2\sigma^2} \qquad \text{range of } X\text{: from } -\infty \text{ to } \infty$$

Mean: μ

Variance: σ^2

For this distribution the variance is independent of the mean. A normal distribution having zero mean and unit variance is called the *standard*

†To show that the mean of normal distribution is μ and the variance of normal distribution is σ^2, the derivatives of moment-generating function are introduced. Moment-generating function is defined as

$$M_X(t) = \int_{-\infty}^{\infty} e^{Xt} f(X)\, dX$$

and the properties of the function are

(1) $\qquad\qquad M_{cf(X)}(t) = M_{f(X)}(ct)$

(2) $\qquad\qquad M_{f(X)+c}(t) = e^{ct} M_{f(X)}(t)$

where c is a constant.

Take the first derivative of $M_x(t)$ (also called the *first moment about the origin*) and let t approach zero will yield the mean of $f(X)$. In the case of normal distribution,

$$f(X) = \frac{1}{\sigma\sqrt{2\pi}} e^{-(1/2)[(X-\mu)/\sigma]^2}$$

Let

$$Y = \frac{X-\mu}{\sigma}$$

then

$$dY = \frac{1}{\sigma}\, dX$$

$$\begin{aligned}
M_Y(t) &= \int_{-\infty}^{\infty} e^{Yt} \frac{1}{\sqrt{2\pi}} e^{-(Y^2/2)}\, dY \\[6pt]
&= \frac{1}{\sqrt{2\pi}} \int_{-\infty}^{\infty} e^{-(Y^2/2)+Yt}\, dY \\[6pt]
&= \frac{1}{\sqrt{2\pi}} \int_{-\infty}^{\infty} e^{-[(Y^2/2)-2(Y/\sqrt{2})(t/\sqrt{2})+t^2/2]+t^2/2}\, dY \\[6pt]
&= \frac{1}{\sqrt{2\pi}} \int_{-\infty}^{\infty} e^{-(1/2)(Y-t)^2+t^2/2}\, dY \\[6pt]
&= \frac{e^{t/2}}{\sqrt{2\pi}} \int_{-\infty}^{\infty} e^{-(1/2)(Y-t)^2}\, dY
\end{aligned}$$

From the standard table of integrals we found

$$\int_{-\infty}^{\infty} e^{-(1/2)Z^2}\, dZ = \sqrt{2\pi}$$

normal distribution. The probability that the random variable of a normal distribution will assume values between $\mu - k\sigma$ and $\mu + k\sigma$ (where k is a constant) may be looked up from a table of areas of the normal curve usually included in the appendices of a statistics textbook.

(d) *Chi-square distribution.* Chi-square (χ^2) distribution is widely used in connection with radial error and testing goodness-of-fit problems. The function is

$$f(\chi^2) = \frac{(\chi^2)^{(\eta/2)-1}e^{-(\chi^2/x)}}{2^{\eta/2}\Gamma^{\eta/2}}$$

where $\Gamma(X)$ denotes the gamma or factorial function of X, which has the property $\Gamma(X + 1) = X\Gamma(X)$, and η is the degrees of freedom, which equals the number of independent variables involved. Chi-square distribution may be interpreted as the sum of the squares of the standard normal variates:

$$\chi^2(\eta) = \sum_{i=1}^{\eta} z_i^2 = \sum_{i=1}^{\eta} \left(\frac{X_i - \mu}{\sigma}\right)^2$$

or conversely, the square of a standard normal variable possesses a chi-square distribution with one degree of freedom.

Let $Z = Y - t$, $dZ = dY$

$$M_y(t) = \frac{e^{t^2/2}}{\sqrt{2\pi}}\sqrt{2\pi} = e^{t^2/2}$$

or

$$M_{(1/\sigma)(X-\mu)}(t) = e^{t^2/2}$$

Since $1/\sigma$ is a constant,

$$M_{X-\mu}\left(\frac{t}{\sigma}\right) = e^{t^2/2}$$

$$M_{X-\mu}(t) = e^{(\sigma t)^2/2}$$

Also $(-\mu)$ is a constant:

$$M_{X-\mu}(t) = e^{-\mu t}M_X(t) = e^{\sigma^2 t^2/2}$$

$$M_X(t) = e^{\mu t + (\sigma^2 t^2/2)}$$

$$\text{Mean} = \left.\frac{dM_X(t)}{dt}\right|_{t=0} = \left. e^{-\mu t + (\sigma^2 t^2/2)}(\mu + \sigma^2 t)\right|_{t=0} = \mu$$

Take the second derivative of $M_{X-\mu}(t)$ (also called the *second moment about the mean*) and let t approach zero will yield the variance of $f(X)$. In the case of normal distribution,

$$\text{Variance} = \left.\frac{d^2 M_{X-\mu}(t)}{dt^2}\right|_{t=0} = \frac{d^2}{dt^2}[e^{\sigma^2 t^2/2}]_{t=0}$$

$$= \frac{d}{dt}[e^{\sigma^2 t^2/2}\cdot\sigma^2 t]_{t=0} = [e^{\sigma^2 t^2/2}(\sigma^2) + \sigma^2 t\cdot e^{\sigma^2 t^2/2}(\sigma^2 t)]_{t=0}$$

$$= \sigma^2$$

In small samples, σ^2 is substituted by sample variance s^2:

$$\eta s^2 = \sum_{i=1}^{r} (X_i - \bar{X})^2 = \sum_{i=1}^{n} [(X_i - \mu) - (\bar{X} - \mu)]^2$$

$$= \sum_{i=1}^{n} (\bar{X}_i - \mu)^2 - n(\bar{X} - \mu)^2$$

where $\bar{X}$ is the sample mean and $\eta = n - 1$ (n is the number of observations). Dividing both sides by σ^2,

$$\frac{\eta s^2}{\sigma^2} = \sum_{i=1}^{n} \left(\frac{X_i - \mu}{\sigma}\right)^2 - \frac{n(\bar{X} - \mu)^2}{\sigma^2}$$

$$= \sum_{i=1}^{n} \left(\frac{X_i - \mu}{\sigma}\right)^2 - \left(\frac{\bar{X} - \mu}{\sigma/\sqrt{n}}\right)^2$$

Using the moment-generating function,

$$M_{\eta s^2/\sigma^2}(t) = \frac{M_{\sum_{i=1}^{n} [(X_i - \mu)/\sigma]^2}(t)}{M_{[(\bar{X} - \mu)/(\sigma/\sqrt{n})]^2}(t)} \qquad \begin{array}{l}(n \text{ degrees of freedom}) \\ \\ (1 \text{ degree of freedom})\end{array}$$

Thus $\eta s^2/\sigma^2$ possesses a χ^2 distribution with $\eta = (n - 1)$ degrees of freedom.

(e) *Student's t distribution.* When sample is small and population variance is unknown, standard normal distribution cannot be used. Student's t distribution with the same mean but larger variance is used instead. (The name "Student" comes from a pseudonym used by William S. Gossett, who developed the procedure in the early 1900's.)
    The function is

$$f(t) = c \left(1 + \frac{t^2}{\eta}\right)^{-(1/2)(\eta + 1)}$$

where c, a constant, $= \Gamma[(\eta + 1)/2]/\sqrt{\eta\pi}2^{\eta/2}\Gamma(\eta/2)$ and η is the degree of freedom. The variable t may be interpreted as the ratio of $z\sqrt{n}/\sqrt{\chi_\eta^2}$ where z is the standard normal variate and χ_η^2 is a χ^2 variate with $\eta = n - 1$ degrees of freedom.

(f) *The F distribution.* In order to compare the variances of different samples (when the samples sizes are small) and determine where the variances are significantly different or may be accepted as the same, the F distribution is used. The function is

$$f(F) = k \frac{F^{(1/2)(\eta_1 - 2)}}{(\eta_2 + \eta_1 F)^{(1/2)(\eta_1 \cap \eta_2)}}$$

where k, a constant, $= \dfrac{\eta_1^{\eta_1/2}\eta_2^{\eta_2/2}\Gamma(\eta_1 + \eta_2/2)}{\Gamma(\eta_1/2)\Gamma(\eta_2/2)}$.

The variable of the F distribution may be interpreted as the ratio of two χ^2 distributions:

$$F = \frac{\chi^2_{\eta_1}/\eta_1}{\chi^2_{\eta_2}/\eta_2}$$

where η_1 is the degrees of freedom of $\chi^2_{\eta_1}$ distribution and η_2 is the degrees of freedom of $\chi^2_{\eta_2}$, distribution.

Probability Functions of Two or More Random Variables

Suppose there are two variables in consideration, one variable X, which is in Poisson distribution.

$$f(X) = e^{-\lambda}\frac{\lambda^X}{X!}, \qquad X = 0, 1, 2, \ldots, \infty$$

The other variable Y is dependent of X and the joint probability distribution of X and Y is given as

$$f(X, Y) = e^{-\lambda}\frac{\lambda^X}{X!}\binom{X}{Y}p^Y(1 - p)^{X-Y}$$

$$X = 0, 1, 2, \ldots, \infty, \qquad Y = 0, 1, \ldots, X$$

Then the marginal probability of Y can be computed as

$$f(Y) = \sum_{X=Y}^{\infty} f(X, Y) = \sum_{X=Y}^{\infty} e^{-\lambda}\frac{\lambda^X}{X!}\binom{X}{Y}p^Y(1 - p)^{X-Y}$$

$$= e^{-\lambda}\sum_{X=Y}^{\infty}\frac{\lambda^X}{X!}\frac{X!}{Y!(X - Y)!}p^Y(1 - p)^{X-Y}$$

$$= \frac{e^{-\lambda}p^Y}{Y!}\sum_{X=Y}^{\infty}\frac{\lambda^X(1 - p)^{X-Y}}{(X - Y)!}$$

$$= \frac{e^{-\lambda}p^Y}{Y!}\left\{\lambda^Y + \frac{\lambda^{Y+1}(1 - p)}{1!} + \frac{\lambda^{Y+2}(1 - p)^2}{2!}\cdots\right\}$$

$$= \frac{e^{-\lambda}(\lambda p)^Y}{Y!}\left\{1 + \frac{\lambda(1 - p)}{1!} + \frac{\lambda^2(1 - p)^2}{2!}\cdots\right\}$$

$$= \frac{e^{-\lambda}(\lambda p)^Y}{Y!}e^{\lambda(1-p)} = \frac{e^{-\lambda p}(\lambda p)^Y}{Y!}, \qquad Y = 0, 1, \ldots, \infty$$

which is a Poisson distribution with parameter equals to λp.
   The conditional probability distributions then are

$$f(X \mid Y) = \frac{f(X, Y)}{f(Y)} = \frac{e^{-\lambda} \dfrac{\lambda^X}{X!} \dbinom{X}{Y} p^Y (1 - p)^{X - Y}}{\dfrac{e^{-\lambda p}(\lambda p)^Y}{Y!}}.$$

$$= \frac{e^{-\lambda(1 - p)} \lambda^{X - Y}(1 - p)^{X - Y}}{(X - Y)!}$$

$$= \frac{e^{-\lambda(1 - p)}[\lambda(1 - p)]^{X - Y}}{(X - Y)!}, \qquad X = Y, Y + 1, Y + 2, \ldots$$

which is a Poisson distribution with parameters equal to $\lambda(1 - p)$.

$$f(Y \mid X) = \frac{f(X, Y)}{f(X)} = \frac{e^{-\lambda} \dfrac{\lambda^X}{X!} \dbinom{X}{Y} p^Y (1 - p)^{X - Y}}{e^{-\lambda} \dfrac{\lambda^X}{X!}}$$

$$= \binom{X}{Y} p^Y (1 - p)^{X - Y}, \qquad Y = 0, 1, \ldots, X$$

which is a binomial distribution with parameters equal to X and p.

For continuous probability distribution, given a joint distribution of two variables $f(X, Y), 0 < X < \infty, 0 < Y < X$ the marginal distributions of Y can be computed by the formula

$$f(Y) = \int_{X = Y}^{\infty} f(X, Y)\, dX$$

and the conditional distributions by

$$f(X \mid Y) = \frac{f(X, Y)}{f(Y)}, f(Y \mid X) = \frac{f(X, Y)}{f(X)}$$

1-3. GOODNESS OF FIT

Since the properties of the theoretical probability distributions are known, it may be convenient to compare the observed frequencies of a variable with the expected frequencies of a theoretical distribution. If they are compatible, we may assume the frequency distribution of the variable can be approximated by its theoretical counterpart and its properties become known.

One of the methods generally used to test the compatibility is the *chi-square test*:

$$\chi^2 = \sum_{i=1}^{k} \frac{(r_i - f_i)^2}{f_i}$$

where k is the number of different values that the variable may assume,

r the observed frequencies, and f the expected frequencies of a theoretical distribution. When the observed frequencies agree perfectly with the expected frequencies, χ^2 will be zero. Increasingly large values of χ^2 indicate poor agreement. Chi-square tables are included in most statistics textbooks with different degrees of freedom [in the above formula, degrees of freedom is $k - 1$)]. The χ^2 value beyond which we will reject compatibility of the observed frequency and the expected frequency is determined by the degree of confidence required.

EXAMPLE:

The experiment of rolling a single die. The random variable may assume six different values, 1, 2, 3, 4, 5, and 6. The theoretical distribution is a uniform distribution $f = \frac{1}{6}$. If we roll the die 60 times, the expected frequency of the variable assuming each of the six values is 10. Suppose the following frequencies are actually observed:

	1	2	3	4	5	6
r	8	13	11	9	7	12

Then the χ^2 value is

$$\chi^2 = \frac{(8 - 10)^2}{10} + \frac{(13 - 10)^2}{10} + \frac{(11 - 10)^2}{10}$$
$$+ \frac{(9 - 10)^2}{10} + \frac{(7 - 10)^2}{10} + \frac{(12 - 10)^2}{10}$$

$$= 2.8$$

From χ^2 distribution table, we find that with degrees of freedom equal to 5 and 5 percent error probability of rejecting the true compatibility hypothesis, the critical χ^2 value is 11.07. Since the computed χ^2 value is smaller than 11.07 we may assume that the observed frequencies agree with the expected frequencies and the die is an "honest" die.

1-4. INDUCTIVE STATISTICS

1. Estimation

(a) *Point estimate.* This is a number computed from sample values that serves as an approximation of the parameter being estimated. Sample proportion is generally used as an estimate of the population proportion:

$$\frac{X}{n} = \text{est}(p) = p'$$

where n is the sample size; sample mean is used as an estimate of the population mean:

$$\overline{X} = \text{est}(\mu)$$

Central-Limit Theorem. The theorem states that if a random variable X has a distribution with mean μ and standard deviation σ, the variable

$$z = \frac{\overline{X} - \mu}{\sigma/\sqrt{n}}$$

has a distribution that approaches the standard normal distribution as n becomes infinite.

(b) *Interval estimate.* Based on the central-limit theorem, an interval may be computed from sample values, that the probability of the interval's containing the true value of the parameter is specified. The interval is called the *confidence interval.*

Estimation of the Population Proportion. The interval which includes p with a specified probability is

$$p' \pm z_0 \cdot \sqrt{\frac{p'(1 - p')}{n}}$$

where z_0 is a standard normal variable set up according to the specified probability. For example, if we need a 95 percent probability to include p, then z_0 is 1.96. However, this estimate is valid only when $np > 5$ for $p < \frac{1}{2}$ and $n(1 - p) > 5$ for $p > \frac{1}{2}$.

Estimation of the Population Mean μ. The interval which includes μ with a specified probability is

$$\overline{X} \pm z_0 \frac{\sigma}{\sqrt{n}}$$

When σ is unknown and n is large (30 or more) then substitute σ with the sample standard deviation S:

$$\overline{X} \pm z_0 \frac{S}{\sqrt{n}}$$

If the sample is small (less than 30), then student t distribution should be used:

$$\overline{X} \pm t_0 \frac{S}{\sqrt{n}}$$

For example, if a 95 percent confidence interval is desired, when sample size is 10, t_0 is equal to 2.26. Note that the interval is larger compared to z_0.

2. Testing Hypotheses

In many instances we do not know the true value of a parameter, such as mean or proportion, so we make guesses or hypotheses. Hypotheses may differ. If we have two different hypotheses about the true value of a parameter we need some way of testing them to find out which has the greater probability of being true.

When we test a hypothesis H_0 against an alternative hypothesis H_1, two types of error may occur:

Facts Decisions	H_0 true	H_1 true
H_0 accepted H_1 accepted	Correct decision Type I error	Type II error Correct decision

The probability of making type I error is called α and the probability of making type II error is called β. Though we cannot eliminate the errors completely, we may control the probabilities of making these errors by taking an appropriate number of sample observations and by setting appropriate critical regions.

Testing a Mean. For adequate sample size, use standard normal distribution. The formula for transformation is

$$z = \frac{\overline{X} - \mu}{\sigma_{\overline{X}}}$$

where $\sigma_{\overline{X}} = \sigma/\sqrt{n}$. If z falls in the critical region, reject H_0 is true, otherwise accept H_0. (See Fig. 1-1.)

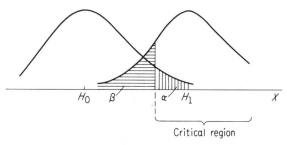

Fig. 1-1

EXAMPLE:

$$H_0: \mu = 100$$
$$H_1: \mu > 100$$

Sample mean: $\overline{X} = 102$
Sample standard deviation: $s = 5$
Sample size: $n = 100$

Since the sample size is large enough, we may use s as an estimate of the population standard deviation σ:

$$\hat{\sigma}_{\overline{X}} = \frac{s}{\sqrt{n}} = \frac{1}{2}$$

$$z = \frac{\overline{X} - \mu}{\hat{\sigma}_{\overline{X}}} = \frac{102 - 100}{^1/_2} = 4$$

If we set α equal to .05, which indicates that we want to avoid making type I error with 95 percent confidence, then the critical region is on the right-hand side of $z_0 = 1.645$.

Since 4 is in the critical region, the decision would be rejecting the hypothesis $H_0: \mu = 100$. (See Fig. 1-2.)

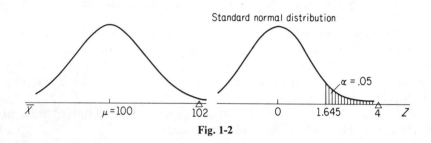

Fig. 1-2

For small sample, use student t distribution:

$$t = \frac{\overline{X} - \mu}{s_{\overline{X}}}$$

where $s_{\overline{X}} = s/\sqrt{n}$.

EXAMPLE:

Testing a mean with a small sample:

$$H_0: \mu = 10(\mu_0)$$
$$H_1: \mu \neq 10(\mu_1) \quad \text{(two-tailed critical region)}$$

A small sample $n = 25$ is taken, the sample mean is $\overline{X} = 11$, and the sample variance is $s^2 = 49$. The transformation is

$$t_0 = \frac{\overline{X} - \mu_0}{s/\sqrt{n}} = \frac{11 - 10}{7/5} = .71$$

Let the error probability $\alpha = .05$, the decision point according to the t distribution table with 24 degrees of freedom is

$$t = 2.06 \quad \text{or} \quad -2.06$$

Since .71 is not in the critical region, we have no evidence of rejecting $H_0: \mu = 10$.

Testing a Proportion. For adequate sample size, approximate normal distribution may be used. The formula for transformation is

$$z = \frac{p' - p}{\sqrt{\dfrac{p(1 - p)}{n}}}$$

EXAMPLE:

$$H_0: p = .6$$
$$H_1: p < .6$$

Sample size: $n = 400$
Sample proportion: $p' = X/n = .58$

$$z = \frac{.58 - .6}{\sqrt{\dfrac{(.6)(.4)}{400}}} = -\frac{.02}{.0245} = -.82$$

If we set α equal to .05, the critical region will be on the left-hand side of $z_0 = -1.645$. Since $-.82$ is not in the critical region, the decision would be accepting hypothesis $H_0: p = .6$. (See Fig. 1-3.)

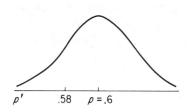

Fig. 1-3

Testing Variance

EXAMPLE:
    Test a hypothetical value of population variance σ^2 against an alternative hypothesis:

$$H_0: \sigma^2 = 30$$
$$H_1: \sigma^2 > 30$$

If we take a sample of size 25 and the sample variance is 40, $\eta s^2/\sigma^2$ possesses a χ^2 distribution with 24 degrees of freedom. From the chi-square distribution table, when error probability is .05, the decision point or critical value of χ^2 is 36.4.
    Now in this problem the sample χ^2 value is

$$\chi_0^2 = \frac{\eta s^2}{\sigma^2} = \frac{24 \cdot 40}{30} = 32$$

The hypothesis $H_0: \sigma^2 = 30$ is accepted.

EXAMPLE:
    Testing the equality of variances,

$$H_0: \sigma_x^2 = \sigma_y^2$$
$$H_1: \sigma_x^2 > \sigma_y^2$$

Take samples $n_x = 10$, $n_y = 10$, and find sample variances $s_x^2 = 30$, $s_y^2 = 5$. From the F distribution table, with $(9, 9)$ degrees of freedom and error probability 5 percent, the critical value of F is

$$F = 3.18$$

In this example the F value is

$$F_0 = \frac{s_x^2}{s_y^2} = \frac{30}{5} = 6$$

Since F_0 is in the critical region, we reject H_0: $\sigma_x^2 = \sigma_x^2$ in favor of H_1: $\sigma_x^2 > \sigma_y^2$.

Operating Characteristic. What is stated above only gives us the probability of making a type I error. We may set α very small, so that the probability of making type I error could be minimized. However, this may increase the probability of making type II error. Thus, it is also necessary to study the size of the type II error. This may be done by computing the *operating characteristic curve*.

EXAMPLE:

Suppose we need to test the difference of two means. The two hypotheses are

$$H_0: \mu_1 - \mu_2 = 0$$
$$H_1: \mu_1 - \mu_2 = 2$$

Sample sizes: $n_1 = 100$, $n_2 = 100$
Sample variances: $s_1^2 = 9$, $s_2^2 = 16$
Sample means: $X_1 = 30$, $X_2 = 29$

The formula for transforming the original value to standard normal variate is

$$z = \frac{(\overline{X}_1 - \overline{X}_2) - (\mu_1 - \mu_2)}{\sigma_{X_1 - X_2}}$$

where

$$\sigma_{\overline{X}_1 - \overline{X}_2} = \sqrt{\frac{s_1^2}{n_1} + \frac{s_2^2}{n_2}}$$

In this example,

$$z = \frac{1 - 0}{\sqrt{\dfrac{9}{100} + \dfrac{16}{100}}} = 2$$

If α is set equal to .025, the critical region is on the right of $z = 1.96$. Since 2 is in the critical region, the decision would be to accept H_1: $\mu_1 - \mu_2 = 2$.

But now we can also calculate the probability of making type II error, β, when using this decision rule. The value 1.96, when transformed to the $(\overline{X}_1 - \overline{X}_2)$ scale, becomes

$$(\mu_1 - \mu_2) + 1.96\sigma_{\bar{x}_1 - \bar{x}_2} = 0 + (1.96)\left(\sqrt{\frac{9}{100} + \frac{16}{100}}\right) = .98$$

$$z = \frac{.98 - 2}{\sqrt{\frac{9}{100} + \frac{16}{100}}} = -2.04$$

From a standard normal distribution table, we can find that $\beta = .5 - .4793 = .0207$. (See Fig. 1-4.)

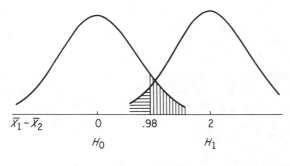

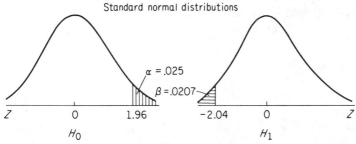

Fig. 1-4

If the alternative hypotheses of $(\mu_1 - \mu_2)$ are many, we can follow the above procedure to compute β for each alternative hypothesis, thus obtain an operating characteristic curve as shown in Fig. 1-5.

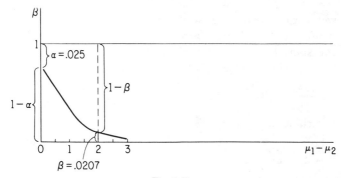

Fig. 1-5

If the sample size remains the same, choosing a larger critical region means decreasing the β value at the expense of increasing the α value; or vice versa. When we need to decrease both the α value and the β value, we will have to take larger samples.

3. Analysis of Variance

Analysis of variance ($\Sigma x^2/n$) is a method to test whether two or more samples differ significantly with respect to some property. The simplest type of an analysis of variance model is to classify observations into different groups on the basis of a single property and use the ratio of the variance between the groups and the average variance within the groups to test whether these groups differ significantly with respect to that property. The ratio is known as the F ratio, which is associated with the F distribution. The testing procedure can best be seen through an example.

EXAMPLE:

Bath soaps made of the same formula are put in three different wrappings and sold at the same price. The result of eight months sales is as follows (assuming the sales data are normally distributed with equal variance):

Soap A Sales			Soap B Sales			Soap C Sales		
X_1	x_1	x_1^2	X_2	x_2	x_2^2	X_3	x_3	x_3^2
100	0	0	120	15	225	90	−8	64
98	−2	4	115	10	100	100	2	4
102	2	4	105	0	0	90	−8	64
95	−5	25	100	−5	25	115	17	289
90	−10	100	110	5	25	89	−9	81
110	10	100	105	0	0	105	7	49
105	5	25	95	−10	100	100	2	4
100	0	0	90	−15	225	95	−3	9
800		258	840		700	784		564

Where lowercase character x_i denotes deviation, $x_i = X_i - \bar{X}$.

We want to test the hypotheses to determine whether different wrappings of the same bath soap have any effect on its sales. The group means are

$$\bar{X}_1 = \frac{\Sigma X_1}{n} = 100 \qquad \bar{X}_2 = \frac{\Sigma X_2}{n} = 105 \qquad \bar{X}_3 = \frac{\Sigma X_3}{n} = 98$$

The group variances:

$$s_1^2 = \frac{\Sigma x_1^2}{n-1} = 36.8 \qquad s_2^2 = \frac{\Sigma x_2^2}{n-1} = 100 \qquad s_3^2 = \frac{\Sigma x_3^2}{n-1} = 80.5$$

The average variance within the three groups is

$$V_1 = \frac{s_1^2 + s_2^2 + s_3^2}{3} = 72.4$$

The total mean of all the observations is

$$\bar{\bar{X}} = \frac{\bar{X}_1 + \bar{X}_2 + \bar{X}_3}{3} = 101$$

The variance of all the observations is

$$\sigma_{\bar{X}}^2 = \frac{(\bar{X}_1 - \bar{\bar{X}})^2 + (\bar{X}_2 - \bar{\bar{X}})^2 + (\bar{X}_3 - \bar{\bar{X}})^2}{3 - 1} = 13$$

Since the variance of sample means is equal to the variance of the variable divided by the sample size ($\sigma_{\bar{X}}^2 = \sigma^2/n$), the variance between these groups is therefore:

$$V_2 = n\sigma_{\bar{X}}^2 = 8 \times 13 = 104$$

The F ratio then can be computed as

$$F = \frac{V_2}{V_1} = \frac{104}{72.4} = 1.44$$

The degrees of freedom for the numerator are 2 ($c - 1$, where c is the number of the groups), the degrees of freedom for the denominator are 21 [$c(r - 1)$, where r is the number of observations in each group], and from the F distribution table, the 5 percent critical value of F corresponding to the degrees of freedom (2, 21) is 3.45. Apparently, the computed F value 1.44 is smaller than 3.47. The analysis thus indicates that we have no significant evidence to reject the hypothesis that different wrappings have no effect on the sales of the bath soap.

For testing samples with more than one classification variable e.g., the effect of different formulas and different wrappings on the sale of bath soap, the total variance is decomposed into more than two components. In the case of two variables of classification, the total variance is decomposed into the row variance (one classification), the column variance (the other classification), and the residual variance.

$$\sum_{i=1}^{r} \sum_{j=1}^{c} (X_{ij} - \bar{\bar{X}})^2 = \sum_{i=1}^{r} \sum_{j=1}^{c} (\bar{X}_i - \bar{\bar{X}})^2$$

$$+ \sum_{i=1}^{r} \sum_{j=1}^{c} (\bar{X}_j - \bar{\bar{X}})^2 + \sum_{i=1}^{r} \sum_{j=1}^{c} (X_{ij} - \bar{X}_i - \bar{X}_j + \bar{\bar{X}})^2$$

where r is the number of rows, c is the number of columns, X_{ij} are the observations, $\bar{X}_i$ is the mean of the ith row, $\bar{X}_j$ is the mean of the jth column, and $\bar{\bar{X}}$ is the total mean.

Thus the row variance is

$$V_r = c \frac{\sum_{i=1}^{r} (\bar{X}_i - \bar{\bar{X}})^2}{r - 1}$$

the column variance is

$$V_c = r \frac{\sum_{j=1}^{c} (\bar{X}_j - \bar{\bar{X}})^2}{c - 1}$$

and the residual variance is

$$V_e = \frac{\sum_{i=1}^{r} \sum_{j=1}^{c} (X_{ij} - \bar{X}_i - \bar{X}_j + \bar{\bar{X}})^2}{(r - 1)(c - 1)}$$

The F ratio for testing the hypothesis to determine whether the column means are equal is

$$F_1 = \frac{V_c}{V_e} = \frac{r(r - 1) \sum_{j=1}^{c} (\bar{X}_j - \bar{\bar{X}})^2}{\sum_{i=1}^{r} \sum_{j=1}^{c} (X_{ij} - \bar{X}_i - \bar{X}_j + \bar{\bar{X}})^2}$$

where the degrees of freedom for the numerator are $c - 1$ and the degrees of freedom for the denominator are $(r - 1)(c - 1)$. And the F ratio for testing the hypothesis that the row means are equal is

$$F_2 = \frac{V_r}{V_e} = \frac{c(c - 1) \sum_{i=1}^{r} (\bar{X}_i - \bar{\bar{X}})^2}{\sum_{i=1}^{r} \sum_{j=1}^{c} (X_{ij} - \bar{X}_i - \bar{X}_j + \bar{\bar{X}})^2}$$

where the degrees of freedom for the numerator are $r - 1$ and the degrees of freedom for the denominator are $(r - 1)(c - 1)$.

A numerical example is as follows. A soap manufacturer produces four different kinds of bath soap and uses three different kinds of wrappings on each of them before putting them on the market, the annual sales of the soap are:

Formula \ Wrapping	A	B	C
1	3,105	3,092	3,118
2	2,880	2,905	2,895
3	3,001	3,014	2,995
4	2,612	2,603	2,598

We use F ratios to test whether different formulas and different wrappings have significant effect on the sales volume,

$$\sum_{i=1}^{4} \sum_{j=1}^{3} X_{ij} = 34{,}818 \qquad \sum_{i=1}^{4} \sum_{j=1}^{3} X_{ij}^2 = 101{,}445{,}842$$

$$\sum_{j=1}^{3}\left(\sum_{i=1}^{4} X_{ij}\right)^2 = 404,097,836 \qquad \sum_{i=1}^{4}\left(\sum_{j=1}^{3} X_{ij}\right)^2 = 304,334,694$$

$$\sum_{j=1}^{3} (\bar{X}_j - \bar{\bar{X}})^2 = \frac{404,097,836}{4^2} - \frac{(34,818)^2}{3 \cdot 4^2} = 15$$

$$\sum_{i=1}^{4} (\bar{X}_i - \bar{\bar{X}})^2 = \frac{304,334,694}{3^2} - \frac{(34,818)^2}{4 \cdot 3^2} = 140,160$$

$$\sum_{i=1}^{4}\sum_{j=1}^{5} (X_{ij} - \bar{\bar{X}})^2 = 101,445,842 - \frac{(34,818)^2}{4 \cdot 3} = 421,420$$

$$\sum_{i=1}^{4}\sum_{j=1}^{5} (X_{ij} - \bar{X}_i - \bar{X}_j + \bar{\bar{X}})^2 = 421,420 - 3(140,160) - 4(15) = 880$$

To test the column variance,

$$F_1 = \frac{4 \cdot 3 \cdot 15}{880} = 0.2$$

with degrees of freedom $(2, 6)$. From the F distribution table, we will find that the 5 percent critical value of F corresponding the degrees of freedom $(3, 6)$ is 5.14. Since F_1 is smaller than 5.14 (not in the critical region), we have no reason to reject the hypothesis that different wrappings have no effect on sales. To test the row variance,

$$F_2 = \frac{3 \cdot 2 \cdot 140,160}{880} = 995.6$$

with degrees of freedom $(3, 6)$. From the F distribution table, we will find that the 5 percent critical value of F corresponding the degrees of freedom $(2, 6)$ is 4.76. Since F_2 is greater than 4.76 (in the critical region), we reject the hypothesis that different formulas have no effect on sales.

4. Analysis of Covariance

The method of testing the effect of one variable separately from the effects of a second variable, while the second variable is represented by actual measurement of each individual instead of by several categories, is called the analysis of covariance ($\Sigma xy/n$). The second variable is usually referred to as the control variable. Similar to analysis of variance, the analysis of covariance procedure also leads to a test for difference in means by separation of a total sum of products (total covariation) into within-groups sum of products (within-groups covariation) and between-groups sum of products (between-groups covariation). However, the test is performed on the difference in means of residuals, where the residuals are the differences of the actual measurement of the first variable and a regression quantity based on the associated second variable.

$$\sum_{i=1}^{g}\sum_{j=1}^{n}(X_{ij}-\overline{\overline{X}})(Y_{ij}-\overline{\overline{Y}}) = \sum_{i=1}^{g}\sum_{j=1}^{n}(X_{ij}-\overline{X}_i)(Y_{ij}-\overline{Y}_i)$$

$$\text{(total covariation)} \qquad\qquad \text{(within-groups covariation)}$$

$$+ n\sum_{i=1}^{g}(\overline{X}_i-\overline{\overline{X}})(\overline{Y}_i-\overline{\overline{Y}})$$

$$\text{(between-groups covariation)}$$

where g is the number of groups, n is the number of observations in each group, $\overline{X}_i$, $\overline{Y}_i$ are the group means and $\overline{\overline{X}}$, $\overline{\overline{Y}}$ are the total means. The equation may be reduced to the following for easier computation:

$$\sum_{i=1}^{g}\sum_{j=1}^{n}X_{ij}Y_{ij} - \frac{\left(\sum_{i=1}^{g}\sum_{j=1}^{n}X_{ij}\right)\left(\sum_{i=1}^{g}\sum_{j=1}^{n}Y_{ij}\right)}{n\times g}$$

$$\text{(total covariation)}$$

$$= \left[\sum_{i=1}^{g}\sum_{j=1}^{n}X_{ij}Y_{ij} - \frac{\sum_{i=1}^{g}\left(\sum_{j=1}^{n}X_{ij}\times\sum_{j=1}^{n}Y_{ij}\right)}{n}\right]$$

$$\text{(within-groups covariation)}$$

$$+ \left[\frac{\sum_{i=1}^{g}\left(\sum_{j=1}^{n}X_{ij}\times\sum_{j=1}^{n}Y_{ij}\right)}{n} - \frac{\left(\sum_{i=1}^{g}\sum_{j=1}^{n}X_{ij}\right)\left(\sum_{i=1}^{g}\sum_{j=1}^{n}Y_{ij}\right)}{n\times g}\right]$$

$$\text{(between-groups covariation)}$$

Next, by treating X as the control variable, the linear regression coefficient of Y on X is computed by the following,

$$y = \hat{b}x + e$$

$$\hat{b} = \frac{\Sigma xy}{\Sigma x^2}$$

where $y = Y - \overline{\overline{Y}}$, $x = X - \overline{\overline{X}}$, and e is the residual or the difference of actual observation of Y and regression quantity of Y based on X,

$$\begin{aligned}
\Sigma e^2 &= \Sigma(y - \hat{y})^2 \\
&= \Sigma(y - \hat{b}x)^2 \\
&= \Sigma y^2 - 2\hat{b}\Sigma xy + \hat{b}^2\Sigma x^2 \\
&= \Sigma y^2 - \frac{(\Sigma xy)^2}{\Sigma x^2}
\end{aligned}$$

The formulas for computing the sums of products (covariations) are listed in the table on page 33.

The sum of products divided by degrees of freedom gives the mean square.

	Degrees of Freedom	Σx^2	Σy^2	Σxy
Total variation or covariation	$ng - 1$	$\Sigma_i \Sigma_j X_{ij}^2 - \dfrac{(\Sigma_i \Sigma_j X_{ij})^2}{ng}$	$\Sigma_i \Sigma_j Y_{ij}^2 - \dfrac{(\Sigma_i \Sigma_j Y_{ij})^2}{ng}$	$\Sigma_i \Sigma_j X_{ij} Y_{ij} - \dfrac{(\Sigma_i \Sigma_j X_{ij})(\Sigma_i \Sigma_j Y_{ij})}{ng}$
Between groups	$g - 1$	$\dfrac{\Sigma_i (\Sigma_j X_{ij})^2}{n} - \dfrac{(\Sigma_i \Sigma_j X_{ij})^2}{ng}$	$\dfrac{\Sigma_i (\Sigma_j Y_{ij})^2}{n} - \dfrac{(\Sigma_i \Sigma_j Y_{ij})^2}{ng}$	$\dfrac{\Sigma_i (\Sigma_j X_{ij} \times \Sigma_j Y_{ij})}{n} - \dfrac{(\Sigma_i \Sigma_j X_{ij})(\Sigma_i \Sigma_j Y_{ij})}{ng}$
Within groups	$g(n - 1)$	The difference of "Total variation or covariation" and "Between groups variation or covariation"		

$$\Sigma e^2 = \Sigma y^2 - \frac{(\Sigma xy)^2}{\Sigma x^2}$$

	Degrees of Freedom	
Total covariation	$ng - 2$	$\left[\Sigma_i \Sigma_j Y_{ij}^2 - \dfrac{(\Sigma_i \Sigma_j Y_{ij})^2}{ng} \right] - \dfrac{\left[\Sigma_i \Sigma_j X_{ij} Y_{ij} - \dfrac{(\Sigma_i \Sigma_j X_{ij})(\Sigma_i \Sigma_j Y_{ij})}{ng} \right]}{\Sigma_i \Sigma_j X_{ij}^2 - \dfrac{(\Sigma_i \Sigma_j X_{ij})^2}{ng}}$
Between groups	$g - 1$	$\left[\dfrac{\Sigma_i (\Sigma_j Y_{ij})^2}{n} - \dfrac{(\Sigma_i \Sigma_j Y_{ij})^2}{ng} \right] - \dfrac{\left[\dfrac{\Sigma_i (\Sigma_j X_{ij} \times \Sigma_j Y_{ij})}{n} - \dfrac{(\Sigma_i \Sigma_j X_{ij})(\Sigma_i \Sigma_j Y_{ij})}{ng} \right]}{\dfrac{\Sigma_i (\Sigma_j X_{ij})^2}{n} - \dfrac{(\Sigma_i \Sigma_j X_{ij})^2}{ng}}$
Within groups	$g(n - 1) - 1$	The difference of "Total covariation" and "Between groups covariation"

The F value for the analysis of covariance is the ratio of the between-groups mean square and the within-groups mean square.

A numerical example will illustrate the computation procedure.

EXAMPLE:

Let X be the original sales of a commodity in 12 different locations and Y be the sales after a sales promotion campaign has been conducted. Groups 1, 2, and 3 represent three different sales promotion programs. The data are shown in the accompanying table.

Group 1		Group 2		Group 3	
X	Y	X	Y	X	Y
4	12	5	15	2	6
3	10	4	14	3	7
2	9	4	13	4	9
3	11	6	16	2	7
12	42	19	58	11	29

The sums of products are:
1. for ΣX^2 (original sales)

Total variation: $4^2 + 3^2 + 2^2 + 3^2 + 5^2 + 4^2 + 4^2 + 6^2$

$$+ 2^2 + 3^2 + 4^2 + 2^2 - \frac{(12 + 19 + 11)^2}{4 \cdot 3}$$

$$= 164 - \frac{1{,}764}{12} = 17$$

Between-groups variation: $\dfrac{12^2 + 19^2 + 11^2}{4} - \dfrac{(12 + 19 + 11)^2}{4 \cdot 3}$

$$= \frac{626}{4} - \frac{1{,}764}{12} = 9.5$$

Within-groups variation: $17 - 9 \cdot 5 = 7.5$

2. For ΣY^2 (sales after promotion)

Total variation: $12^2 + 10^2 + 9^2 + 11^2 + 15^2 + 14^2 + 13^2$

$$+ 16^2 + 6^2 + 7^2 + 9^2 + 7^2 - \frac{(42 + 58 + 29)^2}{4 \cdot 3}$$

$$= 1{,}507 - \frac{16{,}641}{12} = 120.25$$

Between-groups variation: $\dfrac{42^2 + 58^2 + 29^2}{4} - \dfrac{(42 + 58 + 29)^2}{4 \cdot 3}$

$$= \frac{5{,}969}{4} - \frac{16{,}641}{12} = 105.5$$

$$(\text{d.f.} = 2)$$

Within-groups variation: $120.25 - 105.5 = 14.75$ (d.f. $= 9$)

3. for ΣXY

Total covariation: $4(12) + 3(10) + 2(9) + 3(11) + 5(15)$

$\qquad + 4(14) + 4(13) + 6(16) + 2(6) + 3(7)$

$$+ 4(9) + 2(7) - \frac{(12 + 19 + 11)(42 + 58 + 29)}{4 \cdot 3}$$

$$= 491 - \frac{5{,}418}{12} = 39.5$$

Between-groups covariation: $\dfrac{12(42)}{4} + \dfrac{19(58)}{4}$

$$+ \frac{11(29)}{4} - \frac{(12 + 19 + 11)(42 + 58 + 29)}{4 \cdot 3}$$

$$= \frac{1{,}925}{4} - \frac{5{,}418}{12} = 29.75$$

Within-groups covariation: $39.5 - 29.75 = 9.75$

4. for Σe^2

Total covariation: $120.25 - \dfrac{39.5}{17} = 117.93$

Between-groups covariation: $105.5 - \dfrac{29.75}{9.5} = 102.37$ (d.f. $= 2$)

Within-groups covariation: $117.93 - 102.37 = 15.56$ (d.f. $= 8$)

$$F = \frac{102.37/2}{15.56/8} = \frac{51.18}{1.94} = 26.4$$

Compare the F value with $F_{.95}(2, 8) = 4.46$, $F_{.99}(2, 8) = 8.65$, there are significant differences in Y means among the groups after the Y values have been adjusted by the regression of Y on X in each group. (This indicates that the three different sales promotion programs do have different effect on sales, even after the location effect on sales has been removed.) Following the analysis of variance of the Y values only without using the X values, the F ratio would be

$$\frac{105.5/2}{14.75/9} = \frac{52.75}{1.64} = 32.1$$

The larger value of F in this case is the result of overlooking the effect of X on Y. (Locational effect on sales has not been removed.)

SELECTED BIBLIOGRAPHY

1. R. A. Fisher, *Statistical Methods for Research Workers*. Edinburgh: Oliver and Boyd, 1944.

2. D. A. S. Fraser, *Statistics: An Introduction.* New York: Wiley, 1958.

3. P. G. Hoel, *Introduction to Mathematical Statistics*, 3rd ed.   New York: Wiley, 1964.

4. A. M. Mood, *Introduction to the Theory of Statistics.* New York: McGraw-Hill, 1950.

5. E. L. Peterson, *Statistical Analysis and Optimization of Systems.* New York: Wiley, 1961.

6. R. Schalaifer, *Probability and Statistics for Business Decisions.* New York: McGraw-Hill, 1959.

EXERCISES

1-1. Assume that two-thirds of the students in a college are males and one-third are females, and that the probability that a male student being an engineering major is one-third and a female student only one-twentieth. State the probability that:
   (a) A student selected at random will be an engineering student
   (b) A student selected at random will be a male engineering student
   (c) A student selected at random will be a female engineering student
   (d) An engineering student selected at random will be a male student
   (e) An engineering student selected at random will be a female student

1-2. Derive the formula of the mean and variance of a discrete random variable whose distribution is binomial. *Hint.* Mean $= \Sigma x f(x)$; variance $= \Sigma x^2 f(x)$.

1-3. Derive the formula of the mean and variance of a continuous random variable whose distribution is normal. *Hint.* Mean $= \int x f(x)\,dx$; variance $= \int x^2 f(x)\,dx$.

1-4. Given that a continuous variable X is distributed rectangularly between 0 and a, find the uniform distribution function of $(2X + 5)$.

1-5. An urn contains 100 balls:
   (a) Three-fifths of all the balls are round. Among these round balls, half are black and half are white.
   (b) The remaining balls are egg-shaped. Among these egg-shaped balls, four-tenths are black and six-tenths are white.
   A ball is drawn from the urn. What is the probability of the ball being white? If the ball is known to be egg-shaped, what is the probability of the ball being white?

1-6. Assume that the weight (X) of college football players is normally distributed with mean equals to 180 lb and standard deviation 20 lb. Use standard normal distribution table to calculate the probability that:
   (a) $X < 170$ lb,
   (b) $170 < X < 190$ lb.

1-7. If you want to investigate the sales of meat in a town which has approximately 500 supermarkets, how would you take samples? What technique would you use to analyze the sample data and draw conclusion about the population's demand for meat? State your reason.

1-8. A random sample is taken in a city which shows that the number of automobile accidents per week are as the following: 8, 10, 15, 12, 6, 18, 7, 9, 11, 14. Use the χ^2 test to determine whether we may assume that the number of accidents are the same over the weeks.

1-9. A random sample of 500 polls taken in a city shows that 350 of them support a certain legislature. What is the 95 percent confidence interval for the proportion of the population supporting the legislature?

1-10. A random sample of 20 students taken in a college yields the following information:

(a) The average height of the sample $\bar{X} = 5$ ft 8 in.;

(b) The sample standard deviation $S = 3$ in.

Use the Student's t distribution to determine the 95 percent confidence interval for the average height μ of the entire student body of the college.

1-11. A poll of the television audience in a neighborhood shows that 1,000 of 1,200 men liked a certain program, whereas only 800 of 1,000 women liked it. Is the difference of opinion significant?

1-12. Given sample size $n = 100$, sample mean $\bar{X} = 102$, and sample standard deviation $S = 15$. Test the following hypotheses of the population mean: $H_0: \mu = 100$, $H_1: \mu = 105$. Which hypothesis should be accepted with the probability of making type I error controlled at $\alpha = .05$? Also find the probability of making type II error, β, if the above decision rule is used.

chapter 2

A Review of Linear Algebra

Empirical investigation of economic relationship involves the collection and manipulation of a large number of data. Matrix provides a way of orderly arraying the numbers, and facilitates computation to a great extent—especially in the present era of giant digital computers. In this chapter we review the fundamentals of linear algebra, which deals with the operations on matrices.

2-1. MATRICES AND MATRIX OPERATIONS

An ordered collection of numbers written in columns or rows is called a *vector*. A rectangular array of elements arranged in rows or columns is called a *matrix* (plural *matrices*).

EXAMPLE:

$$A = \begin{bmatrix} a_{11} & a_{12} & \cdots & a_{1n} \\ a_{21} & a_{22} & \cdots & a_{2n} \\ \vdots & & & \\ a_{m1} & a_{m2} & \cdots & a_{mn} \end{bmatrix}$$ is a (m by n) matrix.

1. Square Matrix

A matrix with equal number of rows and columns.

2. Unit Matrix (Identity Matrix)

A square matrix with units in the principal diagonal and zeros everywhere else.

EXAMPLE:

$$I = \begin{bmatrix} 1 & 0 & \cdots & 0 \\ 0 & 1 & \cdots & 0 \\ \vdots & & & \\ 0 & 0 & \cdots & 1 \end{bmatrix}$$

3. Diagonal Matrix

A square matrix which has elements, not necessarily equal, in the principal diagonal, and zeros everywhere else.

4. Symmetric Matrix

A square matrix whose symmetric off-diagonal elements are all equal —that is,

$$a_{ij} = a_{ji} \quad \text{for} \quad i, j = 1, 2, \ldots, n$$

5. Triangular Matrix

A triangular matrix is a square matrix with elements in the principal diagonal and one side of the principal diagonal. The elements on the other side of the principal diagonal are all zeros.

$$A = \begin{bmatrix} a_{11} & a_{12} & \cdots & a_{1n} \\ 0 & a_{22} & \cdots & a_{2n} \\ \vdots & & & \\ 0 & 0 & \cdots & a_{nn} \end{bmatrix}$$

6. Transpose of a Matrix

The transpose of a matrix is the interchange of rows and columns of a matrix.

EXAMPLE:

$$A = \begin{bmatrix} a_{11} & a_{12} \\ a_{21} & a_{22} \\ a_{31} & a_{32} \end{bmatrix} \qquad A^T = \begin{bmatrix} a_{11} & a_{21} & a_{31} \\ a_{12} & a_{22} & a_{32} \end{bmatrix}$$

Rules of transposing matrices

$$(A^T)^T = A$$
$$(A + B)^T = A^T + B^T$$
$$(AB)^T = B^T A^T$$

7. Addition and Subtraction of Matrices

If two or more matrices of the same order—that is, with equal number of rows and columns—we may add or subtract their corresponding elements.

EXAMPLE:

$$A = \begin{bmatrix} a_{11} & a_{12} \\ a_{21} & a_{22} \\ a_{31} & a_{32} \end{bmatrix} \qquad B = \begin{bmatrix} b_{11} & b_{12} \\ b_{21} & b_{22} \\ b_{31} & b_{32} \end{bmatrix}$$

$$D = A + B = \begin{bmatrix} a_{11} + b_{11} & a_{12} + b_{12} \\ a_{21} + b_{21} & a_{22} + b_{22} \\ a_{31} + b_{31} & a_{32} + b_{32} \end{bmatrix}$$

8. Scalar Multiplication

When a matrix is multiplied by a scalar, each element of the matrix is multiplied by the scalar.

EXAMPLE:

$$kA = k \begin{bmatrix} a_{11} & a_{12} \\ a_{21} & a_{22} \\ a_{31} & a_{32} \end{bmatrix} = \begin{bmatrix} ka_{11} & ka_{12} \\ ka_{21} & ka_{22} \\ ka_{31} & ka_{32} \end{bmatrix}$$

9. Matrix Multiplication

A first matrix of order $(m \times n)$ and a second matrix of order $(n \times k)$ may be multiplied to produce a third matrix of order of $(m \times k)$ by the following rule:

$$D = AB$$

where A is the first matrix, B is the second matrix and D is the product;

$$d_{ij} = \sum_{t=1}^{n} a_{it} b_{tj} \qquad (i = 1, 2, \ldots, m; j = 1, 2, \ldots, k)$$

Since the number of columns of the first matrix must be equal to the number of rows of the second matrix, the product BA may not exist. And $AB \neq BA$ except for symmetric matrices.

EXAMPLE:

$$A = \begin{bmatrix} a_{11} & a_{12} \\ a_{21} & a_{22} \\ a_{31} & a_{32} \end{bmatrix} \qquad B = \begin{bmatrix} b_{11} & b_{12} & b_{13} \\ b_{21} & b_{22} & b_{23} \end{bmatrix}$$

$$AB = \begin{bmatrix} a_{11}b_{11} + a_{12}b_{21} & a_{11}b_{12} + a_{12}b_{22} & a_{11}b_{13} + a_{12}b_{23} \\ a_{21}b_{11} + a_{22}b_{21} & a_{21}b_{12} + a_{22}b_{22} & a_{21}b_{13} + a_{22}b_{23} \\ a_{31}b_{11} + a_{32}b_{21} & a_{31}b_{12} + a_{32}b_{22} & a_{31}b_{13} + a_{32}b_{23} \end{bmatrix}$$

$$BA = \begin{bmatrix} b_{11}a_{11} + b_{12}a_{21} + b_{13}a_{31} & b_{11}a_{12} + b_{12}a_{22} + b_{13}a_{32} \\ b_{21}a_{11} + b_{22}a_{21} + b_{23}a_{31} & b_{21}a_{12} + b_{22}a_{22} + b_{23}a_{32} \end{bmatrix}$$

Thus

$$AB \neq BA$$

10. Determinant of a Matrix

Associated with any square matrix is a scalar quantity called the *determinant* of the matrix.

The determinant of a 2 × 2 matrix is defined as

$$\begin{vmatrix} a_{11} & a_{12} \\ a_{21} & a_{22} \end{vmatrix} = a_{11}a_{22} - a_{12}a_{21}$$

The determinant of a higher-order $n \times n$ square matrix is computed by the formula

$$|A| = \sum_{j=1}^{n} a_{ij}c_{ij}$$

where c_{ij} are the cofactors of the minors in A, $c_{ij} = (-1)^{i+j}|M_{ij}|$ and $|M_{ij}|$ is the determinant of the minor. (A *minor* is a matrix within a matrix with fewer rows and columns.)

EXAMPLE:

$$\begin{vmatrix} a_{11} & a_{12} & a_{13} \\ a_{21} & a_{22} & a_{23} \\ a_{31} & a_{32} & a_{33} \end{vmatrix} = a_{11}(-1)^{1+1}\begin{vmatrix} a_{22} & a_{23} \\ a_{32} & a_{33} \end{vmatrix} + a_{12}(-1)^{1+2}\begin{vmatrix} a_{21} & a_{23} \\ a_{31} & a_{33} \end{vmatrix}$$

$$+ a_{13}(-1)^{1+3}\begin{vmatrix} a_{21} & a_{22} \\ a_{31} & a_{32} \end{vmatrix}$$

$$= a_{11}a_{22}a_{33} - a_{11}a_{23}a_{32} - a_{12}a_{21}a_{33}$$
$$+ a_{12}a_{23}a_{31} + a_{13}a_{21}a_{32} - a_{13}a_{22}a_{31}$$

11. Adjoint of a Matrix

The adjoint of a matrix is equal to the transpose of a matrix whose elements are replaced by its cofactors.

EXAMPLE:

Let c_{ij} $(i, j = 1, 2, \ldots, n)$ be the cofactors of matrix A. The adjoint of matrix A is

$$\text{adj } A = \begin{bmatrix} c_{11} & c_{21} & \cdots & c_{n1} \\ c_{12} & c_{22} & \cdots & c_{n2} \\ \vdots & & & \\ c_{1n} & c_{2n} & \cdots & c_{nn} \end{bmatrix}$$

12. The Inverse Matrix

Matrix inversion is similar to the operation of division. However, we write $1/A$ as A^{-1} and it applies only to some square matrices. Let A^{-1} be the inverse matrix of A, the following property exists:

$$A^{-1}A = I$$
$$AA^{-1} = I$$

where I is the unit matrix of equal order to A.

Two methods are commonly employed to find the inverse matrix.

(a) The first method is computed from the adjoint and determinant of the matrix. Since

$$|A| = \sum_{j=1}^{n} a_{ij}c_{ij}$$

and

$$(\text{adj } A) = [c_{ij}]^T$$

$$A \cdot \frac{1}{|A|}(\text{adj } A) = \frac{1}{|A|} \begin{bmatrix} a_{11} & a_{12} & \cdots & a_{1n} \\ a_{21} & a_{22} & \cdots & a_{2n} \\ \vdots & & & \\ a_{n1} & a_{n2} & \cdots & a_{nn} \end{bmatrix} \begin{bmatrix} c_{11} & c_{21} & \cdots & c_{n1} \\ c_{12} & c_{22} & \cdots & c_{n2} \\ \vdots & & & \\ c_{1n} & c_{2n} & \cdots & c_{nn} \end{bmatrix}^{\dagger}$$

$$= \frac{1}{|A|} \begin{bmatrix} |A| & 0 & \cdots & 0 \\ 0 & |A| & \cdots & 0 \\ \vdots & & & \\ 0 & 0 & \cdots & |A| \end{bmatrix} = I$$

†Note that

$$\sum_{j=1}^{n} a_{ij}c_{kj} = 0 \qquad \text{when } i \neq k$$
$$= |A| \qquad \text{when } i = k$$

Therefore

$$A^{-1} = \frac{1}{|A|} (\text{adj } A)$$

Thus only a nonsingular square matrix—that is, a matrix having a non-zero determinant—can have inverse matrix.

EXAMPLE:

$$A = \begin{bmatrix} 1 & 3 \\ 2 & 4 \end{bmatrix}, \qquad |A| = 4 \times 1 - 3 \times 2 = -2$$

Cofactors matrix:

$$\begin{bmatrix} 4 & -2 \\ -3 & 1 \end{bmatrix}, \qquad \text{adj } A = \begin{bmatrix} 4 & -3 \\ -2 & 1 \end{bmatrix}$$

$$A^{-1} = -\tfrac{1}{2} \begin{bmatrix} 4 & -3 \\ -2 & 1 \end{bmatrix} = \begin{bmatrix} -2 & \tfrac{3}{2} \\ 1 & -\tfrac{1}{2} \end{bmatrix}$$

Check:

$$A^{-1}A = \begin{bmatrix} -2 & \tfrac{3}{2} \\ 1 & -\tfrac{1}{2} \end{bmatrix} \begin{bmatrix} 1 & 3 \\ 2 & 4 \end{bmatrix} = \begin{bmatrix} (-2+3) & (-6+6) \\ (1-1) & (3-2) \end{bmatrix}$$

$$= \begin{bmatrix} 1 & 0 \\ 0 & 1 \end{bmatrix} = I$$

(b) The second method is to find the row-operations matrix which will reduce the matrix to be inverted into a unit matrix of the same order. The row-operations matrix is then the inverse matrix.

EXAMPLE:

$$A = \begin{bmatrix} 2 & 3 \\ 5 & 6 \end{bmatrix} \qquad [A:I] = \begin{bmatrix} 2 & 3 & \vdots & 1 & 0 \\ 5 & 6 & \vdots & 0 & 1 \end{bmatrix}$$

Step 1. Divide the first row of $[A:I]$ by a_{11}, which is 2.

$$\begin{bmatrix} 1 & \tfrac{3}{2} & \vdots & \tfrac{1}{2} & 0 \\ 5 & 6 & \vdots & 0 & 1 \end{bmatrix}$$

Step 2. Subtract from the second row by a_{21} multiples of the transformed first row, which is 5 times of the transformed first row.)

$$\begin{bmatrix} 1 & \tfrac{3}{2} & \vdots & \tfrac{1}{2} & 0 \\ 0 & -\tfrac{3}{2} & \vdots & -\tfrac{5}{2} & 1 \end{bmatrix}$$

Step 3.   Divide the transformed second row by its a_{22}, which is $-\frac{3}{2}$.

$$\begin{bmatrix} 1 & \frac{3}{2} & \vdots & \frac{1}{2} & 0 \\ 0 & 1 & \vdots & \frac{5}{2} & -\frac{2}{3} \end{bmatrix}$$

Step 4.   Subtract from the transformed first row by a_{12} multiples of the transformed second row, (which is $\frac{3}{2}$ times of the transformed second row.)

$$\begin{bmatrix} 1 & 0 & \vdots & -2 & 1 \\ 0 & 1 & \vdots & \frac{5}{3} & -\frac{2}{3} \end{bmatrix}$$

Since we have performed the same row operations on both A and I, the result must be $[I:A^{-1}]$.

   Check:

$$A A^{-1} = \begin{bmatrix} 2 & 3 \\ 5 & 6 \end{bmatrix} \begin{bmatrix} -2 & 1 \\ \frac{5}{3} & -\frac{2}{3} \end{bmatrix}$$

$$= \begin{bmatrix} (-4+5) & (2-2) \\ (-10+10) & (5-4) \end{bmatrix} = \begin{bmatrix} 1 & 0 \\ 0 & 1 \end{bmatrix} = I$$

Properties of inverse matrices:

$$(A^{-1})^{-1} = A$$
$$(AB)^{-1} = B^{-1}A^{-1}$$
$$(A^{T})^{-1} = (A^{-1})^{T}$$

13. Orthogonal Matrix

A nonsingular matrix is orthogonal if its inverse and transpose are the same.

$$A^{-1} = A^{T} \quad \text{and} \quad A^{T}A = I$$

Properties of an orthogonal matrix:
(a) The value of the determinant $|A| = 1$ or -1.
(b) The sum of squares of elements in any row or column of the matrix is unity:

$$\sum_{j=1}^{n} a_{ij}^{2} = 1 \quad \text{for any } i = 1, 2, \ldots, n$$

(c) The sum of elements in any row or column of the matrix, each multiplied by the corresponding element in another row, is zero:

$$\sum_{j=1}^{n} a_{ij}a_{tj} = 0 \quad \text{for any } i, t = 1, 2, \ldots, n \quad \text{and} \quad i \neq t$$

EXAMPLE:

$$A = \begin{bmatrix} 0 & 1 \\ 1 & 0 \end{bmatrix}, \qquad |A| = -1$$

$$a_{11}^2 + a_{12}^2 = 1, \qquad a_{21}^2 + a_{22}^2 = 1, \qquad a_{11}a_{21} + a_{12}a_{22} = 0$$

Thus A is an orthogonal matrix:

$$A^T = \begin{bmatrix} 0 & 1 \\ 1 & 0 \end{bmatrix}, \qquad A^T A = \begin{bmatrix} 0 & 1 \\ 1 & 0 \end{bmatrix}\begin{bmatrix} 0 & 1 \\ 1 & 0 \end{bmatrix} = \begin{bmatrix} 1 & 0 \\ 0 & 1 \end{bmatrix} = I$$

14. Rank of a Matrix, $\rho(A)$

Rank of a matrix is indicated by the maximum number of linearly independent columns or rows, whichever is the smaller. It may also be indicated by the largest nonvanishing determinant.

EXAMPLES:

(1) $\begin{bmatrix} 1 & 3 \\ 2 & 2 \\ 3 & 1 \end{bmatrix}$ has the rank of 2.

(2) $\begin{bmatrix} 1 & 2 & 3 \\ 2 & 3 & 2 \\ 3 & 4 & 1 \end{bmatrix} = \begin{bmatrix} 1 & 0 & 3 \\ 2 & 0 & 2 \\ 3 & 0 & 1 \end{bmatrix}$ has the rank of 2.

(3) $\begin{bmatrix} 4 & 10 \\ 2 & 5 \end{bmatrix}$ (determinant = 0) has the rank of 1.

15. Trace of a Matrix, tr(A)

Trace of a matrix is defined as the sum of the principal diagonal elements of a matrix.

EXAMPLES:

(1) $A = \begin{bmatrix} 1 & 5 & 3 \\ 2 & 6 & 7 \\ 3 & 4 & 8 \end{bmatrix}$ tr$(A) = 1 + 6 + 8 = 15$

(2) $U = \begin{bmatrix} u_1 \\ u_2 \end{bmatrix}$ $A = \begin{bmatrix} a_{11} & a_{12} \\ a_{21} & a_{22} \end{bmatrix}$

$$(AUU^T) = \begin{bmatrix} a_{11} & a_{12} \\ a_{21} & a_{22} \end{bmatrix} \begin{bmatrix} u_1 \\ u_2 \end{bmatrix} [u_1 \quad u_2] = \begin{bmatrix} a_{11} & a_{12} \\ a_{21} & a_{22} \end{bmatrix} \begin{bmatrix} u_1^2 & u_1 u_2 \\ u_2 u_1 & u_2^2 \end{bmatrix}$$

$$= \begin{bmatrix} a_{11} u_1^2 + a_{12} u_2 u_1 & a_{11} u_1 u_2 + a_{12} u_2^2 \\ a_{21} u_1^2 + a_{22} u_2 u_1 & a_{21} u_1 u_2 + a_{22} u_2^2 \end{bmatrix}$$

$$\text{tr}\,(AUU^T) = a_{11} u_1^2 + a_{12} u_2 u_1 + a_{21} u_1 u_2 + a_{22} u_2^2 \dagger$$

2-2. CHARACTERISTIC ROOTS AND VECTORS

If A is a square matrix, λ is a scalar and

$$AX = \lambda X \quad \text{or} \quad (A - \lambda I) X = 0$$

then λ is called a *characteristic root* of A, and X the respective characteristic vector. They are also called *eigenvalues* and *eigenvectors*, or *latent roots and vectors*.

EXAMPLES:
(a)

$$A = \begin{bmatrix} a_{11} & a_{12} \\ a_{21} & a_{22} \end{bmatrix}, \quad X = \begin{bmatrix} X_1 \\ X_2 \end{bmatrix}$$

$$AX = \lambda X$$

$$\begin{bmatrix} a_{11} & a_{12} \\ a_{21} & a_{22} \end{bmatrix} \begin{bmatrix} X_1 \\ X_2 \end{bmatrix} = \lambda \begin{bmatrix} X_1 \\ X_2 \end{bmatrix}$$

$$a_{11} X_1 + a_{12} X_2 = \lambda X_1$$
$$a_{21} X_1 + a_{22} X_2 = \lambda X_2$$

or

$$(a_{11} - \lambda) X_1 + a_{12} X_2 = 0$$
$$a_{21} X_1 + (a_{22} - \lambda) X_2 = 0$$

†Note:

$$(U^T A U) = [u_1 \quad u_2] \begin{matrix} a_{11} & a_{12} \\ a_{21} & a_{22} \end{matrix} \begin{matrix} u_1 \\ u_2 \end{matrix}$$

$$= [a_{11} u_1 + a_{21} u_2 \quad a_{12} u_1 + a_{22} u_2] \begin{matrix} u_1 \\ u_2 \end{matrix}$$

$$= a_{11} u_1^2 + a_{21} u_2 u_1 + a_{12} u_1 u_2 + a_{22} u_2^2$$

$$= \text{tr}\,(AUU^T)$$

$$\begin{bmatrix} (a_{11} - \lambda) & a_{12} \\ a_{21} & (a_{22} - \lambda) \end{bmatrix} \begin{bmatrix} X_1 \\ X_2 \end{bmatrix} = \begin{bmatrix} 0 \\ 0 \end{bmatrix}$$

$$(A - \lambda I) X = 0$$

For there to exist a solution, since $X \neq 0$, matrix $(A - \lambda I)$ has to be singular and thus its determinant equal to zero:

$$|A - \lambda I| = 0$$

$$\begin{vmatrix} (a_{11} - \lambda) & a_{12} \\ a_{21} & (a_{22} - \lambda) \end{vmatrix} = 0$$

$$(a_{11} - \lambda)(a_{22} - \lambda) - a_{12}a_{21} = 0$$

$$\lambda^2 - (a_{11} + a_{22})\lambda + (a_{11}a_{22} - a_{12}a_{21}) = 0$$

$$\lambda_1 = \tfrac{1}{2}[(a_{11} + a_{22}) + \sqrt{(a_{11} + a_{22})^2 - 4(a_{11}a_{22} - a_{12}a_{21})}]$$

$$\lambda_2 = \tfrac{1}{2}[(a_{11} + a_{22}) - \sqrt{(a_{11} + a_{22})^2 - 4(a_{11}a_{22} - a_{12}a_{21})}]$$

λ_1, λ_2 may be real roots or conjugate complex. If A is symmetric, that is $a_{12} = a_{21}$, then λ_1, λ_2 will always be real.

$$\lambda_1 = \tfrac{1}{2}[(a_{11} + a_{22}) + \sqrt{(a_{11} - a_{22})^2 + 4a_{12}^2}]$$

$$\lambda_2 = \tfrac{1}{2}[(a_{11} + a_{22}) - \sqrt{(a_{11} - a_{22})^2 + 4a_{12}^2}]$$

(b)

$$A = \begin{bmatrix} 2 & -1 & -1 \\ -1 & 2 & -1 \\ -1 & -1 & 2 \end{bmatrix}, \qquad X = \begin{bmatrix} X_1 \\ X_2 \\ X_3 \end{bmatrix}$$

$$(A - \lambda I) = \begin{bmatrix} (2 - \lambda) & -1 & -1 \\ -1 & (2 - \lambda) & -1 \\ -1 & -1 & (2 - \lambda) \end{bmatrix}$$

$$|A - \lambda I| = (2 - \lambda)^3 - 1 - 1 - (2 - \lambda) - (2 - \lambda) - (2 - \lambda)$$

$$= -\lambda^3 + 6\lambda^2 - 9\lambda = 0$$

$$\lambda(\lambda - 3)^2 = 0$$

Thus the characteristic roots are $\lambda_1 = 3$, $\lambda_2 = 3$, $\lambda_3 = 0$. When $\lambda = 0$,

$$(A - \lambda I) X = \begin{bmatrix} 2 & -1 & -1 \\ -1 & 2 & -1 \\ -1 & -1 & 2 \end{bmatrix} \begin{bmatrix} X_1 \\ X_2 \\ X_3 \end{bmatrix} = \begin{bmatrix} 0 \\ 0 \\ 0 \end{bmatrix}$$

$$2X_1 - X_2 - X_3 = 0$$

$$-X_1 + 2X_2 - X_3 = 0$$

$$-X_1 - X_2 + 2X_3 = 0$$

and $(X_1 = 1, X_2 = 1, X_3 = 1)$ is the characteristic vector. When $\lambda = 3$,

$$(A - \lambda I) X = \begin{bmatrix} -1 & -1 & -1 \\ -1 & -1 & -1 \\ -1 & -1 & -1 \end{bmatrix} \begin{bmatrix} X_1 \\ X_2 \\ X_3 \end{bmatrix} = \begin{bmatrix} 0 \\ 0 \\ 0 \end{bmatrix}$$

$$X_1 + X_2 + X_3 = 0$$

Possible characteristic vectors for the two equal roots are

$$(X_1 = 1, X_2 = -1, X_3 = 0) \quad \text{and} \quad (X_1 = 1, X_2 = 1, X_3 = -2)$$

In some cases, matrix A may be reduced to scalar quantities by post-multiplying an orthogonal matrix and premultiplying again by the inverse of the orthogonal matrix. The product is a diagonal matrix, with the elements in the diagonal equal to the characteristic roots. The orthogonal matrix for this example is

$$P = \begin{bmatrix} \dfrac{1}{\sqrt{2}} & \dfrac{1}{\sqrt{6}} & \dfrac{1}{\sqrt{3}} \\ -\dfrac{1}{\sqrt{2}} & \dfrac{1}{\sqrt{6}} & \dfrac{1}{\sqrt{3}} \\ 0 & -\dfrac{2}{\sqrt{6}} & \dfrac{1}{\sqrt{3}} \end{bmatrix}$$

$$P^{-1} = P^T = \begin{bmatrix} \dfrac{1}{\sqrt{2}} & -\dfrac{1}{\sqrt{2}} & 0 \\ \dfrac{1}{\sqrt{6}} & \dfrac{1}{\sqrt{6}} & -\dfrac{2}{\sqrt{6}} \\ \dfrac{1}{\sqrt{3}} & \dfrac{1}{\sqrt{3}} & \dfrac{1}{\sqrt{3}} \end{bmatrix}$$

$$P^{-1}AP = \begin{bmatrix} \dfrac{1}{\sqrt{2}} & -\dfrac{1}{\sqrt{2}} & 0 \\ \dfrac{1}{\sqrt{6}} & \dfrac{1}{\sqrt{6}} & -\dfrac{2}{\sqrt{6}} \\ \dfrac{1}{\sqrt{3}} & \dfrac{1}{\sqrt{3}} & \dfrac{1}{\sqrt{3}} \end{bmatrix} \begin{bmatrix} 2 & -1 & -1 \\ -1 & 2 & -1 \\ -1 & -1 & 2 \end{bmatrix} \begin{bmatrix} \dfrac{1}{\sqrt{2}} & \dfrac{1}{\sqrt{6}} & \dfrac{1}{\sqrt{3}} \\ -\dfrac{1}{\sqrt{2}} & \dfrac{1}{\sqrt{6}} & \dfrac{1}{\sqrt{3}} \\ 0 & -\dfrac{2}{\sqrt{6}} & \dfrac{1}{\sqrt{3}} \end{bmatrix}$$

$$= \begin{bmatrix} 3 & 0 & 0 \\ 0 & 3 & 0 \\ 0 & 0 & 0 \end{bmatrix} = \begin{bmatrix} \lambda_1 & 0 & 0 \\ 0 & \lambda_2 & 0 \\ 0 & 0 & \lambda_3 \end{bmatrix}$$

SELECTED BIBLIOGRAPHY

1. A. C. Aitken, *Determinants and Matrices*. Edinburgh: Oliver and Boyd, 1942.
2. G. Hadley, *Linear Algebra*. Reading, Mass., Addison-Wesley, 1961.
3. E. D. Nering, *Linear Algebra and Matrix Theory*. New York: Wiley, 1963.

EXERCISES

2-1. Given

$$A = \begin{bmatrix} 1 & 3 & 7 \\ 8 & 5 & 2 \\ 4 & 6 & 9 \end{bmatrix} \qquad B = \begin{bmatrix} 2 & 9 & 8 \\ 6 & 7 & 4 \\ 3 & 10 & 5 \end{bmatrix}$$

Calculate $A + B$, $B - A$, AB, BA.

2-2. Given

$$A = \begin{bmatrix} 2 & 6 & 4 \\ 7 & 2 & 8 \end{bmatrix} \qquad B = \begin{bmatrix} 9 & 0 & 7 \\ 5 & -4 & 8 \\ 6 & 3 & 2 \end{bmatrix} \qquad C = \begin{bmatrix} 3 \\ 9 \\ 6 \end{bmatrix}$$

Calculate $[AB]^T$, $B^T A^T$, $[AC]^T$ and $C^T A^T$.

2-3. Calculate the determinant, the adjoint, and the inverse of the following matrix.

$$A = \begin{bmatrix} 4 & -1 & 2 \\ 8 & 7 & 5 \\ 3 & 0 & 9 \end{bmatrix}$$

2-4. Find the characteristic roots and the corresponding characteristic vectors of the following matrix.

$$A = \begin{bmatrix} 1 & 0 & -\frac{1}{2} \\ 0 & 1 & -\frac{1}{2} \\ -\frac{1}{2} & -\frac{1}{2} & 1 \end{bmatrix}$$

2-5. Verify that the following matrix is an orthogonal matrix.

$$A = \begin{bmatrix} -\frac{1}{3} & \frac{2}{3} & -\frac{2}{3} \\ \frac{2}{3} & -\frac{1}{3} & -\frac{2}{3} \\ \frac{2}{3} & \frac{2}{3} & \frac{1}{3} \end{bmatrix}$$

(a) Calculate the value of the determinant.
(b) Calculate the sum of squares of the elements in each row and column.
(c) Calculate the sum of elements in each row (or column) multiplied by the corresponding elements in another row (or column).
(d) Find A^T and A^{-1}. Are they the same?

chapter 3

Linear Models

The simplest relationship that can exist between two sets of variables is a *linear relationship*; it may be expressed functionally as $Y = a + b_1 X_1 + b_2 X_2 + \cdots + b_n X_n$. If the values of the parameters a, b_1, $b_2, \ldots, b_n$ can be estimated, then given a set of values for X_1, $X_2, \ldots, X_n$, we can find the value of the respective Y. One of the methods used to find the "best-fit" line through the sample points taken from the real world is the least-squares regression method. We will start with the case of two variables.

3-1. TWO-VARIABLE LINEAR-REGRESSION MODEL

Let Y be a variable whose value is determined by another variable X. We call X the explanatory variable and Y the explained variable or the variable to be explained. First we test whether we can accept the hypothesis that a linear relationship exists between the two variables. We take a sample of X_i, $Y_i (i = 1, \ldots, n)$ and calculate the linear correlation coefficient r.

$$r = \frac{\Sigma x_i y_i}{n s_x s_y} \quad \text{or} \quad \frac{\text{cov}(x, y)}{s_x s_y} \tag{3-1}$$

where

$$x = X - \bar{X} \quad y = Y - \bar{Y} \quad \left(\bar{X} = \frac{\Sigma X_i}{n} \quad \bar{Y} = \frac{\Sigma Y_i}{n} \right)$$

and

$$s_x = \sqrt{\frac{\Sigma x_i^2}{n}}^\dagger \quad s_y = \sqrt{\frac{\Sigma y_i^2}{n}}^\dagger$$

†When sample size is small in comparison to the entire population, the standard deviations should be adjusted to $s_x = \sqrt{\Sigma x_i^2/(n-1)}$ and $s_y = \sqrt{\Sigma y_i^2/(n-1)}$.

If x_i and y_i are of the same sign, negative or positive, the sum of the product $\Sigma x_i y_i$ will be large; otherwise it will be small.

Figure 3-1 shows that if the sample points cluster in quadrants I and III, it indicates intuitively that a positive correlation exists between X and Y. (If the sample points cluster in quadrants II and IV, it shows a negative correlation between X and Y, and $\Sigma x_i y_i$ will have a negative value.) In the other case, if they scatter evenly in all four quadrants there does not seem to be any correlation between the two variables, and the value of $\Sigma x_i y_i$ will approach zero.

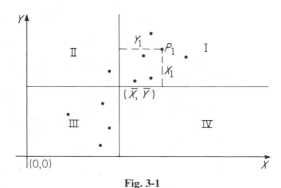

Fig. 3-1

The correlation coefficients between different sets of variables may need to be compared with each other to examine their degrees of correlation. However, X and Y may be in different units; for example, Y may be in dollars and X may be in pounds. Also, the sample size may be different in different cases. Larger sample size will make the value of $\Sigma x_i y_i$ larger. So in order to make r unit free, x is divided by s_x, y is divided by s_y, and the whole term is divided by n to eliminate the effect of different sample size.

When r approaches zero, there is no linear correlation between Y and X, and when r is different from zero we may test its significance by transforming r to an approximately normal variate by the following formula:

$$z = \frac{1}{2} \log \left(\frac{1 + r}{1 - r} \right)$$

The mean value of this transformed variable z is

$$\mu_z = \frac{1}{2} \log \left(\frac{1 + \rho}{1 - \rho} \right)$$

where ρ is the true value of the linear correlation coefficient and the standard deviation of the distribution of z is

$$\sigma_z = \frac{1}{\sqrt{n-3}}$$

for sample size n larger than 30.

We then may use the classical statistical method to test the hypothesis that ρ equals zero (which means no linear correlation between Y and X) against an alternative hypothesis that ρ does not equal zero (which means there is a linear correlation between Y and X).

After we have decided to accept the hypothesis that the relationship between Y and X is linear, we then want to estimate the coefficients of the linear equation. The equation may be expressed as

$$\hat{Y} = a + bX$$

where a is the intercept of the line of the Y-axis, and b is the slope of the line. $\hat{Y}$ is used because the true values of X and Y may not fall on the line. We use Y to denote the true Y value and write

$$Y = a + bX + u$$

where u is the difference between the true Y value and the Y value as specified by the line given X. (See Fig. 3-2.)

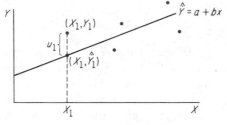

Fig. 3-2

The value u may represent either the net effect of the variables not included in the equation or errors of observation and measurement, or it may be a basic and unpredictable element of randomness, etc. In this chapter we assume u_i are independent random variables with zero mean and constant variance; that is,

$$E(u_i) = 0, \qquad E(u_i^2) = \sigma_u^2 \quad \text{for} \quad i = 1, 2, \ldots, n$$

and

$$E(u_i u_j) = 0 \quad \text{for} \quad i \neq j \quad (i, j = 1, 2, \ldots, n)$$

In the final chapter we discuss the problems that may arise when these assumptions do not hold, and outline ways to correct them.

Now in general we cannot observe all the values of X and Y, but can take only a limited number of samples. From the sample values we estimate the true regression line. We write the estimated values of a and b as $\hat{a}$ and $\hat{b}$. Again, the true sample values of X and Y may not fall on the estimated regression line; thus we write

$$Y = \hat{Y} + e = \hat{a} + \hat{b}X + e \tag{3-2}$$

where $\hat{Y}$ is the Y value specified by the estimated regression line given X and e is the difference between the true sample value of Y and Y. (See Fig. 3-3.)

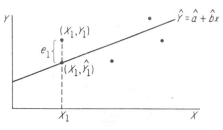

Fig. 3-3

The Least-Squares Estimators

Suppose we take n pairs of values of X and Y and denote these values by

$$(X_1, Y_1), (X_2, Y_2), \ldots, (X_n, Y_n)$$

Then

$$e_i = Y_i - \hat{Y}_i \quad (i = 1, \ldots, n)$$

The principle of least squares is to make Σe_i^2 as small as possible:

$$\Sigma e_i^2 = \Sigma(Y_i - \hat{Y}_i)^2 = \Sigma(Y_i - \hat{a} - \hat{b}X_i)^2$$

A necessary condition that Σe_i^2 be the minimum is that the partial derivatives with respect to a and b should equal to zero.

$$\frac{\partial}{\partial \hat{a}} \Sigma e_i^2 = -2\Sigma(Y_i - \hat{a} - \hat{b}X_i)$$

$$\frac{\partial}{\partial \hat{b}} \Sigma e_i^2 = -2\Sigma X_i(Y_i - \hat{a} - \hat{b}X_i)$$

When they are set equal to zeros, the following equations are obtained:

$$\Sigma Y_i = n\hat{a} + \hat{b}\Sigma X_i \tag{3-3}$$

$$\Sigma X_i Y_i = \hat{a}\Sigma X_i + \hat{b}\Sigma X_i^2 \tag{3-4}$$

These equations are called *normal equations*. Solving for $\hat{b}$,

$$\hat{b} = \frac{\begin{vmatrix} n & \Sigma Y \\ \Sigma X & \Sigma XY \end{vmatrix}}{\begin{vmatrix} n & \Sigma X \\ \Sigma X & \Sigma X^2 \end{vmatrix}} = \frac{n\Sigma XY - (\Sigma X)(\Sigma Y)}{n\Sigma X^2 - (\Sigma X)^2}$$

$$\hat{a} = \overline{Y} - \hat{b}\overline{X}$$

Let $x = X - \bar{X}$ and $y = Y - \bar{Y}$. Then the normal equations become

$$\Sigma(y + \bar{Y}) = n\hat{a} + \hat{b}\Sigma(x + \bar{X})$$
$$\Sigma(x + \bar{X})(y + \bar{Y}) = \hat{a}\Sigma(x + \bar{X}) + \hat{b}\Sigma(x + \bar{X})^2$$

And since

$$\Sigma x = 0 \qquad \Sigma y = 0$$

the equations are simplified to

$$\bar{Y} = \hat{a} + \hat{b}\bar{X} \tag{3-3a}$$
$$\Sigma xy + n\bar{X}\bar{Y} = \hat{a}n\bar{X} + \hat{b}n\bar{X}^2 + \hat{b}\Sigma x^2 \tag{3-4a}$$

or

$$\Sigma xy = \hat{b}\Sigma x^2$$

Thus

$$\hat{b} = \frac{\Sigma xy}{\Sigma x^2} \tag{3-5}$$

$$\hat{a} = \bar{Y} - \hat{b}\bar{X} \tag{3-6}$$

where $\hat{a}$ and $\hat{b}$ are the least-squares point estimators of a and b. Comparing $\hat{b}$ to the linear correlation coefficient r,

$$\hat{b} = \frac{\Sigma xy}{\Sigma x^2} = \frac{\Sigma xy}{ns_x^2} = \frac{\Sigma xy}{ns_x^2} \cdot \frac{s_y}{s_y} = r\frac{s_y}{s_x} \tag{3-7}$$

Also because

$$y = \hat{y} + e \quad \text{(since } Y = \hat{Y} + e \text{ and } \bar{Y} = \hat{a} + \hat{b}\bar{X})$$
$$\Sigma y^2 = \Sigma\hat{y}^2 + \Sigma e^2 + 2\Sigma\hat{y}e$$
$$= \Sigma\hat{y}^2 + \Sigma e^2 + 2\Sigma(\hat{b}x)(y - \hat{b}x)$$
$$= \Sigma\hat{y}^2 + \Sigma e^2 + 2\hat{b}\Sigma xy - 2\hat{b}^2\Sigma x^2$$
$$= \Sigma\hat{y}^2 + \Sigma e^2 + 2\hat{b}(\hat{b}\Sigma x^2) - 2\hat{b}^2\Sigma x^2$$
$$= \Sigma\hat{y}^2 + \Sigma e^2$$

Therefore

$$r^2 = \hat{b}^2\frac{s_x^2}{s_y^2} = \frac{\hat{b}^2\Sigma x^2}{\Sigma y^2} = \frac{\Sigma\hat{y}^2}{\Sigma y^2}$$

or

$$r^2 = \frac{\Sigma y^2 - \Sigma e^2}{\Sigma y^2} = 1 - \frac{\Sigma e^2}{\Sigma y^2} \tag{3-8}$$

The quantity r^2 is called the *coefficient of determination*. It can be expressed as the ratio of the explained variation and the total variation of Y, or as one minus the ratio of the residual or unexplained variation and the total variation of Y. The maximum value of r^2 is 1 when Σe^2 is zero.

In order to make interval estimates of a and b, we need to find the variances of $\hat{a}$ and $\hat{b}$. First

$$\hat{b} = \frac{\Sigma xy}{\Sigma x^2} = \frac{\Sigma x(Y - \overline{Y})}{\Sigma x^2} = \frac{\Sigma x Y}{\Sigma x^2} - \frac{\overline{Y}\Sigma x}{\Sigma x^2}$$

$$= \frac{\Sigma x Y}{\Sigma x^2}$$

$$= \frac{\Sigma x}{\Sigma x^2}(a + bX + u)$$

$$= a\frac{\Sigma x}{\Sigma x^2} + b\frac{\Sigma xX}{\Sigma x^2} + \frac{\Sigma xu}{\Sigma x^2}$$

$$= b\frac{\Sigma x}{\Sigma x^2}(x + \overline{X}) + \frac{\Sigma xu}{\Sigma x^2}$$

$$= b\frac{\Sigma x^2}{\Sigma x^2} + b\overline{X}\frac{\Sigma x}{\Sigma x^2} + \frac{\Sigma xu}{\Sigma x^2}$$

$$= b + \frac{\Sigma xu}{\Sigma x^2}$$

Here we note

$$E(\hat{b}) = E\left[b + \left(\frac{\Sigma xu}{\Sigma x^2}\right)\right]$$

$$= b + E\left(\frac{\Sigma xu}{\Sigma x^2}\right)$$

Since we assume X have fixed values and $E(u) = 0$, then $E(\hat{b}) = b$. The least-squares estimator is unbiased. Also,

$$\hat{b} - b = \frac{\Sigma xu}{\Sigma x^2}$$

$$\text{var}(\hat{b}) = E(\hat{b} - b)^2 = E\left(\frac{\Sigma xu}{\Sigma x^2}\right)^2$$

Assume fixed X values, then Σx^2 is a constant, and

$$\text{var}(\hat{b}) = \frac{1}{(\Sigma x^2)^2}E(x_1^2 u_1^2 + \cdots + x_n^2 u_n^2$$

$$+ 2x_1 x_2 u_1 u_2 + \cdots + 2x_{n-1} x_n u_{n-1} u_n)$$

We further assume that u_i are independent variables with zero mean and constant variance ($E(u_i) = 0$, $E(u_i^2) = \sigma_u^2$ for all i and $E(u_i u_j) = 0$ for $i \neq j; i,j = 1, 2, \ldots, n$). Then

$$E(x_i^2 u_i^2) = x_i^2 \sigma_u^2$$

$$\text{var}(\hat{b}) = \frac{\sigma_u^2}{(\Sigma x^2)^2}\Sigma x^2 = \frac{\sigma_u^2}{\Sigma x^2} \tag{3-9}$$

and

$$\hat{a} = \bar{Y} - \hat{b}\bar{X}$$

$$= \frac{\Sigma Y}{n} - \frac{\Sigma xy}{\Sigma x^2}\,\bar{X}$$

$$= \frac{\Sigma Y}{n} - \bar{X}\left[\frac{\Sigma x(Y - \bar{Y})}{\Sigma x^2}\right]$$

$$= \frac{\Sigma Y}{n} - \bar{X}\frac{\Sigma xY}{\Sigma x^2}$$

$$= \Sigma\left[\frac{1}{n} - \left(\bar{X}\frac{x}{\Sigma x^2}\right)\right]Y$$

$$= \Sigma\left[\frac{1}{n} - \left(\bar{X}\frac{x}{\Sigma x^2}\right)\right](a + bX + u)$$

$$= \frac{n}{n}a - a\bar{X}\frac{\Sigma x}{\Sigma x^2} + b\frac{\Sigma X}{n} - b\bar{X}\frac{\Sigma xX}{\Sigma x^2} + \Sigma\left(\frac{1}{n} - \bar{X}\frac{x}{\Sigma x^2}\right)u$$

$$= a + b\bar{X} - b\bar{X}\frac{\Sigma x(x + \bar{X})}{\Sigma x^2} + \Sigma\left(\frac{1}{n} - \bar{X}\frac{x}{\Sigma x^2}\right)u$$

$$= a + b\bar{X} - b\bar{X}\frac{\Sigma x^2}{\Sigma x^2} + \Sigma\left(\frac{1}{n} - \bar{X}\frac{x}{\Sigma x^2}\right)u$$

$$= a + \Sigma\left(\frac{1}{n} - \bar{X}\frac{x}{\Sigma x^2}\right)u$$

Thus

$$\hat{a} - a = \Sigma\left(\frac{1}{n} - \bar{X}\frac{x}{\Sigma x^2}\right)u$$

$$\text{var}(\hat{a}) = E(\hat{a} - a)^2$$

$$= E\left[\Sigma\left(\frac{1}{n} - \bar{X}\frac{x}{\Sigma x^2}\right)u\right]^2$$

$$= \left[\frac{n}{n^2} - \frac{2\bar{X}}{n}\left(\frac{\Sigma x}{\Sigma x^2}\right) + \bar{X}^2\frac{\Sigma x^2}{(\Sigma x^2)^2}\right]\sigma_u^2$$

$$= \left(\frac{1}{n} + \frac{\bar{X}^2}{\Sigma x^2}\right)\sigma_u^2$$

$$= \left(\frac{\Sigma x^2 + n\bar{X}^2}{n\Sigma x^2}\right)\sigma_u^2$$

$$= \left(\frac{\Sigma(X - \bar{X})^2 + n\bar{X}^2}{n\Sigma x^2}\right)\sigma_u^2$$

$$= \left(\frac{\Sigma X^2 - 2\bar{X}\Sigma X + n\bar{X}^2 + n\bar{X}^2}{n\Sigma x^2} \right) \sigma_u^2$$

$$= \frac{\Sigma X^2}{n\Sigma x^2} \sigma_u^2 \tag{3-10}$$

Note also

$$E(\hat{a}) = a + E\left(\frac{\Sigma u}{n} - \bar{X}\frac{\Sigma xu}{\Sigma x^2} \right)$$

When we assume $E(u_i) = 0$ and X have fixed values, $E(\Sigma xu) = 0$, $E(\hat{a}) = a$, and $\hat{a}$ is an unbiased estimator of a.

The covariance of $\hat{a}$ and $\hat{b}$ is given by

$$\text{cov } (\hat{a}, \hat{b}) = E(\hat{a} - a)(\hat{b} - b)$$

$$= E\left[\Sigma\left(\frac{1}{n} - \bar{X}\frac{x}{\Sigma x^2} \right) u \frac{\Sigma xu}{\Sigma x^2} \right]$$

$$= E\left[\frac{\Sigma xu^2}{n\Sigma x^2} - \bar{X}\frac{\Sigma x^2 u^2}{(\Sigma x^2)^2} \right]$$

$$= \left[\frac{\Sigma x}{n\Sigma x^2} - \bar{X}\frac{1}{\Sigma \bar{x}^2} \right] \sigma_u^2$$

$$= -\frac{\bar{X}}{\Sigma x^2} \sigma_u^2 \tag{3-11}$$

Using the t distribution with $n - 2$ degrees of freedom, the interval esti-mates of a and b can be expressed as

$$\hat{a} \pm t_{\alpha/2} \cdot \sqrt{\text{var } (\hat{a})} = \hat{a} \pm t_{\alpha/2} \frac{\sqrt{\Sigma X^2}}{\sqrt{n\Sigma x^2}} \sigma_u \tag{3-12}†$$

$$\hat{b} \pm t_{\alpha/2} \cdot \sqrt{\text{var } (\hat{b})} = \hat{b} \pm t_{\alpha/2} \frac{1}{\sqrt{\Sigma x^2}} \sigma_u \tag{3-13}†$$

where $t_{\alpha/2}$ specifies the level of confidence (for sample size larger than 30, the standard normal distribution may be used).

[Note: The joint distribution for t and X_i is

$$h(t, X_i) = g(t \mid X_i) f(X_i)$$

where $g(t \mid X_i)$ are the conditional distributions of t given X_i. But

---

†The confidence intervals of a and b specified in Eqs. 3-11 and 3-12 involve student's t distribution on the assumption of fixed X_i; that is,

$$P(-t_{\alpha/2} < t < t_{\alpha/2}) = 1 - \alpha$$

where t_i is some function of the observations on X and Y.

$$1 - \alpha = P(-t_{\alpha/2} < t < t_{\alpha/2})$$

$$= \int_{-t_{\alpha/2}}^{t_{\alpha/2}} g(t \mid X_i) \, dt$$

$$= \int_{-\infty}^{\infty} \cdots \int_{-\infty}^{\infty} \int_{-t_{\alpha/2}}^{t_{\alpha/2}} g(t \mid X_i) f(X_i) \, dt \, dX_i$$

Since

$$\int_{-\infty}^{\infty} \cdots \int_{-\infty}^{\infty} f(X_i) \, dX_i = 1$$

$$1 - \alpha = \int_{-\infty}^{\infty} \cdots \int_{-\infty}^{\infty} \int_{-t_{\alpha/2}}^{t_{\alpha/2}} h(t, X_i) \, dt \, dX_i$$

Thus Eqs. 3-12 and 3-13 are still valid when X_i are random variables, provided that the conditional distribution of Y given X fulfills the assumption of homoscedasticity, $(E(u_i) = 0, E(u_i^2) = \sigma_u^2$ for all i and $E(u_i u_j) = 0$ for $i \neq j; i, j = 1, 2, \ldots, n).]$

Empirically, however, the variance of the disturbance term σ_u^2 is usually unknown and has to be estimated from the sample-error term e. Thus σ_u^2 is replaced by $\hat{\sigma}_u^2$ in the formulas, and $\hat{\sigma}_u^2$ is computed as the following. Since

$$Y_i = a + bX_i + u_i$$

and

$$\bar{Y} = a + b\bar{X} + \bar{u}$$

Hence

$$y_i = bx_i + (u_i - \bar{u})$$

Also

$$e_i = y_i - \hat{b}x_i$$

$$= -(\hat{b} - b) x_i + (u_i - \bar{u})$$

$$\Sigma e^2 = (\hat{b} - b)^2 \Sigma x^2 + \Sigma (u - \bar{u})^2 - 2(\hat{b} - b) \Sigma x(u - \bar{u})$$

$$E(\Sigma e^2) = E[(\hat{b} - b)^2 \Sigma x^2 + \Sigma (u - \bar{u})^2 - 2(\hat{b} - b) \Sigma x(u - \bar{u})]$$

Since

$$E[(\hat{b} - b)^2 \Sigma x^2] = \left(\frac{\sigma_u^2}{\Sigma x^2}\right) \Sigma x^2$$

$$= \sigma_u^2$$

$$E[\Sigma (u - \bar{u})^2] = E[\Sigma u^2 + n\bar{u}^2 - 2\bar{u}\Sigma u]$$

$$= E\left(\Sigma u^2 - \frac{(\Sigma u)^2}{n}\right)$$

$$= \frac{(n - 1)}{n} E(\Sigma u^2)$$

$$= (n - 1) \sigma_u^2$$

$$E[(\hat{b} - b) \Sigma x(u - \bar{u})] = E\left[\left(\frac{\Sigma xu}{\Sigma x^2}\right)(\Sigma xu - \bar{u}\Sigma x)\right]$$

$$= E\left[\frac{\Sigma x^2 u^2}{\Sigma x^2}\right]$$

$$= \sigma_u^2$$

Thus

$$E(\Sigma e^2) = \sigma_u^2 + (n - 1)\sigma_u^2 - 2\sigma_n^2 = (n - 2)\sigma_u^2$$

An unbiased estimator of σ_u^2 should be

$$\hat{\sigma}_u^2 = \frac{\Sigma e^2}{n - 2} \tag{3-14}$$

$\hat{\sigma}_u = \sqrt{\Sigma e^2/(n - 2)}$ is called the *standard error of estimate*. [In the case of m variables, $\hat{\sigma}_u = \sqrt{\Sigma e^2/(n - m)}$.]

Testing the Significance of b

After we estimate b from sample data, we need to test whether b is significantly different from zero.

$$H_0: b = 0$$
$$H_1: b \neq 0$$

We may use t test:

$$t_0 = \frac{\hat{b} - 0}{\sqrt{\text{var}(\hat{b})}} = \frac{\hat{b}}{\hat{\sigma}_u/\sqrt{\Sigma x^2}} = \frac{\hat{b}\sqrt{\Sigma x^2}}{\hat{\sigma}_u}$$

With specified error probability α, if t_0 falls in the critical region of the t distribution of $(n - 2)$ degrees of freedom, we will reject H_0 and accept b as significant, otherwise, b is not significant. The same test may be applied to the linear correlation coefficient r. In the case of r,

$$t_0 = \frac{r\sqrt{n - 2}}{\sqrt{1 - r^2}} \qquad \text{(with } n - 2 \text{ degrees of freedom)}$$

which is identical to the t test for $\hat{b}$,

$$\frac{r\sqrt{n - 2}}{\sqrt{1 - r^2}} = \hat{b}\frac{sx}{sy}\frac{\sqrt{n - 2}}{\sqrt{1 - r^2}} = \hat{b}\frac{\sqrt{\Sigma x^2}}{\sqrt{\Sigma y^2}}\frac{\sqrt{n - 2}}{\sqrt{1 - r^2}}$$

But

$$\hat{\sigma}_u^2 = \frac{\Sigma e^2}{n - 2} = \frac{\Sigma(y - \hat{b}x)^2}{n - 2}$$

$$= \frac{\Sigma\hat{y}^2 - 2\hat{b}\Sigma xy + \hat{b}^2\Sigma x^2}{n - 2} \qquad \left(\hat{b} = \frac{\Sigma xy}{\Sigma x^2}, \quad \Sigma xy = \hat{b}\Sigma x^2\right)$$

$$= \frac{\Sigma y^2 - \hat{b}^2 \Sigma x^2}{n - 2}$$

$$= \frac{\Sigma y^2 - r^2 \Sigma y^2}{n - 2}$$

$$= \frac{\Sigma y^2 (1 - r^2)}{n - 2}$$

Thus

$$\frac{1}{\hat{\sigma}_u} = \frac{\sqrt{n - 2}}{\sqrt{\Sigma y^2} \sqrt{1 - r^2}} \quad \text{and} \quad \frac{r \sqrt{n - 2}}{\sqrt{1 - r^2}} = \frac{\hat{b} \sqrt{\Sigma x^2}}{\hat{\sigma}_u}$$

Analysis-of-Variance Test

As stated previously, analysis of variance uses F ratio for testing the significance of an estimate and F distribution may be interpreted as the ratio of the two chi-square distributions.

Since $(\hat{b} - b)/\sqrt{\text{var}(\hat{b})}$ follows standard normal distribution, its square $[(\hat{b} - b)^2 \Sigma x^2]/\sigma_u^2$ has the χ^2 distribution with 1 degree of freedom. And $\Sigma e^2/\sigma_u^2$ has the χ^2 distribution with $n - 2$ degrees of freedom. Thus the analysis of variance test for the hypothesis $b = 0$ is

$$F = \frac{\hat{b}^2 \Sigma x^2}{\Sigma e^2/(n - 2)}$$

where the total variation of Y is Σy^2, the variation explained by X is $\Sigma \hat{y}^2 = \hat{b}^2 \Sigma x^2$ and the residual variation is Σe^2.

Source of Variation	Sum of Squares	Degrees of Freedom	Mean Square
X	$\Sigma \hat{y}^2 = \hat{b}^2 \Sigma x^2$	1	$\Sigma \hat{y}^2$
Residual	Σe^2	$n - 2$	$\Sigma e^2/(n - 2)$
Total	$\Sigma y^2 = \Sigma \hat{y}^2 + \Sigma e^2$	$n - 1$	

With specified α, if F_0 falls in the critical region of the F distribution with degrees of freedom $(1, n - 2)$, we will reject the hypothesis $b = 0$ and accept the hypothesis that b is significantly different from zero, otherwise, accept the hypothesis that b is not significant.

Maximum-Likelihood Estimators

The above interval estimates of a and b using the least-squares method are based on the assumption that the X_i values are fixed. In practical applications, however, X_i may also be a random variable.

Let $f(X_i)$, $i = 1, 2, \ldots, n$ be the probability distribution of X_i, and assume that the conditional probability distribution of the Y_i given X_i

are normal and independent with expected values $(a + bX_i)$ and constant variance σ_u^2. Then the joint distribution of X_i and Y_i can be expressed as

$$L = f(X_i) \cdots f(X_n) \cdots f(Y_1 \mid X_1) \cdots f(Y_n \mid X_n)$$

$$= f(X_1) \cdots f(X_n) \cdot \frac{1}{(2\pi\sigma_u^2)^{n/2}}$$

$$\cdot \exp\left[-\frac{1}{2\sigma_u^2} \Sigma(Y_i - a - bX_i)^2\right] \qquad (3\text{-}15)$$

Since the logarithm of a function has the maximum value at the same position as the original function, we take the logarithm of L, which is

$$\log L = \log f(X_1) + \cdots + \log f(X_n) - \left(\frac{n}{2}\right)\log 2\pi$$

$$- \left(\frac{n}{2}\right)\log \sigma_u^2 - \frac{1}{2\sigma_u^2} \Sigma(Y_i - a - bX_i)^2$$

Partially differentiating $\log L$ with respect to a, b, and σ_u^2 gives

$$\frac{\partial \log L}{\partial a} = \frac{1}{\sigma_u^2} \Sigma(Y_i - a - bX_i)$$

$$\frac{\partial \log L}{\partial b} = \frac{1}{\sigma_u^2} \Sigma X_i(Y_i - a - bX_i)$$

$$\frac{\partial \log L}{\partial \sigma_u^2} = -\frac{n}{2\sigma_u^2} + \frac{1}{2\sigma_u^4} \Sigma(Y_i - a - bX_i)^2$$

Equating them to zero, we obtain the maximum-likelihood estimators of a and b:

$$\hat{b} = \frac{n\Sigma XY - (\Sigma X)(\Sigma Y)}{n\Sigma X^2 - (\Sigma X)^2} \quad \text{or} \quad \frac{\Sigma xy}{\Sigma x^2} \qquad (3\text{-}16)$$

$$\hat{a} = \bar{Y} - \hat{b}\bar{X} \qquad (3\text{-}17)$$

$$\hat{\sigma}_u^2 = \frac{1}{n} \Sigma(Y_i - \hat{a} - \hat{b}X_i)^2 \qquad (3\text{-}18)$$

They are the same as the least-squares estimators.

Prediction. Given an X value, X_0, we want to predict the Y value. The starting point would be the point on the regression line:

$$\hat{Y}_0 = \hat{a} + \hat{b}X_0$$

However, prediction involves uncertainty, and we will obtain more information from an interval estimate with a specified level of confidence. Therefore we need to know the variance of $\hat{Y}_0$.

$$\text{var}(\hat{Y}_0) = E[\hat{Y}_0 - E(\hat{Y}_0 \mid X_0)]^2$$

$$= E[\hat{a} + \hat{b}X_0 - (a + bX_0)]^2$$

$$= E[(\hat{a} - a) + (\hat{b} - b) X_0]^2$$

$$= \text{var}(\hat{a}) + X_0^2 \text{var}(\hat{b}) + 2X_0 \text{cov}(\hat{a}, \hat{b})$$

$$= \frac{\Sigma X^2}{n\Sigma x^2} \sigma_u^2 + X_0^2 \frac{\sigma_u^2}{\Sigma x^2} - 2X_0 \frac{\bar{X}}{\Sigma x^2} \sigma_u^2$$

$$= \sigma_u^2 \left[\frac{\Sigma(x + \bar{X})^2}{n\Sigma x^2} + \frac{X_0^2}{\Sigma x^2} - 2 \frac{X_0 \bar{X}}{\Sigma x^2} \right]$$

$$= \sigma_u^2 \left[\frac{1}{n} + \frac{\bar{X}^2}{\Sigma x^2} + \frac{X_0^2}{\Sigma x^2} - \frac{2X_0 \bar{X}}{\Sigma x^2} \right]$$

$$= \sigma_u^2 \left[\frac{1}{n} + \frac{(X_0 - \bar{X})^2}{\Sigma x^2} \right] \tag{3-19}$$

Using t distribution with $n - 2$ degrees of freedom, we have the interval estimate of $\hat{Y}_0$, which is

$$(\hat{a} + \hat{b}X_0) \pm t_{\alpha/2}\hat{\sigma}_u \sqrt{\frac{1}{n} + \frac{(X_0 - \bar{X})^2}{\Sigma x^2}} \tag{3-20}$$

If we want to predict the actual Y value instead of the Y value on the regression line, then the variance of Y_0 will be

$$\text{var}(Y_0) = E(Y_0 - \hat{Y}_0)^2$$

$$= E[(a + bX_0 + u_0) - (\hat{a} + \hat{b}X_0)]^2$$

$$= E(u_0^2) + E[(\hat{a} - a) + (\hat{b} - b)\bar{X}_0]^2$$

$$= \sigma_u^2 \left[1 + \frac{1}{n} + \frac{(X_0 - \bar{X})^2}{\Sigma x^2} \right] \tag{3-21}$$

Thus the interval estimate of Y_0 is

$$(\hat{a} + \hat{b}X_0) \pm t_{\alpha/2}\hat{\sigma}_u \sqrt{1 + \frac{1}{n} + \frac{(X_0 - \bar{X})^2}{\Sigma x^2}} \tag{3-22}$$

Bayesian Estimates of Parameters

Based on the Bayes' formula presented in Chapter 1, another approach is developed for estimating the value of the parameters.

Suppose a relationship represented by

$$Y = bX + u$$

and the error term is assumed to follow a normal distribution

$$P(u) \sim N(0, \sigma_u^2) \quad \text{or} \quad \frac{1}{(\sqrt{2\pi}\,\sigma_u)^n} e^{-(\Sigma u^2/2\sigma_u^2)}$$

Also, the a priori distribution of the parameter, $P(b)$, is known. According to the multiplication theorem of probability,

$$P(Y, b) = P(b) \cdot P(Y \mid b)$$

Since $P(u)$ is normally distributed, $P(Y \mid b)$ must also be normally distributed and may be estimated from sample observations of Y and X, $[1/(\sqrt{2\pi}\,\sigma_y)^n]\,e^{-[\Sigma(y-bx)^2/2\sigma_y^2]}$. After the joint distribution of $P(Y, b)$ is determined, the marginal distribution of Y may be found by the following, $P(Y) = \int P(Y, b)\,db$ (integrated over the range within which b may take possible values). Then the a posteriori distributions of b can be obtained conditional to Y,

$$P(b \mid Y) = \frac{P(Y, b)}{P(Y)}$$

From the distribution of b given empirical observations of Y, we may select the Baysian estimate of b. $\hat{b}$ may be the mean of the distribution, if we use the criteria of minimizing the variance of $\hat{b}$ estimates.

3-2. THREE-VARIABLE LINEAR-REGRESSION MODEL

Let Y be a variable whose value is determined by two other variables X_2 and X_3. If the relationship can be approximated by a linear plane, it can be expressed by the following equation:

$$\hat{Y} = b_1 + b_2 X_2 + b_3 X_3$$

where $\hat{Y}$ is used because the true values of X_2, X_3, and Y may not lie on the plane. We use Y to denote the true value and write

$$Y = b_1 + b_2 X_2 + b_3 X_3 + u$$

where u is the difference between Y and $\hat{Y}$.

Now in general we cannot observe all values of X_2, X_3, and Y, but can observe only a finite number of samples. From the sample values we may apply methods such as least squares to estimate the parameters of the equation.

Again, the true sample values of X_2, X_3, and Y may not fall on the estimated regression plane; thus we write

$$Y = \hat{Y} + e$$
$$= \hat{b}_1 + \hat{b}_2 X_2 + \hat{b}_3 X_3 + e$$

where e is the difference between the observed value of Y and the Y value on the estimated regression plane. If we use the deviations of X_2, X_3, and Y from their respective means, it can be expressed as

$$y = \hat{y} + e$$
$$= \hat{b}_2 x_2 + \hat{b}_3 x_3 + e \tag{3-23}$$

The Least-Squares Estimators

Suppose we take n observations on X_2, X_3, and Y and denote them as

$$(X_{21}, X_{31}, Y_1) \cdots (X_{2n}, X_{3n}, Y_n)$$

Then

$$e_i = Y_i - \hat{Y}_i (i = 1, 2, \ldots, n)$$
$$e_i^2 = (Y_i - \hat{Y}_i)^2$$
$$= (Y_i - \hat{b}_1 - \hat{b}_2 X_{2i} - \hat{b}_3 X_{3i})^2$$

The partial derivatives with respect to $\hat{b}_1$, $\hat{b}_2$, and $\hat{b}_3$ are

$$\frac{\partial}{\partial \hat{b}_1} \Sigma e_i^2 = -2\Sigma (Y_i - \hat{b}_1 - \hat{b}_2 X_{2i} - \hat{b}_3 X_{3i})$$

$$\frac{\partial}{\partial \hat{b}_2} \Sigma e_i^2 = -2\Sigma X_{2i}(Y_i - \hat{b}_1 - \hat{b}_2 X_{2i} - \hat{b}_3 X_{3i})$$

$$\frac{\partial}{\partial \hat{b}_3} \Sigma e_i^2 = -2\Sigma X_{3i}(Y_i - \hat{b}_1 - \hat{b}_2 X_{2i} - \hat{b}_3 X_{3i})$$

Equating these to zero and letting $a_{1.23}$, $b_{12.3}$, and $b_{13.2}$ be the least-squares estimates of $\hat{b}_1$, $\hat{b}_2$, and $\hat{b}_3$ respectively, we obtain

$$\Sigma Y_i = n a_{1.23} + b_{12.3} \Sigma X_{2i} + b_{13.2} \Sigma X_{3i}$$
$$\Sigma X_{2i} Y_i = a_{1.23} \Sigma X_{2i} + b_{12.3} \Sigma X_{2i}^2 + b_{13.2} \Sigma X_{2i} X_{3i}$$
$$\Sigma X_{3i} Y_i = a_{1.23} \Sigma X_{3i} + b_{12.3} \Sigma X_{2i} X_{3i} + b_{13.2} \Sigma X_{3i}^2$$

Solving for $b_{12.3}$, $b_{13.2}$, $a_{1.23}$ and using deviation terms of X_2, X_3, and Y,

$$(x_2 = X_2 - \overline{X}_2 \quad x_3 = X_3 - \overline{X}_3 \quad y = Y - \overline{Y})$$

we obtain

$$b_{12.3} = \frac{(\Sigma x_2 y)(\Sigma x_3^2) - (\Sigma x_3 y)(\Sigma x_2 x_3)}{(\Sigma x_2^2)(\Sigma x_3^2) - (\Sigma x_2 x_3)^2} \tag{3-24}$$

$$b_{13.2} = \frac{(\Sigma x_3 y)(\Sigma x_2^2) - (\Sigma x_2 y)(\Sigma x_2 x_3)}{(\Sigma x_2^2)(\Sigma x_3^2) - (\Sigma x_2 x_3)^2} \tag{3-25}$$

$$a_{1.23} = \overline{Y} - b_{12.3} \overline{X}_2 - b_{13.2} \overline{X}_3 \tag{3-26}$$

Since the formula for the simple correlation coefficient between two variables is

$$r = \frac{\Sigma xy}{n s_x s_y}$$

we may write

$$r_{12} = \frac{\Sigma x_2 y}{n s_1 s_2} \qquad r_{13} = \frac{\Sigma x_3 y}{n s_1 s_3} \qquad r_{23} = \frac{\Sigma x_2 x_3}{n s_2 s_3}$$

and Eqs. 3-24 and 3-25 may be written as

$$b_{12.3} = \frac{r_{12} - r_{13} r_{23}}{1 - r_{23}^2} \frac{s_1}{s_2} \tag{3-27}$$

$$b_{13.2} = \frac{r_{13} - r_{12} r_{23}}{1 - r_{23}^2} \frac{s_1}{s_3} \tag{3-28}$$

The variances of the estimators are

$$\text{var}(b_{12.3}) = \frac{\Sigma x_{1.23}^2}{(n-3)\Sigma x_{23}^2}$$

$$\text{var}(b_{13.2}) = \frac{\Sigma x_{1.23}^2}{(n-3)\Sigma x_{32}^2}$$

where

$$x_{1.23} = y - b_{12.3}x_2 - b_{13.2}x_3$$

$$x_{23} = x_2 - \hat{b}_{23}x_3$$

and

$$x_{32} = x_3 - \hat{b}_{32}x_2$$

Test the significance of the relationship between the variables Y, X_2, and X_3.

F test:

Source of Variation	Degrees of Freedom	Mean Square
Explained by X_2 and X_3 $(b_{12.3}\Sigma x_2 y + b_{13.2}\Sigma x_3 y)$	2	$(b_{12.3}\Sigma x_2 y + b_{13.2}\Sigma x_3 y)/2$
Residual or unexplained (Σe^2)	$n-3$	$\Sigma e^2/(n-3)$
Total variation of $Y(\Sigma y^2)$	$n-1$	

The F ratio is

$$F = \frac{(b_{12.3}\Sigma x_2 y + b_{13.2}\Sigma x_3 y)/2}{\Sigma e^2/(n-3)} \qquad (\text{d.f.} = 2, n-3)$$

Compare the F ratio with the critical value found in the F-distribution table. If the F ratio is greater than the critical value, we conclude that a significant relationship exists between the three variables.

Stepwise F tests:

Source of Variation	Degrees of Freedom	Mean Square
Explained by $X_2(\hat{b}_2\Sigma x_2 y)$	1	$\hat{b}_2\Sigma x_2 y[\hat{b}_2 = (\Sigma x_2 y/\Sigma x_2^2)]$
Addition of X_3	1	$(b_{12.3}\Sigma x_2 y + b_{13.2}\Sigma x_3 y)$ $- (\hat{b}_2\Sigma x_2 y)$
Explained by X_2 and X_3 $(b_{12.3}\Sigma x_2 y + b_{13.2}\Sigma x_3 y)$	2	$(b_{12.3}\Sigma x_2 y + b_{13.2}\Sigma x_3 y)/2$
Residual (Σe^2)	$n-3$	$\Sigma e^2/(n-3)$
Total variation of $Y(\Sigma y^2)$	$n-1$	

The significance of the additional X_3 effect is tested by

$$F = \frac{(b_{12.3}\Sigma x_2 y + b_{13.2}\Sigma x_3 y) - (\hat{b}_2 \Sigma x_2 y)}{\Sigma e^2/(n - 3)} \quad (\text{d.f.} = 1, n - 3)$$

or

Source of Variation	Degrees of Freedom	Mean Square
Explained by X_3 $(\hat{b}_3 \Sigma x_3 y)$	1	$\hat{b}_3 \Sigma x_3 y[\hat{b}_3 = (\Sigma x_3 y/\Sigma x_3^2)]$
Addition of X_2	1	$(b_{12.3}\Sigma x_2 y + b_{13.2}\Sigma x_3 y)$ $- (\hat{b}_3 \Sigma x_3 y)$
Explained by X_2 and X_3 $(b_{12.3}\Sigma x_2 y + b_{13.2}\Sigma x_3 y)$	2	$(b_{12.3}\Sigma x_2 y + b_{13.2}\Sigma x_3 y)/2$
Residual (Σe^2)	$n - 3$	$\Sigma e^2/(n - 3)$
Total variation of Y (Σy^2)	$n - 1$	

The significance of the additional X_2 effect is tested by

$$F = \frac{(b_{12.3}\Sigma x_2 y + b_{13.2}\Sigma x_3 y) - (\hat{b}_3 \Sigma x_3 y)}{\Sigma e^2/(n - 3)} \quad (\text{d.f.} = 1, n - 3)$$

t test: The net effect of X_2 and X_3 can also be tested by t values:

$$t_2 = \frac{b_{12.3}}{\sqrt{\dfrac{\Sigma e^2}{n - 3}} \sqrt{a_{22}}} \quad (\text{d.f.} = n - 3)$$

where $a_{22} = \Sigma x_3^2/[\Sigma x_2^2 \Sigma x_3^2 - (\Sigma x_2 x_3)^2]$ and

$$t_3 = \frac{b_{13.2}}{\sqrt{\dfrac{\Sigma e^2}{n - 3}} \sqrt{a_{33}}} \quad (\text{d.f.} = n - 3)$$

where $a_{33} = \Sigma x_2^2/[\Sigma x_2^2 \Sigma x_3^2 - (\Sigma x_2 x_3)^2]$. If t_2 and t_3 are greater than the respective critical values found in the t-distribution table, the regression coefficients $b_{12.3}$ and $b_{13.2}$ are accepted as significantly different from zero, which indicates significant relationships exist between X_2 and Y, X_3, and Y.

The Coefficient of Multiple Correlation

To measure the linear correlation between X_2, X_3, and Y we use the coefficient of multiple correlation $R_{1.23}$. The square of $R_{1.23}$ is called the *coefficient of determination*, $R_{1.23}^2$. It is the ratio of the explained variation and the total variation of Y.

$$R_{1.23}^2 = \frac{\Sigma \hat{y}^2}{\Sigma y^2}$$

or

$$= 1 - \frac{\Sigma e^2}{\Sigma y^2}$$

Since

$$\Sigma e^2 = \Sigma e(y - \hat{b}_2 x_2 - \hat{b}_3 x_3)$$
$$= \Sigma ey - \hat{b}_2 \Sigma ex_2 - \hat{b}_3 \Sigma ex_3$$

and in the least-squares process,

$$\frac{\partial \Sigma e_i^2}{\partial \hat{b}_2} = -\Sigma e_i x_2 = 0 \qquad \frac{\partial \Sigma e_i^2}{\partial \hat{b}_3} = -\Sigma e_i x_3 = 0$$

Thus

$$\Sigma ex_2 = 0 \qquad \text{and} \qquad \Sigma ex_3 = 0$$

Therefore

$$\Sigma e^2 = \Sigma ey$$
$$= \Sigma(y - b_{12.3} x_2 - b_{13.2} x_3) y$$
$$= \Sigma y^2 - b_{12.3} \Sigma x_2 y - b_{13.2} \Sigma x_3 y$$

We can then write

$$R_{1.23}^2 = 1 - \frac{\Sigma e^2}{\Sigma y^2}$$

$$= 1 - \frac{\Sigma y^2 - b_{12.3} \Sigma x_2 y - b_{13.2} \Sigma x_3 y}{\Sigma y^2}$$

$$= \frac{b_{12.3} \Sigma x_2 y + b_{13.2} \Sigma x_3 y}{\Sigma y^2} \qquad (3\text{-}29)$$

or, using simple correlation coefficients,

$$R_{1.23}^2 = \frac{r_{12}^2 + r_{13}^2 - 2r_{12}r_{13}r_{23}}{1 - r_{23}^2} \qquad (3\text{-}30)$$

Testing the significance of $R_{1.23}^2$.

Whether $R_{1.23}^2$ is significantly different from zero may be tested by the F ratio,

$$F = \frac{R_{1.23}^2 (n - m)}{(1 - R_{1.23}^2)(m - 1)} \qquad \begin{array}{l} [(m - 1) \text{ degrees of freedom}] \\ [(n - m) \text{ degrees of freedom}] \end{array}$$

where n is the sample size and m is the number of variables. In the case of three-variable model,

$$F(2, n - 3) = \frac{R_{1.23}^2 (n - 3)}{(1 - R_{1.23}^2)(3 - 1)}$$

If F is in the critical region of the F distribution with degrees of freedom $(2, n - 3)$, the null hypothesis that $R_{1.23}^2$ is equal to zero will be rejected and we may accept the hypothesis that the multiple correlation is significant.

Partial-Correlation Coefficients

We may ask whether an observed correlation between Y and X_2 is primarily due to the fact that each is influenced by the third variable X_3, or whether there is a significant net correlation between Y and X_2. Thus we need to remove the influence of X_3 from both Y and X_2 and see what correlation exists between the residuals. We call this measure the *partial-correlation coefficient* between Y and X_2 with X_3 held constant, and use the symbol $r_{12.3}$. The square of $r_{12.3}$, written as $(r_{12.3}^2)$, may be defined as the percent of variation in Y unexplained by X_3 that can be explained by adding X_2 to the model.

Let the linear regression of Y on X_3 be expressed as

$$Y_i = a_{13} + b_{13}X_{3i} + v_i$$

and the linear regression of X_2 on X_3 as

$$X_{2i} = a_{23} + b_{23}X_{3i} + w_i$$

Using deviation terms,

$$v = y - b_{13}x_3$$
$$w = x_2 - b_{23}x_3$$

The partial-correlation between Y and X_2 with X_3 held constant then can be found by the following:

$$r_{12.3} = \frac{\Sigma vw}{\sqrt{\Sigma v^2} \cdot \sqrt{\Sigma w^2}}$$

$$= \frac{\Sigma(y - b_{13}x_3) \cdot (x_2 - b_{23}x_3)}{\sqrt{\Sigma(y - b_{13}x_3)^2} \cdot \sqrt{\Sigma(x_2 - b_{23}x_3)^2}}$$

$$= \Sigma x_2 y - b_{13}\Sigma x_2 x_3 - b_{23}\Sigma x_3 y + b_{13}b_{23}\Sigma x_3^2 \Big/$$
$$\sqrt{\Sigma y^2 - 2b_{13}\Sigma x_3 y + b_{13}^2 \Sigma x_3^2}$$
$$\cdot \sqrt{\Sigma x_2^2 - 2b_{23}\Sigma x_2 x_3 + b_{23}^2 \Sigma x_3^2}$$

$$= ns_1 s_2 r_{12} - \left(r_{13}\frac{s_1}{s_3}\right) ns_2 s_3 r_{23} - \left(r_{23}\frac{s_2}{s_3}\right) ns_1 s_3 r_{13}$$
$$+ r_{13}\frac{s_1}{s_3} \cdot r_{23}\frac{s_2}{s_3} \cdot ns_3^2 \Big/$$
$$\sqrt{ns_1^2 - 2\left(r_{13}\frac{s_1}{s_3}\right) ns_3 s_1 r_{13} + \left(r_{13}\frac{s_1}{s_3}\right)^2 ns_3^2}$$
$$\cdot \sqrt{ns_2^2 - 2\left(r_{23}\frac{s_2}{s_3}\right) ns_2 s_3 r_{23} + \left(r_{23}\frac{s_2}{s_3}\right)^2 ns_3^2}$$

$$= \frac{n s_1 s_2 (r_{12} - r_{13} r_{23})}{n s_1 s_2 \sqrt{1 - r_{13}^2} \cdot \sqrt{1 - r_{23}^2}}$$

$$= \frac{r_{12} - r_{13} r_{23}}{\sqrt{1 - r_{13}^2} \cdot \sqrt{1 - r_{23}^2}} \tag{3-31}$$

Similarly,

$$r_{13.2} = \frac{r_{13} - r_{12} r_{23}}{\sqrt{1 - r_{12}^2} \cdot \sqrt{1 - r_{23}^2}} \tag{3-32}$$

$$r_{23.1} = \frac{r_{23} - r_{12} r_{13}}{\sqrt{1 - r_{12}^2} \cdot \sqrt{1 - r_{13}^2}} \tag{3-33}$$

This three-variable model can be further extended to linear models with more than three variables. However, since the computation will be more complicated when the number of variables increases, the use of matrix notation is preferable.

3-3. LINEAR-REGRESSION MODEL IN MATRIX FORM

The normal equations of the three-variable linear model are

$$b_{12.3} \Sigma x_2^2 + b_{13.2} \Sigma x_2 x_3 = \Sigma x_2 y$$
$$b_{12.3} \Sigma x_2 x_3 + b_{13.2} \Sigma x_3^2 = \Sigma x_3 y$$

and are expressed in matrix form as

$$\begin{bmatrix} \Sigma x_2^2 & \Sigma x_2 x_3 \\ \Sigma x_2 x_3 & \Sigma x_3^2 \end{bmatrix} \begin{bmatrix} b_{12.3} \\ b_{13.2} \end{bmatrix} = \begin{bmatrix} \Sigma x_2 y \\ \Sigma x_3 y \end{bmatrix}$$

or in general terms as

$$X^T X \hat{B} = X^T Y$$

where

$$X^T = \begin{bmatrix} x_{21} & x_{22} & \cdots & x_{2n} \\ x_{31} & x_{32} & \cdots & x_{3n} \\ \vdots & & & \\ x_{m1} & x_{m2} & \cdots & x_{mn} \end{bmatrix}$$

$$X = \begin{bmatrix} x_{21} & x_{31} & \cdots & x_{m1} \\ x_{22} & x_{32} & \cdots & x_{m2} \\ \vdots & & & \\ x_{2n} & x_{3n} & \cdots & x_{mn} \end{bmatrix}$$

$$\hat{B} = \begin{bmatrix} b_{12.34\ldots m} \\ b_{13.24\ldots m} \\ \vdots \\ b_{1m.23\ldots(m-1)} \end{bmatrix}$$

and

$$Y = \begin{bmatrix} y_1 \\ y_2 \\ \vdots \\ y_n \end{bmatrix}$$

In the foregoing, n is the number of observations on each variable, and m is the number of variables (1 explanatory variable and $(m - 1)$ explained variables). In order to solve the normal equations to obtain estimators of the coefficients, n must be equal to or greater than m. Continue with the matrix notation.

$$\hat{B} = (X^T X)^{-1}(X^T Y) \tag{3-34}$$

Now

$$Y = X\hat{B} + e$$

where e is a vector of the error terms:

$$e = Y - X\hat{B}$$
$$e^T e = (Y - X\hat{B})^T(Y - X\hat{B})$$
$$= Y^T Y - \hat{B}^T X^T Y$$

The total variation in Y is $Y^T Y$, and the residual or unexplained variation is

$$e^T e = Y^T Y - \hat{B}^T X^T Y$$

Thus the variation explained by $X_2, \ldots, X_m$ is $\hat{B}^T X^T Y$.

The coefficient of determination is expressed by the ratio of the explained variation and the total variation which is

$$R^2 = \frac{\hat{B}^T X^T Y}{Y^T Y} \tag{3-35}$$

The significance of the kth regression coefficient $\hat{b}_k$ may be tested by

$$t_k = \frac{\hat{b}_k}{\sqrt{\sum_{i=1}^{n} e_i^2/(n - m)} \sqrt{a_{kk}}} \qquad (n - m) \text{ degrees of freedom}$$

where a_{kk} is the kth element in the main diagonal of $(X^T X)^{-1}$.†   The

†An extension of two variables case

$$t = \frac{\hat{b}}{\sqrt{\operatorname{var}(b)}} = \frac{\hat{b}}{\hat{\sigma}_u / \sqrt{\Sigma x^2}} = \frac{\hat{b}}{\sqrt{\Sigma e^2/(n - 2)} \sqrt{(\Sigma x^2)^{-1}}}$$

significance of R^2 may be tested by

$$F = \frac{R^2(n - m)}{(1 - R^2)(m - 1)} \qquad (m - 1, n - m) \text{ degrees of freedom}$$

Analysis of variance:

Source of Variation	Sum of Squares	Degrees of Freedom	Mean Square
$X_2, X_3, \ldots, X_m$	$\hat{B}^T X^T Y = Y^T Y \cdot R^2$	$m - 1$	$\hat{B}^T X^T Y/(m - 1)$
Residual	$e^T e = Y^T Y(1 - R^2)$	$n - m$	$e^T e/(n - m)$
Total	$Y^T Y$	$n - 1$	

Generalized Least Squares

The least-squares estimate of parameters of a linear equation presented above is based on the following assumption:

$$E(U) = 0$$

$$E(UU^T) = \sigma_\mu^2 I = \begin{bmatrix} \sigma_\mu^2 & 0 & \cdots & 0 \\ 0 & \sigma_\mu^2 & & \\ 0 & & & \sigma_\mu^2 \end{bmatrix}$$

Which assumes that the error term μ_i have zero mean and constant variance σ_μ^2. The off-diagonal terms, $E(u_i u_j) = 0$ for $i \neq j$, indicate that the u_i values are pairwise uncorrelated. However, when $E(UU^T) = V \neq \sigma_\mu^2 I$, that is $\{E(u_i^2)$ is not constant, $E(u_i u_j)$ does not equal to zero when $i \neq j\}$, then the least-squares method will not give the least variance estimate. The revision of the ordinary least-squares estimation method is called *generalized least squares*. It may be applied to cases with serially correlated disturbance terms (u_i). Assume,

$$Y = XB + U$$

and let the new estimator,

$$\hat{B} = AY \quad (AY \text{ are linear estimates of } B),$$

$$V = E(UU^T) = \begin{bmatrix} E(u_1^2) & E(u_1 u_2) & '' \\ E(u_2 u_1) & E(u_2^2) & '' \\ \vdots & & \\ '' & '' & E(u_n^2) \end{bmatrix} \quad \begin{array}{l} \text{is the variance and} \\ \text{covariance matrix} \end{array}$$

If $\hat{B}$ is unbiased,

$$E(\hat{B}) = E(AY) = B$$

However,

$$E(AY) = E\{A(XB + U)\}$$

$$= AE(XB) + AE(U)$$

$$= AXB$$

Thus for $E(\hat{B}) = B$, $AX = I$ (condition for unbiasedness).

Now for $\hat{B}$ to be an efficient estimator (least variance), the variance of $\hat{B}$ has to be minimized:

$$E\{(\hat{B} - B)^T(\hat{B} - B)\} = E\{(AY - B)^T(AY - B)\}$$

$$= E\{(AXB + AU - B)^T(AXB + AU - B)\} = E\{(AU)^T(AU)\}$$

$$= E(U^T A^T A U) = \text{tr}(A^T A U U^T) \quad \text{or} \quad \text{tr}(A^T A V)$$

minimize $\{\text{tr}(A^T A V) - \lambda(AX - I)\}$, where λ is a matrix of Lagrange multipliers.

Equating the partial derivative with respect to A to zero, we obtain the minimum condition,

$$2AV = \lambda X^T$$

Postmultiplied by $V^{-1}X$,

$$2AVV^{-1}X = \lambda X^T V^{-1} X \quad \text{or} \quad 2AX = \lambda X^T V^{-1} X$$

Since $AX = I$,

$$\lambda = 2(X^T V^{-1} X)^{-1}$$

Thus

$$AV = (X^T V^{-1} X)^{-1} X^T \quad \text{or} \quad A = (X^T V^{-1} X) X^T V^{-1}$$

and the unbiased and efficient estimate is

$$\hat{B} = AY = (X^T V^{-1} X)^{-1} X^T V^{-1} Y$$

which applies to general situations where the variance-covariance matrix may assume any value.

EXAMPLES: (The sample values of the variables are arbitrary and are only for illustrating the computational procedure):

TWO-VARIABLE LINEAR REGRESSION MODEL

	Y	X	XY	y	x	xy	X^2	y^2	x^2	bx	$(y - \hat{b}x)^2$
1	100	15	1,500	−42.5	−30.5	1,296.25	225	1,806.25	930.25	−51.545	81.812
2	110	27	2,970	−32.5	−18.5	601.25	729	1,056.25	342.25	−31.265	1.525
3	115	32	3,680	−27.5	−13.5	371.25	1,024	756.25	182.25	−22.815	21.949
4	120	35	4,200	−22.5	−10.5	236.25	1,225	506.25	110.25	−17.745	22.610
5	130	40	5,200	−12.5	− 5.5	68.75	1,600	156.25	30.25	− 9,295	10.272
6	145	46	6,670	2.5	0.5	1.25	2,116	6.25	0.25	.845	2.739
7	150	55	8,250	7.5	9.5	71.25	3,025	56.25	90.25	16.055	73.188
8	170	60	10,200	27.5	14.5	348.75	3,600	756.25	210.25	24.505	8.970
9	185	65	12,025	42.5	19.5	828.75	4,225	1,806.25	380.25	32.955	91.107
10	200	80	16,000	57.5	34.5	1,983.75	6,400	3,306.25	1,190.25	58.305	0.648

ΣY	ΣX	ΣXY			Σxy	ΣX^2	Σy^2	Σx^2		Σe^2
1,425	455	70,695			5,857.5	24,169	10,212.5	3,466.5		314.82

Solving the normal equations for $\hat{a}$ and $\hat{b}$,

$$\Sigma Y = n\hat{a} + \hat{b}\Sigma X$$
$$\Sigma XY = \hat{a}\Sigma X + \hat{b}\Sigma X^2$$

or

$$\hat{b} = \frac{\Sigma xy}{\Sigma x^2} = \frac{5,857.5}{3,466.5} = 1.69$$

$$\hat{a} = \bar{Y} - \hat{b}\bar{X} = 142.5 - (1.69)(45.5) = 65.61$$

where

$$\bar{Y} = \frac{\Sigma Y}{n} = 142.5$$

$$\bar{X} = \frac{\Sigma X}{n} = 45.5$$

$$x = X - \bar{X}$$

and

$$y = Y - \bar{Y}$$

The equation of the regression line is

$$\hat{Y} = \hat{a} + \hat{b}X$$
$$= 65.61 + 1.69X$$

The correlation coefficient is given by

$$r = \sqrt{1 - \frac{\Sigma e^2}{\Sigma y^2}} = \sqrt{1 - \frac{314.82}{10,212.5}} = .984$$

where

$$e^2 = (y - \hat{b}x)^2$$

or

$$r = \frac{\Sigma xy}{n s_x s_y} = \frac{5,857.5}{10(18.619)(31.957)} = .984$$

where

$$s_x = \sqrt{\frac{\Sigma x^2}{n}} = \sqrt{\frac{3,466.5}{10}} = 18.619$$

$$s_y = \sqrt{\frac{\Sigma y^2}{n}} = \sqrt{\frac{10,212.5}{10}} = 31.957$$

The 95 percent interval estimates of b and a are

$$\hat{b} \pm t_{0.025} \frac{\hat{\sigma}_u}{\sqrt{\Sigma x^2}} = 1.69 \pm 2.3 \frac{(6.2273)}{\sqrt{3,466.5}}$$

$$= 1.69 \pm .24495$$

$$\hat{a} \pm t_{0.025} \sqrt{\frac{\Sigma X^2}{n\Sigma x^2}} \, \hat{\sigma}_u = 65.61 \pm (2.3) \sqrt{\frac{24{,}169}{10 \times 3{,}466.5}} \quad (6.273)$$

$$= 65.61 \pm 12.047 \quad (\alpha = 0.05, \text{ d.f.} = 8)$$

where

$$\hat{\sigma}_u = \sqrt{\frac{\Sigma e^2}{n-2}} = \sqrt{\frac{314.82}{8}} = 6.273$$

Testing the significance of the correlation:

$$t_0 = \frac{r\sqrt{n-2}}{\sqrt{1-r^2}} = \frac{(.984)(8)}{\sqrt{1-.968}}$$

$$= 43.7 \qquad \text{It is significant.}$$

Given $X_0 = 90$, the predicted value of Y_0 with 95 percent confidence is

$$\hat{Y}_0 = (\hat{a} + \hat{b}X_0) \pm t_{0.025}\hat{\sigma}_u \sqrt{1 + \frac{1}{n} + \frac{(X_0 - \overline{X})^2}{\Sigma x^2}}$$

$$= 65.61 + (1.69)(90) \pm (2.3)(6.273) \sqrt{1 + \frac{1}{10} + \frac{(90 - 45.5)^2}{3{,}466.5}}$$

$$= 217.71 \pm 18.63$$

THREE-VARIABLE LINEAR-REGRESSION MODEL

	Y	X_2	X_3	y	x_2	x_3	y^2	x_2^2	x_3^2	$x_2 y$	$x_3 y$	$x_2 x_3$
1	100	15	8	−42.5	−30.5	−21	1,806.25	930.25	441	1,296.25	892.5	640.5
2	110	27	10	−32.5	−18.5	−19	1,056.25	342,25	361	601.25	617.5	351.5
3	115	32	12	−27.5	−13.5	−17	756.25	182.25	289	371.25	467.5	229.5
4	120	35	15	−22.5	−10.5	−14	506.25	110.25	196	236.25	315.0	147.0
5	130	40	20	−12.5	− 5.5	− 9	156.25	30.25	81	68.75	112.5	49.5
6	145	46	30	2.5	0.5	1	6.25	0.25	1	1.25	2.5	0.5
7	150	55	35	7.5	9.5	6	56.25	90.25	36	71.25	45.0	57.0
8	170	60	48	27.5	14.5	19	756.25	210.25	361	398.75	522.5	275.5
9	185	65	52	42.5	19.5	23	1,806.25	380.25	529	828.75	977.5	448.5
10	200	80	60	57.5	34.5	31	3,306.25	1,190.25	961	1,983.75	1,782.5	1,069.5

	ΣY	ΣX_2	ΣX_3				Σy^2	Σx_2^2	Σx_3^2	$\Sigma x_2 y$	$\Sigma x_3 y$	$\Sigma x_2 x_3$
	1,425	455	290				10,212.5	3,466.5	3,256	5,857.5	5,735.0	3,269.0

Solving the normal equations for $a_{1.23}$, $b_{12.3}$, and $b_{13.2}$,

$$b_{12.3}\,\Sigma x_2^2 + b_{13.2}\,\Sigma x_2 x_3 = \Sigma x_2 y$$

$$b_{12.3}\,\Sigma x_2 x_3 + b_{13.2}\,\Sigma x_3^2 = \Sigma x_3 y$$

$$(3{,}466.5)\,b_{12.3} + (3{,}269)\,b_{13.2} = 5{,}857.5$$

$$(3{,}269)\,b_{12.3} + (3{,}256)\,b_{13.2} = 5{,}735$$

$$b_{12.3} = 0.54 \qquad b_{13.2} = 1.22$$

and

$$a_{1.23} = \overline{Y} - b_{12.3}\overline{X}_2 - b_{13.2}\overline{X}_3$$

$$= 142.5 - (0.54)(45.5) - (1.22)(29) = 82.55$$

The equation of the regression plane is

$$\hat{Y} = a_{1.23} + b_{12.3}X_2 + b_{13.2}X_3$$
$$= 82.55 + 0.54X_2 + 1.22X_3$$

	Y	$\hat{Y}$	e	e^2
1	100	100.41	$-.41$	.17
2	110	109.33	.67	.45
3	115	114.47	.53	.28
4	120	119.75	.25	.06
5	130	125.55	1.45	2.10
6	145	143.99	1.01	1.02
7	150	154.95	-4.95	24.50
8	170	173.51	-3.51	12.32
9	185	181.09	3.91	15.29
10	200	198.95	1.05	1.10
				57.29

$$t_2 = \frac{b_{12.3}}{\sqrt{\frac{\Sigma e^2}{n-3}}\sqrt{a_{22}}}$$

$$= \frac{0.54}{\sqrt{\frac{57.29}{7}}\sqrt{\frac{3{,}256}{(3{,}466.5)(3{,}256) - (3{,}269)^2}}} = 2.56$$

$$t_3 = \frac{b_{13.2}}{\sqrt{\frac{\Sigma e^2}{n-3}}\sqrt{a_{33}}}$$

$$= \frac{1.22}{\sqrt{\frac{57.29}{7}}\sqrt{\frac{3{,}466.5}{(3{,}466.5)(3{,}256) - (3{,}269)^2}}} = 5.6$$

Both $b_{12.3}$ and $b_{13.2}$ are significant at 0.05 level ($t_{.025} = 2.365$ with $(10 - 3)$ degrees of freedom). The standard error of estimate is

$$\hat{\sigma}_u = \frac{\Sigma e^2}{n-m} = \frac{57.29}{10-3} = 2.87$$

The multiple-correlation coefficient is given by

$$R_{1.23} = \sqrt{\frac{b_{12.3}\Sigma x_2 y + b_{13.2}\Sigma x_3 y}{\Sigma y^2}}$$

$$= \sqrt{\frac{0.54(5{,}857.5) + 1.22(5{,}735)}{10{,}212.5}} = .997$$

Apply the following F test:

$$F = \frac{(.997)^2(10 - 3)}{(1 - .997^2)(3 - 1)} = 66.92$$

Since

$$F_{0.05}(2, 7) = 4.74, \qquad F_{0.01}(2, 7) = 9.55$$

We may conclude that $R^2_{1.23}$ is significantly different from zero.

$$\left(\text{The mean square is } \frac{Y^T Y \cdot R^2}{m - 1} = \frac{(10,212.5)(.9948)}{3 - 1} = 5079 \cdot 7 \right)$$

or

$$R_{1.23} = \sqrt{\frac{r_{12}^2 + r_{13}^2 - 2r_{12}r_{13}r_{23}}{1 - r_{23}^2}}$$

$$= \sqrt{\frac{(.984)^2 + (.995)^2 - 2(.984)(.995)(.973)}{1 - (.973)^2}} = .997$$

where

$$r_{12} = \frac{\Sigma x_2 y}{n s_1 s_2} = \frac{5,857.5}{(10)(31.96)(18.62)} = .984$$

$$r_{13} = \frac{\Sigma x_3 y}{n s_1 s_3} = \frac{5,735}{(10)(31.96)(18.04)} = .995$$

$$r_{23} = \frac{\Sigma x_2 x_3}{n s_2 s_3} = \frac{3,269}{(10)(18.62)(18.04)} = .973$$

and

$$s_1 = \sqrt{\frac{\Sigma y^2}{n}} = \sqrt{\frac{10,212.5}{10}} = 31.96$$

$$s_2 = \sqrt{\frac{\Sigma x_2^2}{n}} = \sqrt{\frac{3,466.5}{10}} = 18.62$$

$$s_3 = \sqrt{\frac{\Sigma x_3^2}{n}} = \sqrt{\frac{3,256}{10}} = 18.04$$

The partial-correlation coefficients are

$$r_{12.3} = \frac{r_{12} - r_{13}r_{23}}{\sqrt{1 - r_{13}^2} \cdot \sqrt{1 - r_{23}^2}} = \frac{.984 - (.995)(.973)}{\sqrt{(1 - .995^2)(1 - .973^2)}} = .69$$

$$r_{13.2} = \frac{r_{13} - r_{12}r_{23}}{\sqrt{1 - r_{12}^2} \cdot \sqrt{1 - r_{23}^2}} = \frac{.995 - (.984)(.973)}{\sqrt{(1 - .984^2)(1 - .973^2)}} = .92$$

$$r_{23.1} = \frac{r_{23} - r_{12}r_{13}}{\sqrt{1 - r_{12}^2} \cdot \sqrt{1 - r_{13}^2}} = \frac{.973 - (.995)(.984)}{\sqrt{(1 - .984^2)(1 - .995^2)}} = -.34$$

Solve the three-variable linear regression model using matrix notation.

For estimating the parameters,

$$X^T X B = X^T Y \qquad \hat{B} = [X^T X]^{-1}[X^T Y]$$

In this case

$$X^T X = \begin{bmatrix} \Sigma x_2^2 & \Sigma x_2 x_3 \\ \Sigma x_2 x_3 & \Sigma x_3^2 \end{bmatrix} = \begin{bmatrix} 3,466.5 & 3,269 \\ 3,269 & 3,256 \end{bmatrix}$$

$$X^T Y = \begin{bmatrix} \Sigma x_2 y \\ \Sigma x_3 y \end{bmatrix} = \begin{bmatrix} 5,857.5 \\ 5,735.0 \end{bmatrix}$$

$$[X^T X]^{-1} = \frac{1}{\det[X^T X]} \ \text{adj}[X^T X] = \frac{1}{600,563} \begin{bmatrix} 3,256 & -3,269 \\ -3,269 & 3,466.5 \end{bmatrix}$$

$$= \begin{bmatrix} 00542157941 & -.00544322577 \\ -.00544322577 & .00577208386 \end{bmatrix}$$

$$\hat{B} = \begin{bmatrix} b_{12.3} \\ b_{13.2} \end{bmatrix} = \begin{bmatrix} .00542157941 & -.00544322577 \\ -.00544322577 & .00577208386 \end{bmatrix} \begin{bmatrix} 5,857.5 \\ 5,735.0 \end{bmatrix}$$

$$= \begin{bmatrix} .54 \\ 1.22 \end{bmatrix}$$

Thus

$$b_{12.3} = .54 \quad \text{and} \quad b_{13.2} = 1.22$$

For computing the multiple-correlation coefficient,

$$R^2 = \frac{\hat{B}^T X^T Y}{Y^T Y}$$

In this case

$$R^2 = \frac{[b_{12.3} \quad b_{13.2}] \begin{bmatrix} \Sigma x_2 y \\ \Sigma x_3 y \end{bmatrix}}{[\Sigma y^2]}$$

$$= \frac{[.54 \quad 1.22] \begin{bmatrix} 5,857.5 \\ 5,735.0 \end{bmatrix}}{10,212.5}$$

$$= \frac{10,159.75}{10,212.5} = 0.9948$$

Thus

$$R \cong .997$$

Iterative Methods of Solution

Among numerical methods of solving simultaneous equations, there are relaxation methods which start from a guessed solution and approach gradually toward a true solution. Some of the relaxation methods, however, have no definite routine defining the way in which one should proceed from one approximate solution to the next approximate solution. Those methods which have definite routine to approach a true solution are called *iterative methods*. In the following, we illustrate one of the iterative methods called the Gauss-Seidel method.

Given a set of simultaneous equations, which may be normal equations where the numbers are the sum of the cross-products of the observed values of the variables, e.g., $\Sigma x_2 y$, $\Sigma x_3 y$, $\Sigma x_3 y$, $\Sigma x_2 x_3$, Σx_2^2, Σx_3^2,

$$13b_1 + 5b_2 - 3b_3 + b_4 = 18$$
$$2b_1 + 12b_2 + b_3 - 4b_4 = 13$$
$$3b_1 - 4b_2 + 10b_3 + b_4 = 29$$
$$2b_1 + b_2 - 3b_3 + 9b_4 = 31$$

We rearrange them in the following form:

$$b_1 = {}^{18}\!/_{13} - {}^{5}\!/_{13}b_2 + {}^{3}\!/_{13}b_3 - {}^{1}\!/_{13}b_4$$
$$b_2 = {}^{13}\!/_{12} - {}^{1}\!/_{6}b_1 - {}^{1}\!/_{12}b_3 + {}^{1}\!/_{3}b_4$$
$$b_3 = {}^{29}\!/_{10} - {}^{3}\!/_{10}b_1 + {}^{2}\!/_{5}b_2 - {}^{1}\!/_{10}b_4$$
$$b_4 = {}^{31}\!/_{9} - {}^{2}\!/_{9}b_1 - {}^{1}\!/_{9}b_2 + {}^{1}\!/_{3}b_3$$

We first start with a trial solution: $b_1 = b_2 = b_3 = 0$; substituting this solution in the first equation, we obtain $b_1 = {}^{18}\!/_{13} = 1.385$. We then substitute $b_1 = 1.385$ and $b_3 = b_4 = 0$ in the second equation and obtain $b_2 = .853$. Substituting $b_1 = 1.385$, $b_2 = .853$, $b_4 = 0$ in the third equation, we get $b_3 = 2.826$. Finally we substitute $b_1 = 1.385$, $b_2 = .853$, $b_3 = 2.826$ in the fourth equation, and obtain $b_4 = 3.984$. This completes the first stage of iteration.

When we continue this iteration procedure, we will get the following results.

	b_1	b_2	b_3	b_4
1st stage	1.385	.853	2.826	3.984
2nd stage	1.402	1.942	2.858	3.870
3rd stage	1.000	1.969	3.001	4.004
4th stage	1.012	1.999	2.996	3.996
5th stage	1.000	1.999	3.000	4.000

The result shown in the 5th stage approaches to the exact answer $b_1 = 1$, $b_2 = 2$, $b_3 = 3$, $b_4 = 4$. Since the Gauss-Seidel method has definite routine of iteration procedure, it can be easily programmed on the computer. The method also may be applied to estimate the parameters of simultaneous equations whose variables are in nonlinear forms. However, there can be one difficulty—sometimes the procedure may not converge and thus the solution cannot be obtained. No simple necessary and sufficient conditions for convergence can be defined.

3-4. SIMULTANEOUS-EQUATION MODELS

In the real world the relationship between economic variables may be very complicated. They may interact upon each other simultaneously. Sometimes therefore we cannot take a single equation and consider it independently. Direct application of ordinary least squares on each individual equation in a simultaneous-equations model will yield biased estimates of parameters. The following is the usual approach in dealing with simultaneous relationships.

1. To specify the model properly:

In general, we must specify as many relations (structural equations) in a model as the total number of endogenous variables included in the model. Endogenous variables are those variables whose values are determined in the model. Exogenous variables are those variables whose values will affect the values of the endogenous variables, but their own values are determined outside the model. The classification of variables into endogenous and exogenous is a relative one, depending upon the extent of the system being studied and the purpose for which the model is built.

2. To estimate the parameters:
   (a) Change the structural equations into reduced-form equations (each equation has only one endogenous variable as the dependent variable and the rest are all exogenous variables) and apply ordinary least squares to estimate the reduced-form coefficients. They may be used for predicting future values of the endogenous variables or computing structural coefficients (if the functional relationship between the reduced-form coefficients and the structural coefficients can be established).
   (b) To estimate the parameters by methods other than the ordinary least squares. There are methods, such as *two-stage least squares* (which after some preliminary adjustment in the data still estimate the coefficients by each equation), and three-stage least squares and *full-information maximum-likelihood method*, which estimates all the parameters in the model simultaneously. All these will be discussed in detail in Chapter 6. Here we list only some models of simultaneous equation systems for illustration.

Model 1. The Cobweb Model

$$Q_d = a + bP + u$$
$$Q_s = c + dP_{-1} + v$$
$$Q_d = Q_s + w$$

where Q_d is the quantity demanded for a given product, Q_s the quantity supplied of the same product, P the price of the product (P_{-1} is the price in the previous period), and u, v, w the error terms of respective equations. The first equation represents the demand relationship of the product, the second the supply relationship, and the last the market-clearance situation.

Model 2. A Saving and Investment Model

$$S = a + bY + u$$
$$I = c + dY + v$$
$$S = I + w$$

where S is saving, Y income, I investment, and u, v, w the error terms of respective equations. The first equation represents the behavior characteristic of saving, the second the behavior characteristic of investment, and the third the balancing of saving and investment in the financial market.

Model 3. A Dynamic Multiplier and Accelerator Model

$$C_t = cY_t + u_t$$
$$I_t = v(Y_t - Y_{t-1}) + v_t$$
$$Y_t = C_t + I_t + A_t + w_t$$

where C is consumption, Y income, I investment, A autonomous expenditure (such as government and foreign investment) and u, v, w the error terms of respective equations. The first equation indicates that consumption is a function of current income, the second indicates that investment is related to the change of income of current period and last period, and the third indicates that income is generated from consumption, investment and autonomous expenditure.

3-5. MULTIPLIERS AND ACCELERATORS

Economic theories propose that whenever an amount of new investment has been injected into an economy, a rippling effect will occur, and eventually the total income generated in the economy will be some multiple of the initial investment. The mathematical derivation of the simplest multiplier is

$$Y = C + I \tag{3-36}$$

which states that income of an economy is equal to its consumption plus investment. Further, it assumes that consumption is a portion of the income:

$$C = cY \tag{3-37}$$

where c is the propensity to consume. Combining Eqs. 3-36 and 3-37, we get

$$Y = cY + I$$

$$Y = \left(\frac{1}{1-c}\right)I$$

The term $(1/1 - c)$ is the simplest form of a multiplier. Thus if we can estimate the propensity to consume, we can also compute the multiplier. In the gross-flow table of the input-output model described later in this chapter, we have a vector C, which indicates that portion of output of each industry group in an economy consumed by the final users. This indicates the propensity to consume goods and services produced by each industry group. Therefore, the multiplier effect of investment in each industry group can be estimated.

For the study of a region's economy, more complicated multipliers may be used, such as the following:

$$\frac{1}{1 - [(c \times R_c) + (i \times R_i)]}$$

where c = propensity to consume
R_c = proportion of the consumption goods produced locally
i = propensity to invest
R_i = proportion of the investment goods produced locally

Economists also observe that when the consumption in an economy increases by a certain amount, the producers, anticipating further increase in demand or merely trying to fulfill backlogs, will tend to enlarge the productive capacity. Thus the rate of investment will be accelerated. The simplest form of this relationship may be specified as

$$I = v(Y_t - Y_{t-1})$$

where v is the investment coefficient indicating the power of the accelerator. Compare the gross-flow tables of an input-output model at different time periods, the lagged relationship will show how the increase in consumption in one period will affect the business investment in subsequent periods.

The combined effect of the multiplier and accelerator on an economy is best illustrated in a feedback or control model, of which the following is an example. Suppose that the relationship between income Y, consumption C, induced investment I and autonomous expenditure A is described by the following three equations:

$$Y_t = C_t + I_t + A_t \tag{3-38}$$

$$C_t = cY_t \tag{3-39}$$

$$I_t = a(Y_{t-1} - Y_{t-2}) = a\Delta Y_{t-1} \tag{3-40}$$

The first equation states that income is the sum of consumption, induced investment, and autonomous expenditure. The second indicates that consumption is related to income; c is the propensity to consume and its relationship with the multiplier is

$$m = \frac{1}{1 - c}$$

The third equation indicates that induced investment is related to the change of the last two periods income, a is the accelerator. The model is given in schematic form in Fig. 3-4. The illustration shows that both I and C act on Y, and Y in turn reacts back on C and I through operators c and $(a\Delta)$ with time lag. And A may be used as a control device to insure that Y, C, and I be kept on some desired levels.

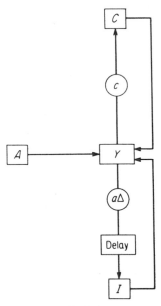

Fig. 3-4

3-6. ELASTICITIES

In studying economic phenomena we are often interested in the sensitivity of the increment change of one variable (X) with respect to another (Y). One of the measurements commonly used for this purpose is *elasticity*. Elasticity E is defined by

$$E = \frac{\dfrac{\Delta Y}{Y}}{\dfrac{\Delta X}{X}}$$

$$= \frac{X}{Y} \cdot \frac{\Delta Y}{\Delta X}$$

When X represents the price of a product and Y the quantity demanded, E is the elasticity of demand (usually negative); when Y represents the quantity supplied, E is the elasticity of supply (usually positive). There are also other elasticities that economists are interested in, such as income elasticity, elasticity of productivity, etc.

To estimate a particular elasticity, we use the following example to introduce the procedure. Suppose we have a demand function as follows:

$$P_t = c X_t^a Y_t^b u_t \qquad (3\text{-}41)$$

where P_t = price during time period t
$\quad\ X_t$ = quantity produced and consumed during time period t
$\quad\ Y_t$ = real income during time period t
$\quad\ u_t$ = random disturbance during time period t
$\quad\ c$ = constant

By transforming Eq. 3-41 to logarithm for time periods t and $(t - 1)$, we obtain

$$\log P_t = \log c + a \log X_t + b \log Y_t + \log u_t \qquad (3\text{-}42)$$

$$\log P_{t-1} = \log c + a \log X_{t-1} + b \log Y_{t-1} + \log u_{t-1} \qquad (3\text{-}43)$$

Taking the difference of Eqs. 3-42 and 3-43, we obtain

$$\Delta \log P_t = a \Delta \log X_t + b \Delta \log Y_t + \Delta \log u_t \qquad (3\text{-}44)$$

Assuming ($\Delta \log u_t$) is an independent variable with zero means and constant variance, we may estimate a and b by the least-squares method. The normal equations are

$$\Sigma(\Delta \log P_t)(\Delta \log X_t) = \hat{a}\Sigma(\Delta \log X_t)^2 + \hat{b}\Sigma(\Delta \log Y_t)(\Delta \log X_t)$$

$$\Sigma(\Delta \log P_t)(\Delta \log Y_t) = \hat{a}\Sigma(\Delta \log Y_t)(\Delta \log X_t) + \hat{b}\Sigma(\Delta \log Y_t)^2$$

Thus

$$\hat{a} = \frac{\begin{vmatrix} \Sigma(\Delta \log P_t)(\Delta \log X_t) & \Sigma(\Delta \log Y_t)(\Delta \log X_t) \\ \Sigma(\Delta \log P_t)(\Delta \log Y_t) & \Sigma(\Delta \log Y_t)^2 \end{vmatrix}}{\begin{vmatrix} \Sigma(\Delta \log X_t)^2 & \Sigma(\Delta \log Y_t)(\Delta \log X_t) \\ \Sigma(\Delta \log Y_t)(\Delta \log X_t) & \Sigma(\Delta \log Y_t)^2 \end{vmatrix}} \qquad (3\text{-}45)$$

$$\hat{b} = \frac{\begin{vmatrix} \Sigma(\Delta \log X_t)^2 & \Sigma(\Delta \log P_t)(\Delta \log X_t) \\ \Sigma(\Delta \log Y_t)(\Delta \log X_t) & \Sigma(\Delta \log P_t)(\Delta \log Y_t) \end{vmatrix}}{\begin{vmatrix} \Sigma(\Delta \log X_t)^2 & \Sigma(\Delta \log Y_t)(\Delta \log X_t) \\ \Sigma(\Delta \log Y_t)(\Delta \log X_t) & \Sigma(\Delta \log Y_t)^2 \end{vmatrix}} \qquad (3\text{-}46)$$

In Eq. 3-44, a represents the ratio of the marginal change of $\Delta \log P$ with respect to $\Delta \log X$. Since

$$\frac{\partial (\log X)}{\partial (\log P)} = \frac{\partial (\log X)}{\partial X} \cdot \frac{\partial X}{\partial P} \cdot \frac{\partial P}{\partial (\log P)}$$

$$= \frac{1}{X} \cdot \frac{\partial X}{\partial P} \cdot \frac{1}{\dfrac{\partial \log P}{\partial P}}$$

$$= \frac{P}{X} \cdot \frac{\partial X}{\partial P}$$

Thus $1/\hat{a}$ is an estimate of the price elasticity and similarity $1/\hat{b}$ is an estimate of the income elasticity.

3-7. INPUT-OUTPUT MODELS

The input-output model was first introduced by Wassily Leontief and is used to describe the economic base of a region or a country at some point of time. The productive sector of the economy is first broken down into a number of industry groups according to the characteristics of the region and the interest of the researcher. The final-user sector is classified at the first level into local use (local investment and local consumption) and export. Then the export sector may be further classified into different regions with which the economy has significant economic relationships.

After the various sectors of the model are specified, data on income and employment are collected to form input-output matrices such as the gross-flow table shown in Fig. 3-5.

Reading by rows, the first n rows indicate the amount of output of each industry group of the region sold to the other industry groups of the same region (matrix Y) or to the local users groups (matrix C) or

Industry Groups	Interindustry – Intermediate Use	Final Use		Total Output
	(1) --- (n)	Local Use	Export	
(1) . . . (n)	Y	C	X	O
Import --------	M			
Primary inputs---	P			
Total input -----	N			

Fig. 3-5

exported to other regions (matrix X). The sum of each row is the total output of the industry group (vector O). Reading by columns, the first n columns indicate the amount of input that the industry at the top purchased from other industry groups in the region plus the import from other regions (matrix M) and the primary inputs employed by the industry group (vector P). The column total represents the total input of the industry group (vector N). Total input of each industry group is assumed to be equal to its total output.

We then compute the input-output coefficients from the original data to obtain input-output matrix A in such a way that the elements of matrix A are equal to

$$A_{ij} = \frac{Y_{ij}}{O_j} \quad (i,j = 1, 2, \ldots, n)$$

where Y_{ij} are elements of matrix Y, and O_j is the total output of the industry groups.

In other words, industry group j, in order to produce a dollar's worth of output, needs to purchase A_{ij} worth of input from industry group i, and import M_j/O_j worth of input from outside and employ P_j/O_j worth of primary inputs such as labor, land and capital (they are the capital-output ratio, labor-output ratio, etc.).

We may also compute the percentages by rows to show the direct effect of the local final users and the outside regions on the production scales of each industry group. For the local final users, the percentages are computed by the following formula:

$$\frac{C_{ik}}{O_i} (i = 1, 2, \ldots, n; k = (n + 1), \ldots, n_k)$$

where C_{ik} is the elements of matrix C and O_i is the total output of industry group i, and for the outside regions, the percentages are X_{il}/O_i ($i = 1, 2, \ldots, n; l = n_k + 1, \ldots, n_l$) where X_{il} is the elements of matrix X.

For estimating the total effect, which includes not only the direct effect described above but also the indirect effect resulting from the continuous interaction of selling and buying activities between the different industry groups in the region, iterative method may be applied to trace the round by round effect from an initial increase of final demand.

Leontief, however, using the following reasoning developed a matrix method to compute the total effect:

$$\text{Total output} - \text{intermediate use} = \text{final use}$$

Using the matrix notation,

$$O - AO = C + X$$
$$(I - A) \cdot O = C + X, \quad O = (I - A)^{-1}C + (I - A)^{-1}X$$

where I is a unit matrix with the same rank as A.

Thus we first calculate $(I - A)^{-1}$, which is known as the *Leontief inverse matrix*. The total effect of the local demand on the production of the industry groups may be obtained by the following computation:

$$(I - A)^{-1}C$$

The total effect of the outside demand is

$$(I - A)^{-1}X$$

This method of survey has the following advantages:

1. It measures the interrelationship or interdependency of the industry groups in a region.
2. It pinpoints the more important local final users and outside regions which have greater effect on a particular industry.
3. The primary input rows indicate the contribution of each industry group to the employment of the primary factors of production including labor.
4. It provides an information base for development or investment planning of the region.

However, it has been often criticized on the ground that

1. It assumes that homogeneity exists among the products in each industry group.
2. It assumes constant proportion of input and output relationship (if dollar is used as the unit of measurement, it has to be adjusted to constant dollar first).
3. It provides no way to estimate how long it will take to have the total effect felt.

Further extensions of the basic input-output model may be made in three ways. One is by breaking down the final-use section into consumers, business investment, government and exports to different regions or nations in order to have a more detailed investigation of the various final demand each with its specific impact on output and primary inputs. Another method is to subdivide an economy into several regions and construct interregional input-output tables for interregional analysis. A more advanced method is to include capital formation data in the model and make period analyses of investment as a function of previous demand and production, thus changing the model to a dynamic one.

A numerical example is given as follows. Suppose the production and sales data of an economy are collected as shown in the accompanying table.

Producing Sector \ Using Sector	Primary Industry	Manu-facturing Industry	Service Industry	Total Intermediate Use
Primary industry...........	50	250	10	310
Manufacturing industry ...	100	500	40	640
Service industry............	70	200	100	370
Total purchases	220	950	150	1,320
Primary inputs	180	550	350	
Total inputs	400	1,500	500	

Producing Sector \ Using Sector	Consump-tion	Invest-ment	Govern-ment	Total Final Use	Total Output
Primary industry...........	60	0	30	90	400
Manufacturing industry ...	500	200	160	860	1,500
Service industry............	100	0	30	130	500
Total purchases					
Primary inputs				GNP 1,080	
Total inputs					2,400

The interindustry input-output coefficients matrix is

$$A = \begin{bmatrix} .125 & .167 & .020 \\ .250 & .333 & .080 \\ .175 & .133 & .200 \end{bmatrix}$$

The primary input and output ratios are

Primary Industry	Manufacturing Industry	Service Industry
.45	.36	.70

The inverse coefficients are calculated as

$$[I - A]^{-1} = \frac{1}{\det[I - A]} \cdot \text{adj}[I - A]$$

$$= \frac{1}{.42} \begin{bmatrix} .523 & .136 & .027 \\ .214 & .697 & .075 \\ .150 & .146 & .542 \end{bmatrix}$$

$$= \begin{bmatrix} 1.245 & .324 & .064 \\ .510 & 1.660 & .179 \\ .357 & .348 & 1.291 \end{bmatrix}$$

where

$$[I - A] = \begin{bmatrix} .875 & -.167 & -.020 \\ -.250 & .667 & -.080 \\ -.175 & -.133 & .800 \end{bmatrix}$$

Check: Let T be the total final use

$$[I - A]^{-1} T = \begin{bmatrix} 1.245 & .324 & .064 \\ .510 & 1.660 & .179 \\ .357 & .348 & 1.291 \end{bmatrix} \begin{bmatrix} 90 \\ 860 \\ 130 \end{bmatrix} = \begin{bmatrix} 397.76 \\ 1,496.77 \\ 499.24 \end{bmatrix} \simeq \begin{bmatrix} 400 \\ 1,500 \\ 500 \end{bmatrix}$$

Assume other things remaining unchanged, the economy wants to raise the consumption level to $\begin{bmatrix} 80 \\ 600 \\ 150 \end{bmatrix}$, which increases the total final use to $\begin{bmatrix} 110 \\ 960 \\ 180 \end{bmatrix}$. In order to support this, the required total output may be calculated as follows:

$$[I - A]^{-1} T_1 = \begin{bmatrix} 1.245 & .324 & .064 \\ .510 & 1.660 & .179 \\ .357 & .348 & 1.291 \end{bmatrix} \begin{bmatrix} 110 \\ 960 \\ 180 \end{bmatrix} = \begin{bmatrix} 459.51 \\ 1,681.92 \\ 605.73 \end{bmatrix}$$

And the new gross-flow table is changed as shown.

Using Sector Producing Sector	Primary Industry	Manu-facturing Industry	Service Industry	Total Intermediate Use
Primary industry........	57.44	280.88	12.12	350.44
Manufacturing industry	114.88	560.08	48.46	723.42
Service industry.........	80.41	233.70	121.15	425.26
Total purchases.........	252.73	1,064.66	181.73	1,499.12
Primary inputs..........	206.78	617.26	424.00	
Total inputs.............	459.51	1,681.92	605.73	

Producing Sector / Using Sector	Con-, sump-tion	Invest-ment	Govern-ment	Total Final Use	Total Output
Primary industry........	80	0	30	110	460.44
Manufacturing industry	600	200	160	960	1,683.42
Service industry.........	150	0	30	180	605.26
Total purchases.........					
Primary inputs..........				GNP 1,250	
Total inputs.............					2,748

Other Techniques and Models of Input-Output Analysis

1. Iterative procedure of estimating the total effect caused by an initial final demand.

In order to satisfy a given final demand, the industry sectors in a region will produce not only goods and services that will directly satisfy the final demand, but also intermediate goods and services that will be used by other industries as inputs to produce other outputs. This multiplier effect can be seen from the consecutive iterations of additional demands of the various industries in the region caused by the initial final demand.

Following is a numerical example to illustrate the iterative procedure.

Given an economy with three industrial sectors and the input-output coefficients are given as follows.

Producing Sector / Using Sector	Primary	Manufacturing	Services
Primary	.2	.2	0
Manufacturing....................	0	.2	0
Services...........................	.1	.2	.1

and the final demand vector is

Producing Sector	Final Demand
Primary	40
Manufacturing....................	100
Services...........................	60

The iterative procedure of estimating the required total output to support this given final demand will be as follows:

In order to produce 40 units of primary goods, the first-round required inputs to the primary industries are: primary .2 × 40 = 8 units, services .1 × 40 = 4 units. In order to produce 100 units of manufacturing goods, the first-round required inputs to the manufacturing industries are: primary .2 × 100 = 20 units, manufacturing .2 × 100 = 20 units, services .2 × 100 = 20 units. In order to produce 60 units of services, the first-round required inputs to the service industries are: services .1 × 60 = 6 units.

Thus in the first round the primary industries are required to produce 8 + 20 = 28 units, the manufacturing industries are required to produce 20 units, and the services industries 4 + 20 + 6 = 30 units.

In the second round, in order to produce 28 units of primary goods, the primary industries require primary inputs of .2 × 28 = 5.6 units and service inputs of .1 × 28 = 2.8 units in order to produce 20 units of manufacturing goods. The manufacturing industries require inputs from primary, manufacturing, and services of .2 × 20 = 4 units each. In order to produce 30 units of services, the service industries require service inputs of .1 × 30 = 3 units. Thus in the second round, the required output of primary industries is 5.6 + 4 = 9.6 units, that of manufacturing 4 units, and that of services 2.8 + 4 + 3 = 9.8 units.

The required inputs to all industry sectors in the succeeding rounds can be computed in the same manner, the result is as follows:

	Primary	Manufacturing	Services
Initial final demand	40	100	60
1st round requirement	28	20	30
2nd round requirement	9.6	4	9.8
3rd round requirement............	2.72	0.8	2.74
4th round requirement............	0.704	0.16	0.706
5th round requirement............	0.1728	0.032	0.173
	81.1968	124.992	103.419

Using the inverse method,

$$A = \begin{bmatrix} .2 & .2 & 0 \\ 0 & .2 & 0 \\ .1 & .2 & .1 \end{bmatrix}$$

$$[I - A]^{-1} = \begin{bmatrix} 5/4 & 5/16 & 0 \\ 0 & 5/4 & 0 \\ 5/36 & 5/16 & 10/9 \end{bmatrix}$$

$$[I - A]^{-1} T = \begin{bmatrix} 5/4 & 5/16 & 0 \\ 0 & 5/4 & 0 \\ 5/36 & 5/16 & 10/9 \end{bmatrix} \begin{bmatrix} 40 \\ 100 \\ 60 \end{bmatrix} = \begin{bmatrix} 81.2 \\ 125 \\ 103.47 \end{bmatrix}$$

Thus five iterations of the above example already bring the estimated required total output close to the analytical solution.

2. The estimation of regional multiplier may be done in a gross term by the following formula using the regional data on employment:

$$\text{Regional multiplier} = \frac{\text{total employment}}{\text{base employment}}$$
(employment in the export industries)

However, if regional input-output table is available, we may estimate the multipliers of income changes in each of the industrial sector. There are two types of multipliers which may be computed. The first one measures the effect of the initial income change on direct and indirect income changes and the second measures the effect of the initial income change on direct, indirect and induced income changes. The following example will illustrate the computation procedure.

Purchasing Industry / Using Industry	Primary	Manu-facturing	Service	Household	Other Final Use	Total Output
Primary..................	50	250	10	60	30	400
Manufacturing.........	100	500	40	500	360	1,500
Service..................	70	200	100	100	30	500
Primary inputs.........	180	550	350			
Total input.............	400	1,500	500			

In order to include the household sector into the interindustry matrix, we make the following adjustment:

Total household consumption = 60 + 500 + 100 = 660

Total primary inputs = 180 + 550 + 350 = 1,080

Household inputs to primary industry = $180 \times \dfrac{660}{1,080} = 110$

Household inputs to manufacturing industry = $550 \times \dfrac{660}{1,080} = 336$

Household inputs to service industry = $350 \times \dfrac{660}{1,080} = 214$

Thus the interindustry matrix including the household sector becomes

Purchasing / Using	Primary	Manu-facturing	Service	House-hold
Primary	50	250	10	60
Manufacturing............................	100	500	40	500
Service......................................	70	200	100	100
Household	110	336	214	0

The input-output coefficients matrix is

$$A' = \begin{bmatrix} .125 & .167 & .020 & 60/660 \\ .250 & .333 & .080 & 500/660 \\ .175 & .133 & .200 & 100/660 \\ 110/400 & 336/1{,}500 & 214/500 & 0 \end{bmatrix}$$

$$= \begin{bmatrix} .125 & .167 & .020 & .091 \\ .250 & .333 & .080 & .759 \\ .175 & .133 & .200 & .151 \\ .275 & .224 & .428 & 0 \end{bmatrix}$$

The fourth row of this matrix represents the direct income-change coefficients of each sector.

The inverse of matrix $[I - A]$, where A is the matrix which does not include the household sector, is

$$[I - A]^{-1} = \begin{bmatrix} 1.245 & .324 & .064 \\ .510 & 1.660 & .179 \\ .357 & .348 & 1.291 \end{bmatrix}$$

The product of

$$[I - A]^{-1} \begin{bmatrix} 110/400 \\ 336/1{,}500 \\ 214/500 \end{bmatrix} = \begin{bmatrix} 1.245 & .324 & .064 \\ .510 & 1.660 & .179 \\ .357 & .348 & 1.291 \end{bmatrix} \begin{bmatrix} .275 \\ .224 \\ .428 \end{bmatrix} = \begin{bmatrix} .445527 \\ .588702 \\ .728675 \end{bmatrix}$$

represents the direct and indirect income-change coefficients of each sector. Since

$$\text{Type I multipliers} = \frac{\text{direct and indirect income change}}{\text{direct income change}}$$

For primary industry

$$\frac{.446}{.275} = 1.62$$

For manufacturing industry

$$\frac{.589}{.224} = 2.62$$

For service industry

$$\frac{.729}{.428} = 1.70$$

The inverse of matrix $I - A'$, where A' is the matrix which includes the household, indicates not only the direct and indirect income changes but also the induced income change.

$$[I - A']^{-1} = \begin{bmatrix} .875 & -.167 & -.02 & -.091 \\ -.25 & .667 & -.08 & -.759 \\ -.175 & -.133 & .8 & -.151 \\ -.275 & -.224 & -.428 & 1 \end{bmatrix}^{-1}$$

$$= \begin{bmatrix} 1.8307 & 0.9072 & 0.6462 & 0.9527 \\ 2.6115 & 3.7623 & 2.2807 & 3.4376 \\ 1.1315 & 1.1206 & 2.0675 & 1.2657 \\ 1.5727 & 1.5719 & 1.5735 & 2.5737 \end{bmatrix}$$

The coefficients in the fourth row represents the direct, indirect, and induced changes of each sector. Since

$$\text{Type II multipliers} = \frac{\text{direct, indirect and induced income change}}{\text{direct income change}}$$

For primary industry

$$\frac{1.5727}{.275} = 5.75$$

For manufacturing industry

$$\frac{1.5719}{.224} = 7.01$$

For service industry

$$\frac{1.5735}{.428} = 3.68$$

In summary:

Sector	Direct Income Change	Indirect Income Change	Direct and Indirect Income Change	Induced Income Change	Direct, Indirect, and Induced Income Change	Type I Multiplier	Type II Multiplier
Primary industry ..	.275	.171	.446	1.127	1.573	1.62	5.75
Manufacturing industry	.224	.365	.589	0.983	1.572	2.62	7.01
Service industry....	.428	.301	.729	0.845	1.574	1.70	3.68

3. An interregional input-output model for analyzing the production and consumption relationship among different regions.

(a) Assumptions of the simplest interregional input-output model:

(1) Two regions 1 and 2, with similarly defined sectors $1, 2, \ldots, n$.
(2) The two regions form a closed economy.
(3) The production technology and the trade relationship in these two regions remain constant.

First we analyze only one sector (k) of region 1 and 2, which may be later generalized to include all sectors.

(b) The input-output coefficients *within* region 1 and 2 of sector j

Region 1:

$$a_{ij}^{(1)} = \frac{\text{output of sector } i \text{ purchased by sector } j \text{ as input in region 1}}{\text{total output of sector } j \text{ in region 1}}$$

$$(i, j = 1, 2, \ldots, n \text{ sectors})$$

Region 2:

$$a_{ij}^{(2)} = \frac{\text{output of sector } i \text{ purchased by sector } j \text{ as input in region 2}}{\text{total output of sector } j \text{ in region 2}}$$

(c) The relationship *between* region 1 and 2, of producing and purchasing product k.

		Purchasing Region		Total Output of Product k	Export of Product k
		1	2		
Producing	1	p_{11}	p_{12}	$O^{(1)} = p_{11} + p_{12}$	p_{12} (from region 1 to 2)
Region	2	p_{21}	p_{22}	$O^{(2)} = p_{21} + p_{22}$	p_{21} (from region 2 to 1)
Import		p_{21}	p_{12}		
		(of region 1 from 2)	(of region 2 from 1)		

Supply of product k:

$$\text{Region 1} = p_{11} + p_{21}$$
$$\text{Region 2} = p_{12} + p_{22}$$

Demand of product k:

$$\text{Region 1} = \sum_j a_{kj}^{(1)} O^{(1)} + Y^{(1)} \quad \text{(interindustry use + final use)}$$

$$(j = 1, 2, \ldots, n)$$

$$\text{Region 2} = \sum_j a_{kj}^{(2)} O^{(2)} + Y^{(2)}$$

Since supply is assumed to equal demand in both regions,

$$\sum_j a_{kj}^{(1)} O^{(1)} + Y^{(1)} = p_{11} + p_{21} = S^{(1)}$$

$$\sum_j a_{kj}^{(2)} O^{(2)} + Y^{(2)} = p_{12} + p_{22} = S^{(2)}$$

(d) (1) The (import/total supply) coefficients are defined as

$$r^{(1)} = \frac{p_{21}}{S^{(1)}} \qquad \text{(of region 1, imported from region 2)}$$

$$r^{(2)} = \frac{p_{12}}{S^{(2)}} \qquad \text{(of region 2, imported from region 1)}$$

(2) The (local produced/total supply) coefficients are defined as

$$1 - r^{(1)} = \frac{p_{11}}{S^{(1)}} \qquad \text{(of region 1)}$$

$$1 - r^{(2)} = \frac{p_{22}}{S^{(2)}} \qquad \text{(of region 2)}$$

Therefore

$$O^{(1)} = p_{11} + p_{12} \qquad \text{(Total output = local use + export)}$$

$$= (1 - r^{(1)}) S^{(1)} + r^{(2)} \cdot S^{(2)}$$

$$= (1 - r^{(1)}) \left(\sum_j a_{ij}^{(1)} O^{(1)} + Y^{(1)} \right) + r^{(2)} \left(\sum_j a_{ij}^{(2)} O^{(2)} + Y^{(2)} \right)$$

$$= (1 - r^{(1)}) \left(\sum_j a_{ij}^{(1)} O^{(1)} \right) + r^{(2)} \left(\sum_j a_{ij}^{(2)} O^{(2)} \right)$$

$$+ (1 - r^{(1)}) Y^{(1)} + r^{(2)} Y^{(2)}$$

The total output of product k in region 1 = the interindustry use of product k in region 1 produced by region 1 + the interindustry use of product k in region 2 produced by region 1 + the final use of product k in region 1 produced by region 1 + the final use of product k in region 2 produced by region 1. (i) The larger the $(1 - r^{(1)})$, the larger the effect of region 1's interindustry use and final use of product k will have on the economy of region 1, (local effect). (ii) The larger the $r^{(2)}$, the larger the effect of region 2's interindustry use and final use of product k will have on the economy of region 1 (interregional effect). Similarly,

$$O^{(2)} = (1 - r^{(2)}) \left(\sum_j a_{ij}^{(2)} O^{(2)} \right) + r^{(1)} \left(\sum_j a_{ij}^{(1)} O^{(1)} \right)$$

$$+ (1 - r^{(2)}) Y^{(2)} + r^{(1)} Y^{(1)}$$

The following is a two-region, two-sector model to illustrate the total effect of the final demand in two regions on the total outputs of the two regions.

Producing		Purchasing			
		Region (1)		Region (2)	
Region	Sector	Sector 1	Sector 2	Sector 1	Sector 2
(1)	1	$(1 - r_1^{(1)})a_{11}^{(1)}$	$(1 - r_1^{(1)})a_{12}^{(1)}$	$r_1^{(1)}a_{11}^{(1)}$	$r_1^{(1)}a_{12}^{(1)}$
	2	$(1 - r_2^{(1)})a_{21}^{(1)}$	$(1 - r_2^{(1)})a_{22}^{(1)}$	$r_2^{(1)}a_{21}^{(1)}$	$r_2^{(1)}a_{22}^{(1)}$
(2)	1	$r_1^{(2)}a_{11}^{(2)}$	$r_1^{(2)}a_{12}^{(2)}$	$(1 - r_1^{(2)})a_{11}^{(2)}$	$(1 - r_1^{(2)})a_{12}^{(2)}$
	2	$r_2^{(2)}a_{21}^{(2)}$	$r_2^{(2)}a_{22}^{(2)}$	$(1 - r_2^{(2)})a_{21}^{(2)}$	$(1 - r_2^{(2)})a_{22}^{(2)}$

The $(1 - r_i^{(1)})a_{ij}^{(1)}$, $r_i^{(1)}a_{ij}^{(1)}$, $r_i^{(2)}a_{ij}^{(2)}$ and $(1 - r_i^{(2)})a_{ij}^{(2)}$ are all coefficients. Let us call this square matrix A. We can then find the inverse matrix $(I - A)^{-1}$. Let the final demand in region (1) and (2) for the products of sector 1 and 2 be as follows.

Region	Sector	Final Use	Shipments
(1)	1	$Y_1^{(1)}$	$(1 - r_1^{(1)}) Y_1^{(1)} + r_1^{(2)} Y_1^{(2)}$
	2	$Y_2^{(1)}$	$(1 - r_2^{(1)}) Y_2^{(1)} + r_2^{(2)} Y_2^{(2)}$
(2)	1	$Y_1^{(2)}$	$(1 - r_1^{(2)}) Y_1^{(2)} + r_1^{(1)} Y_1^{(1)}$
	2	$Y_2^{(2)}$	$(1 - r_2^{(2)}) Y_2^{(2)} + r_2^{(1)} Y_2^{(1)}$

The shipments column indicates the quantity that each region produces to satisfy its own final demand plus the quantity that the same region produces to satisfy other regions demand. Let us call this column vector Y. Then the total outputs required of region (1), sectors 1 and 2 and region (2), sectors 1 and 2 to sustain this demand will be

$$O = (I - A)^{-1} Y$$

The vector O will contain the following elements:

$$O = \begin{bmatrix} O_1^{(1)} \\ O_2^{(1)} \\ O_1^{(2)} \\ O_2^{(2)} \end{bmatrix}$$

The model may be expanded to include more than two regions and/or more than two sectors.

Numerical Example (A Two-Region Two-Sector Model)

Given:

Input-output coefficients:

$$a_{11}^{(1)} = .1, \quad a_{12}^{(1)} = .3, \quad a_{21}^{(1)} = .2, \quad a_{22}^{(1)} = .15$$
$$a_{11}^{(2)} = .05, \quad a_{12}^{(2)} = .2, \quad a_{21}^{(2)} = .3, \quad a_{22}^{(2)} = .1$$

Import/total supply coefficients:

$$r_1^{(1)} = .6, \quad r_2^{(1)} = .1$$
$$r_1^{(2)} = .2, \quad r_2^{(2)} = .3$$

Local produced/total supply coefficients:

$$1 - r_1^{(1)} = .4, \quad 1 - r_2^{(1)} = .9$$
$$1 - r_1^{(2)} = .8, \quad 1 - r_2^{(2)} = .7$$

Final use:

$$Y_1^{(1)} = 100, \quad Y_2^{(1)} = 60$$
$$Y_1^{(2)} = 50, \quad Y_2^{(2)} = 120$$

Then

$$
\begin{bmatrix} O_1^{(1)} \\ O_2^{(1)} \\ O_1^{(2)} \\ O_2^{(2)} \end{bmatrix} =
\begin{bmatrix}
[1 - (.4)(.1)] & [-(.4)(.3)] & [-(.6)(.1)] & [-(.6)(.3)] \\
[-(.9)(.2)] & [1 - (.9)(.15)] & [-(.1)(.2)] & [-(.1)(.15)] \\
[-(.2)(.05)] & [-(.2)(.02)] & [1 - (.8)(.05)] & [-(.8)(.2)] \\
[-(.3)(.3)] & [-(.3)(.1)] & [-(.7)(.3)] & [1 - (.7)(.1)]
\end{bmatrix}^{-1}
$$

$$
\times
\begin{bmatrix}
[(.4)(100) + (.2)(50)] \\
[(.9)(60) + (.3)(120)] \\
[(.8)(50) + (.6)(100)] \\
[(.7)(120) + (.1)(60)]
\end{bmatrix}
=
\begin{bmatrix}
100.37 \\
109.63 \\
133.13 \\
140.09
\end{bmatrix}
$$

4. A dynamic input-output model for analyzing the economic growth of
an economy.

The model is for measuring the capital accumulation from period to
period and the growth of production capacity. It may be used to test
the overall feasibility of investment programs or to determine how investment should be allocated among sectors over time.

Let X_i be the total output of i sector

$$(i = 1, 2, \ldots, n)$$

K_i be the productive capacity in i sector measured in the same unit as
X_i, the output sector i produces.

$$(i = 1, 2, \ldots, n)$$

$$a_{ij} = \frac{\text{output of sector } i \text{ purchased by sector } j \text{ as intermediate input}}{\text{total output of sector } j}$$

$$(i, j = 1, 2, \ldots, n)$$

$$b_{ij} = \frac{\text{output of sector } i \text{ purchased by sector } j \text{ as capital goods}}{\text{total additional productive capacity of sector } j}$$

$$(i, j = 1, 2, \ldots, n)$$

S_{ij} = stock of commodity i needed to produce a level of capacity K in sector j

Then

$$b_{ij} = \frac{S_{ij}^t - S_{ij}^{t-1}}{K_j^t - K_j^{t-1}} = \frac{\Delta S_{ij}^t}{\Delta K_j^t}$$

b_{ij} may be interpreted as the marginal stock-capacity ratio

$$\Delta S_{ij}^t = b_{ij} \Delta K_j^t$$

$$X_i^t = \sum_j a_{ij} X_j^t + \sum_j b_{ij} \Delta K_j^t + Y_i^t$$

(Total output = intermediate demand
+ induced investment demand + final demand)

or

$$X_i^t - \sum_j a_{ij} X_j^t - \Sigma b_{ij} \Delta K_j^t = Y_i^t$$

If productive capacity exceeds total demand, excess or unused capacity will result for the period:

$$U_i^t = K_i^t - X_i^t$$

Of course, U_i^t can also be negative when total demand is greater. (U_i^t also is identical to ΔK_i^t; thus $\Delta K_i^t = K_i^t - X_i^t$ or $K_i^t = \Delta K_i^t + X_i^t$)

$$\begin{aligned}
\Delta U_i^t &= U_i^t - U_i^{t-1} \\
&= K_i^t - X_i^t - (K_i^{t-1} - X_i^{t-1}) \\
&= (K_i^t - K_i^{t-1}) - (X_i^t - X_i^{t-1}) \\
&= \Delta K_i^t - X_i^t + X_i^{t-1} \text{ (or } \Delta K_i^t - \Delta X_i^t)
\end{aligned}$$

The increment of unused capacity is the difference of the increment of capacity and the increment of output.

A two-sector and two-time-period model using the previous equations is constructed as follows.

Output Period:			(1)				(2)			Restric- tions
Production or Capacity Building			P		C		P		C	Final Demand or Capacity
Input Period	Current Output or Capacity	Sector	Sector							
			1	2	1	2	1	2	1	2	
			$X_1^{(1)}$	$X_2^{(1)}$	$\Delta K_1^{(1)}$	$\Delta K_2^{(1)}$	$X_1^{(2)}$	$X_2^{(2)}$	$\Delta K_1^{(2)}$	$\Delta K_2^{(2)}$	
(1)	O	1	1	$-a_{12}^{(1)}$	0	0	0	0	$-b_{11}^{(1)}$	$-b_{12}^{(1)}$	$Y_1^{(1)}$
		2	$-a_{21}^{(1)}$	1	0	0	0	0	$-b_{21}^{(1)}$	$-b_{22}^{(1)}$	$Y_2^{(1)}$
	C	1	-1	0	1	0	0	0	0	0	$-K_1$
		2	0	-1	0	1	0	0	0	0	$-K_2$
(2)	O	1	0	0	0	0	1	$-a_{12}^{(2)}$	0	0	$Y_1^{(2)}$
		2	0	0	0	0	$-a_{21}^{(2)}$	1	0	0	$Y_2^{(2)}$
	C	1	1	0	0	0	-1	0	1	0	ΔU_1
		2	0	1	0	0	0	-1	0	1	ΔU_2

where $a_{ij}^{(1)}$ = input-output coefficients of sectors 1 and 2 in period (1)

$a_{ij}^{(2)}$ = input-output coefficients of sectors 1 and 2 in period (2)

$b_{ij}^{(1)}$ = ratio of the outputs of sectors 1 and 2 in period (1) pur- chased by sectors 1 and 2 as additional production capacity and the total additional capacity of sectors 1 and 2.

$b_{ij}^{(2)}$ are not entered into the table, because in this model we do not consider the capital formation for period 3

$Y_i^{(1)}$ = final demand for outputs of sector 1 and 2 in period (1)

$Y_i^{(2)}$ = final demand for outputs of sector 1 and 2 in period (2)

K_i = initial productive capacity of sector 1 and 2 prior to period 1

ΔU_i = unused productive capacity of sector 1 and 2 resulted in period 2

Let us denote the 8 × 8 coefficient matrix as M and the 8 × 1 final demand restrictions vector as Y. Then we may compute the required production and capacity building for sectors 1 and 2 in periods 1 and 2 by the matrix inverse method,

$$O = M^{-1} Y$$

(We may not want any unused productive capacity. In this case, set all $\Delta U_i = 0$.)

The result vector should include the following elements,

$$O = \begin{bmatrix} X_1^{(1)} \\ X_2^{(1)} \\ K_1^{(1)} \\ K_2^{(1)} \\ X_1^{(2)} \\ X_2^{(2)} \\ K_1^{(2)} \\ K_2^{(2)} \end{bmatrix}$$

$X_1^{(1)}$, $X_2^{(1)}$ output for total use in period 1

$K_1^{(1)}$, $K_2^{(1)}$ capacity building during the previous period for use in period 1

$X_1^{(2)}$, $X_2^{(2)}$ output for total use in period 2

$K_1^{(2)}$, $K_2^{(2)}$ capacity building during period 1 for use in period 2

Numerical Example (A Two-Sector Two-Period Input-Output Model)

Initial capital

$$K_1 = 80, \quad K_2 = 90$$

Final use

$$Y_1^{(1)} = 100, \quad Y_2^{(1)} = 150$$
$$Y_1^{(2)} = 120, \quad Y_2^{(2)} = 180$$

Excess capacity

$$\Delta U_1 = 0, \quad \Delta U_2 = 0$$

Input-output coefficients

$$a_{11}^{(1)} = 0, \quad a_{12}^{(1)} = .6, \quad a_{21}^{(1)} = .4, \quad a_{22}^{(1)} = 0$$
$$a_{11}^{(2)} = 0, \quad a_{12}^{(2)} = .6, \quad a_{21}^{(2)} = .4, \quad a_{22}^{(2)} = 0$$

Stock capacity ratios

$$b_{11}^{(1)} = .5, \quad b_{12}^{(1)} = 2, \quad b_{21}^{(1)} = 3, \quad b_{22}^{(1)} = .6$$

Then

$$\begin{bmatrix} X_1^{(1)} \\ X_2^{(1)} \\ K_1^{(1)} \\ K_2^{(1)} \\ X_1^{(2)} \\ X_2^{(2)} \\ K_1^{(2)} \\ K_2^{(2)} \end{bmatrix} = \begin{bmatrix} 1 & -.6 & 0 & 0 & 0 & 0 & -.5 & -2 \\ -.4 & 1 & 0 & 0 & 0 & 0 & -3 & -.6 \\ -1 & 0 & 1 & 0 & 0 & 0 & 0 & 0 \\ 0 & -1 & 0 & 1 & 0 & 0 & 0 & 0 \\ 0 & 0 & 0 & 0 & 1 & -.6 & 0 & 0 \\ 0 & 0 & 0 & 0 & -.4 & 1 & 0 & 0 \\ 1 & 0 & 0 & 0 & -1 & 0 & 1 & 0 \\ 0 & 1 & 0 & 0 & 0 & -1 & 0 & 1 \end{bmatrix}^{-1} \begin{bmatrix} 100 \\ 150 \\ -80 \\ -90 \\ 120 \\ 180 \\ 0 \\ 0 \end{bmatrix}$$

$$= \begin{bmatrix} 291.93 \\ 294.34 \\ 211.93 \\ 204.34 \\ 300.00 \\ 300.00 \\ 8.07 \\ 5.66 \end{bmatrix}$$

SELECTED BIBLIOGRAPHY

1. R. G. D. Allen, *Mathematical Economics*. London: Macmillan, 1960.
2. H. B. Chenery and P. G. Clark, *Interindustry Economics*. New York: Wiley, 1959.
3. A. S. Goldberger, *Econometric Theory*. New York: Wiley, 1964.
4. F. A. Graybill, *An Introduction to Linear Statistical Models*. New York: McGraw-Hill, 1961.
5. J. Johnston, *Econometric Methods*. New York: McGraw-Hill, 1960.

EXERCISES

3-1. Find the equation of the regression line for the following data ($Y = \hat{a} + \hat{b}x$). Also calculate the linear correlation coefficient r. Is r significantly different from zero?

X	70	65	75	60	70	75	70	65	70	70	75	65
Y	150	130	170	120	160	210	150	140	165	160	180	120

3-2. Find the variances of the intercept ($\hat{a}$) and the slope ($\hat{b}$) of the regression line given in Exercise 3-1. Then determine the 95 percent confidence limits for (a) and (b).

3-3. When X equals 80, make a prediction of the value of Y. Specify confidence limits.

3-4. Find the equation of the regression plane for the following data:

$$(Y = a_{1.23} + b_{12.3}X_2 + b_{13.2}X_3)$$

X_2	15	20	24	12	18	10	25	14	19	27	16	22
X_3	32	40	45	25	35	30	46	40	38	44	32	39
Y	100	150	200	125	220	170	300	180	250	400	225	300

3-5. Calculate the multiple correlation coefficient and partial correlation coefficients for the data given in Exercise 3-4. Discuss the adequacy of using the regression plane to represent the data.

3-6. Use matrix-algebra to estimate the regression coefficients and the multiple correlation coefficients of the data given in Exercise 3-4.

3-7. Given the following data of an economy:

Using Industry or Sector / Producing Industry	Primary Industry	Manu-facturing Industry	Service Industry	Govern-ment	Private Consumer
Primary industry............	100	500	100	200	100
Manufacturing industry	300	1,000	200	400	600
Service industry	200	600	500	300	400

Calculate the input-output coefficients and inverse coefficients. Explain what they represent.

3-8. Assuming that in Exercise 3-7 the foreign trade is negligibly small, what is the contribution (or value added figure) of each industry to the economy? If the demand of the government for the manufactured goods is increased by 10 percent, how do the production and distribution of the economy have to be changed in order to meet this increase? What are the assumptions behind the prediction?

chapter 4

Nonlinear Models

The models we have discussed in the preceding chapter are all based on the assumption that the relationship between the economic variables is linear. However, in the real world we find many relationships that are not linear. If the interval of the function which we are interested in (for example, the price of a commodity can vary only from eighty cents to a dollar) can be approximated by a linear segment, the method described in Chapter 3 may still be applied. But if the relevant interval is definitely nonlinear, then other methods of specification and estimation have to be found.

4-1. TRANSFORMATION OF VARIABLES

One way to avoid the difficulty is to transform the original variables, if possible, from a nonlinear relationship to a linear relationship and then apply the linear-regression method to the transformed variables. The following are a few examples.

An original relationship

$$Y = aX^b \qquad (4\text{-}1)$$

may be transformed to

$$\log Y = \log a + b \log X \qquad (4\text{-}2)$$

Thus the transformed relationship between $\log X$ and $\log Y$ becomes linear.

Or an original relationship;

$$Y = e^{a+bX} \qquad (4\text{-}3)$$

may be transformed to a linear relationship between $\log Y$ and X when written as

$$\log Y = a + bX \qquad (4\text{-}4)$$

The well-known Cobb-Douglas production function $X = cL^a K^b$ may be transformed to

$$\log X = \log c + a \log L + b \log K$$

4-2. THE NONLINEAR-REGRESSION MODEL

Another method is to fit nonlinear functions to original data, using the least-squares method. For example, if the function is in the form of a polynomial:

$$\hat{Y} = a + bX + cX^2 \tag{4-5}$$

and the differences between the actual observations and the points on the curve are

$$e_i = Y_i - \hat{Y}_i$$

$$= Y_i - (a + bX_i + cX_i^2) \qquad (i = 1, 2, \ldots, n)$$

Then

$$\sum_{i=1}^{n} e_i^2 = \sum_{i=1}^{n} (Y_i - a - bX_i - cX_i^2)^2$$

Applying the least-squares method we obtain

$$\frac{\partial \sum e_i^2}{\partial a} = -2\Sigma(Y_i - a - bX_i - cX_i^2)$$

$$\frac{\partial \sum e_i^2}{\partial b} = -2\Sigma X_i(Y_i - a - bX_i - cX_i^2)$$

$$\frac{\partial \sum e_i^2}{\partial c} = -2\Sigma X_i^2(Y_i - a - bX_i - cX_i^2)$$

Setting the partial deviatives equal zero, the resulting normal equations will be

$$\Sigma Y_i = n\hat{a} + \hat{b}\Sigma X_i + \hat{c}\Sigma X_i^2$$

$$\Sigma X_i Y_i = \hat{a}\Sigma X_i + \hat{b}\Sigma X_i^2 + \hat{c}\Sigma X_i^3$$

$$\Sigma X_i^2 Y_i = \hat{a}\Sigma X_i^2 + \hat{b}\Sigma X_i^3 + \hat{c}\Sigma X_i^4$$

Solving for the unknowns $\hat{a}$, $\hat{b}$, $\hat{c}$ we, get the least-squares estimates as follows:

$$\hat{a} = \frac{\begin{vmatrix} \Sigma Y_i & \Sigma X_i & \Sigma X_i^2 \\ \Sigma X_i Y_i & \Sigma X_i^2 & \Sigma X_i^3 \\ \Sigma X_i^2 Y_i & \Sigma X_i^3 & \Sigma X_i^4 \end{vmatrix}}{\begin{vmatrix} n & \Sigma X_i & \Sigma X_i^2 \\ \Sigma X_i & \Sigma X_i^2 & \Sigma X_i^3 \\ \Sigma X_i^2 & \Sigma X_i^3 & \Sigma X_i^4 \end{vmatrix}} \tag{4-6}$$

$$\hat{b} = \frac{\begin{vmatrix} n & \Sigma Y_i & \Sigma X_i^2 \\ \Sigma X_i & \Sigma X_i Y_i & \Sigma X_i^3 \\ \Sigma X_i^2 & |\Sigma X_i^2 Y_i & \Sigma X_i^4 \end{vmatrix}}{\begin{vmatrix} n & \Sigma X_i & \Sigma X_i^2 \\ \Sigma X_i & \Sigma X_i^2 & \Sigma X_i^3 \\ \Sigma X_i^2 & \Sigma X_i^3 & \Sigma X_i^4 \end{vmatrix}} \tag{4-7}$$

$$\hat{c} = \frac{\begin{vmatrix} n & \Sigma X_i & \Sigma Y_i \\ \Sigma X_i & \Sigma X_i^2 & \Sigma X_i Y_i \\ \Sigma X_i^2 & \Sigma X_i^3 & \Sigma X_i^2 Y_i \end{vmatrix}}{\begin{vmatrix} n & \Sigma X_i & \Sigma X_i^2 \\ \Sigma X_i & \Sigma X_i^2 & \Sigma X_i^3 \\ \Sigma X_i^2 & \Sigma X_i^3 & \Sigma X_i^4 \end{vmatrix}} \tag{4-8}$$

After we find the least-squares estimates of the parameters of the equation, we can compute the estimated Y value given the X value, and estimate the coefficient of determination by the following formula:

$$r^2 = \frac{\Sigma \hat{y}_i^2}{\Sigma y_i^2}$$

where $\hat{y}_i = \hat{b} x_i + \hat{c} x_i^2$ and x_i, y_i are deviations from the sample means, or

$$r^2 = 1 - \frac{\Sigma e_i^2}{\Sigma y_i^2} \tag{4-9}$$

EXAMPLE: (To illustrate the computational procedure.)

	Y	X	X^2	X^3	X^4	XY	X^2Y	y	y^2	$(Y - \hat{a} - \hat{b}X - \hat{c}X^2)^2$
1	25	1	1	1	1	25	25	−85	7,225	18.276
2	30	3	9	27	81	90	270	−80	6,400	1.782
3	40	6	36	216	1,296	240	1,440	−70	4,900	19.378
4	55	10	100	1,000	10,000	550	5,500	−55	3,025	171.872
5	80	12	144	1,728	20,736	960	11,520	−30	900	7.344
6	100	14	196	2,744	38,416	1,400	19,600	−10	100	1.464
7	120	15	225	3,375	50,625	1,800	27,000	10	100	159.138
8	160	20	400	8,000	160,000	3,200	64,000	50	2,500	16.728
9	210	25	625	15,625	390,625	5,250	131,250	100	10,000	13.579
10	280	30	900	27,000	810,000	8,400	252,000	170	28,900	.504
	ΣY	ΣX	ΣX^2	ΣX^3	ΣX^4	ΣXY	ΣX^2Y		Σy^2	Σe^2
	1,100	136	2,636	59,716	1,481,780	21,915	512,605		64,050	410.065

Solving the normal equations for $\hat{a}$, $\hat{b}$, and $\hat{c}$,

$$\Sigma Y = n\hat{a} + \hat{b}\Sigma X + \hat{c}\Sigma X^2$$
$$\Sigma XY = \hat{a}\Sigma X + \hat{b}\Sigma X^2 + \hat{c}\Sigma X^3$$
$$\Sigma X^2 Y = \hat{a}\Sigma X^2 + \hat{b}\Sigma X^3 + \hat{c}\Sigma X^4$$

$$1,100 = 10\hat{a} + 136\hat{b} + 2,636\hat{c}$$
$$21,915 = 136\hat{a} + 2,636\hat{b} + 59,716\hat{c}$$
$$512,605 = 2,636\hat{a} + 59,716\hat{b} + 1,481,780\hat{a}$$

$$\hat{a} = 17.31 \qquad \hat{b} = 3.23 \qquad \hat{c} = 0.185$$

The equation of the nonlinear curve is

$$\hat{Y} = \hat{a} + \hat{b}X + \hat{c}X^2$$
$$\hat{Y} = 17.31 + 3.23X + 0.185X^2$$

The correlation coefficient is given by

$$r = \sqrt{1 - \frac{\Sigma e^2}{\Sigma y^2}} = \sqrt{1 - \frac{410.07}{64,050}} = .997$$

4-3. NONLINEAR FUNCTIONS FIT TO TIME-SERIES DATA

There are many instances where we are concerned about the change of a variable through time, such as the change of the national income. Linear-difference equations are often used to approximate these time-dependent functions.

The general form of a first-order linear-difference equation is

$$f(t) = Y_t - aY_{t-1} \tag{4-10}$$

If we let $\bar{Y}$ be the equilibrium value of Y,

$$f(t) = \bar{Y}_t - a\bar{Y}_{t-1} \tag{4-11}$$

and y the deviation from the equilibrium value, we obtain

$$y_t = ay_{t-1}$$

where

$$y_t = Y_t - \bar{Y}_t \qquad y_{t-1} = Y_{t-1} - \bar{Y}_{t-1}$$
$$y_t = a(ay_{t-2}) = a^2 y_{t-2} = \cdots a^t y_0 \tag{4-12}$$

Eventually $y_t = a^t y_0$, where y_0 is the initial deviation from the equilibrium level. Observing the equation, we note that as t increases, the value of y_t depends on the value of the parameter a.

(a) When $\quad a > 1,\quad y_t$ increases steadily and without limit.
(b) When $\quad a = 1,\quad y_t$ is constant.
(c) When $\quad 1 > a > 0,\quad y_t$ decreases steadily toward zero.

(d) When $0 > a > -1$, y_t alternates from negative to positive and vice versa, and decreases toward zero.

(e) When $a = -1$, y_t has constant oscillation.

(f) When $a < -1$, y_t alternates and its magnitude increases without limit.

It is obvious that even though the difference equation is linear, the behavior of Y with respect to time is nonlinear. Given the initial value of Y and the parameter a, we can trace the path of Y through time.

The general form of a second-order linear-difference equation is

$$f(t) = Y_t + aY_{t-1} + bY_{t-2} \qquad (4\text{-}13)$$

The deviation of Y from the equilibrium level $\bar{Y}$ then has the following relationship:

$$y_t + ay_{t-1} + by_{t-2} = 0 \qquad (4\text{-}14)$$

In solving the equation, let $y_t = \lambda^t$; then

$$\lambda^t + a\lambda^{t-1} + b\lambda^{t-2} = 0$$

Therefore

$$\lambda^2 + a\lambda + b = 0 \qquad (4\text{-}15)$$

The solutions are

$$\lambda_1 = \tfrac{1}{2}(-a + \sqrt{a^2 - 4b}) \qquad (4\text{-}16)$$
$$\lambda_2 = \tfrac{1}{2}(-a - \sqrt{a^2 - 4b}) \qquad (4\text{-}17)$$

The value of Y thus depends on a and b.

(a) If $a^2 > 4b$,

$$y_t = A_1\lambda_1^t + A_2\lambda_2^t$$

or

$$Y_t = \bar{Y}_t + A_1\lambda_1^t + A_2\lambda_2^t \qquad (4\text{-}18)$$

where A_1, A_2 are arbitrary constants whose value can be determined by initial values of y_0 and y_1. That is,

$$y_0 = A_1 + A_2 \qquad y_1 = A_1\lambda_1 + A_2\lambda_2$$

When $|\lambda_1| > 1$, Y_t will increase without limit;

$\lambda_1 = \lambda_2 = 0$, Y_t will be constant and equal to $\bar{Y}_t$;

$|\lambda_1| < 1$ ($|\lambda_2|$ also < 1), Y_t will decrease towards $\bar{Y}_t$.

(b) If $a^2 = 4b$, $\lambda_1 = \lambda_2 = -\tfrac{1}{2}a$

$$Y_t = \bar{Y}_t + (A_1 + A_2 t)(-\tfrac{1}{2}a)^t \qquad (4\text{-}19)$$

where A_1, A_2 are arbitrary constants which can be found in terms of initial values of y_0 and y_1. That is,

$$y_0 = A_1 \qquad y_1 = (A_1 + A_2)(-\tfrac{1}{2}a)$$

When $\quad 2 > a > 0,\quad Y_t$ alternates and decreases toward $\bar{\bar{Y}}_t$
$\qquad\qquad a \geq 2,\quad Y_t$ alternates and explodes
$\qquad -2 < a < 0,\quad Y_t$ decreases steadily toward $\bar{\bar{Y}}_t$
$\qquad\qquad a \leq -2,\quad Y_t$ increases steadily and without limit

(c) If $a^2 < 4b$, λ_1 and λ_2 are conjugate complex, and

$$\lambda_1 = -\frac{a}{2} + \frac{1}{2}i\sqrt{4b - a^2} \qquad \lambda_2 = -\frac{a}{2} - \frac{1}{2}i\sqrt{4b - a^2}$$

$$Y_t = \bar{\bar{Y}}_t + A_1\left(-\frac{a}{2} + \frac{1}{2}i\sqrt{4b - a^2}\right)^t + A_2\left(-\frac{a}{2} - \frac{1}{2}i\sqrt{4b - a^2}\right)^t$$

$$(4\text{-}20)$$

where A_1 and A_2 are arbitrary constants. The equation is a sinusoidal function, using sine and cosine curves to depict periodic or cyclical movement through time.

Taylor's theorem states that

$$f(x) = f(c) + \frac{f'(c)}{1!}(x - c) + \frac{f''(c)}{2!}(x - c)^2 \cdots$$

When $c = 0$, it is known as the Maclaurin's series:

$$f(x) = f(0) + \frac{f'(0)}{1!}x + \frac{f''(0)}{2!}x^2 \cdots$$

Applying the theorem to e^{ix}, $\cos x$, and $\sin x$, we obtain

$$e^{ix} = 1 + ix - \frac{x^2}{2!} - i\frac{x^3}{3!} \cdots$$

$$\cos x = 1 - \frac{x^2}{2!} + \frac{x^4}{4!} - \frac{x^6}{6!} \cdots$$

$$\sin x = x - \frac{x^3}{3!} + \frac{x^5}{5!} - \frac{x^7}{7!} \cdots$$

Thus

$$e^{ix} = \cos x + i \sin x \qquad \text{or} \qquad e^{-ix} = \cos x - i \sin x$$

Let $\alpha = -a/2$, $\beta = \frac{1}{2}\sqrt{4b - a^2}$ and transform $\alpha \pm i\beta$ to polar coordinates:

$$\alpha \pm i\beta = r \cos\theta \pm r \sin\theta i$$
$$= r(\cos\theta \pm i \sin\theta)$$
$$= re^{\pm i\theta}$$

Therefore

$$(\alpha \pm i\beta)^t = r^t e^{\pm i\theta t}$$

We may then rewrite Eq. 4-20 as

$$Y_t = \bar{\bar{Y}}_t + A_1(\alpha + i\beta)^t + A_2(\alpha - i\beta)^t$$
$$= \bar{\bar{Y}}_t + r^t[A_1 e^{i\theta t} + A_2 e^{-i\theta t}]$$

$$= \overline{Y}_t + r^t[A_1(\cos \theta t + i \sin \theta t) + A_2(\cos \theta t - i \sin \theta t)]$$
$$= \overline{Y}_t + r^t[(A_1 + A_2)\cos \theta t + i(A_1 - A_2)\sin \theta t]$$

Let $A_1 + A_2 = A \cos e$, $i(A_1 - A_2) = A \sin e$. Then

$$Y_t = \overline{Y}_t + r^t[A \cos e \cos \theta t + A \sin e \sin \theta t]$$
$$= \overline{Y}_t + Ar^t \cos(\theta t - e) \tag{4-21}$$

The arbitrary constants A and e are to be found from the initial values of Y_0 and Y_1.

Since

$$r \cos \theta = \alpha = -\frac{a}{2}$$

and

$$r \sin \theta = \beta = \tfrac{1}{2}\sqrt{4b - a^2}$$

$$\tan \theta = \frac{\beta}{\alpha} = -\frac{\sqrt{4b - a^2}}{a} \qquad \theta = \tan^{-1}\left(-\frac{\sqrt{4b - a^2}}{a}\right)$$

$$r^2 = \alpha^2 + \beta^2 = \frac{a^2}{4} + \frac{(4b - a^2)}{4} = b \qquad r = \sqrt{b}$$

When $r > 1$, Y_t becomes explosive as t increases

$\qquad\quad r < 1$, Y_t comes to the equilibrium level as t increases

and

$\qquad\quad r = 1$, Y_t becomes a regular oscillation of constant amplitude

The periodic function can be better understood by studying Fig. 4-1.

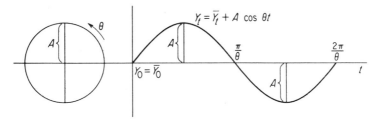

Fig. 4-1

Assume $r = 1$, $e = 0$. The horizontal axis indicates the equilibrium level of Y, $(\overline{Y})$. When $e = 0$, $Y_0 = \overline{Y}_0$. A is the amplitude of the curve, θ the angular velocity, and the time required to complete a cycle of oscillation is given by

$$T = \frac{2\pi}{\theta}$$

SELECTED BIBLIOGRAPHY

1. R. G. D. Allen, *Mathematical Economics*. London: Macmillan, 1960.
2. E. F. Beach, *Economic Models: An Exposition*. New York: Wiley, 1957.
3. J. S. Duesenberry, G. Fromm, L. R. Klein, and E. Kuh (eds.), *The Brookings-SSRC Quarterly Econometric Model of the United States*. Chicago: Rand-McNally and North-Holland Press, 1965.
4. L. R. Klein, R. J. Ball, A. Hazelwood, and P. Vandome, *An Econometric Model of the United Kingdom*. Oxford: Blackwell, 1961.
5. L. R. Klein and A. S. Goldberger, *An Econometric Model of United States, 1929–1952*. Amsterdam: North-Holland, 1955.

EXERCISES

4-1. Transform the following equations into a linear relationship and estimate the regression coefficients (a) and (b) for the given data. $Y = cK^aL^bu$, where c is a constant and u is a random variable.

Y	60	70	75	80	70	65	60	100	105	90	80	95
K	200	240	260	270	250	300	200	350	355	340	320	345
L	40	42	45	48	46	50	48	60	65	62	60	64

4-2. Find the regression coefficients of $Y = a + bX + cX^2$ based on the following data:

X	4	8	7	6	5	3	7	9	10	12	8	15
Y	85	120	115	90	95	80	125	150	160	180	90	200

4-3. Find the correlation coefficient of the relationship expressed in Exercise 4-2. Is it significant? If X equals 20, make a prediction for Y.

4-4. Find the general solution for $y_t = \frac{1}{2} y_{t-1}$ given the initial condition $y_0 = 1$. As t increases, how would y change?

4-5. Find the general solution for $y_t = y_{t-1} - y_{t-2}$, given $y_0 = 1$, $y_1 = \frac{1}{2}$. As t increases, what will be the time path for Y_t?

chapter 5

Computer-Simulation Models†

In real life it often happens that the economic system under study is very complicated. It may be that we have difficulty in specifying the system in exact mathematical forms, or that we have specified the system by a set of mathematical equations, but the existing analytical methods may fail to solve the equations. If such is the case we may use the computer-simulation method to find approximate solutions.

Not only may computer simulation yield solutions for a very complicated system, but the method also has the following advantages.

1. When sampling in the real world is a problem, the computer-simulation method proposes to generate a large number of sample values from a known probability distribution based on theory of randomness.
2. When we can observe only the input and output data of a system without exact knowledge of the system itself, we may use the computer-simulation method to test our hypothesis about the operating characteristics of the system. If the input and output data of the simulation model coincide with the empirical observations, we may conclude that our hypothesis is correct.
3. When a decision maker has to choose the best policy from a number of alternatives and it will take too long or be too costly to try out all the alternatives in real life, computer-simulation provides a way to simulate all alternatives in compressed time and without interrupting the actual operation of the system. The decision maker thus may have more

†Irma Adelman and Frank L. Adelman in "The Dynamic Properties of the Klein Goldberger Model," *Econometrica*, Vol. 27, October 1959, pp. 595–625, have reported the successful use of simulation method in simulating business cycles in the United States.

information obtained from comparing the simulation results of different alternatives to make a sensible choice.
4. By examining the time paths of the variables in the model we may learn
how step by step these variables reach the final state which may enable
us to design control devices to make the variables fall into certain
limits in a specified time period.

5-1. GENERATION OF RANDOM NUMBERS

In order to obtain representative samples from a population we need
a device to assure randomness. In computer simulation this is provided
by a sequence of random numbers. One way to have a sequence of random numbers is to store a random-number table in the memory of the
computer. Because the memory location is numbered and sequenced,
only a few simple instructions in a computer program will enable the
computer to select these random numbers by their proper sequence.
However, to store a random-number table in the memory of a computer
requires hundreds or thousands of locations. This is a very costly require-
ment and limits the available locations for storing computer programs
and other data. Thus we usually use the method of generating pseudo-
random numbers.

There are different ways of generating pseudo-random numbers.
Those most often used are listed as follows.

Additive Method

The method assumes k starting values. k should be larger than 15.
The sequence of pseudo-random numbers is then generated according to
the formula

$$R_{i+1} \equiv R_i + R_{i-k+1} \, (\text{modulo } m) \qquad (5\text{-}1)$$

The formula indicates a congruence relationship. Modulo m means
$R_{i+1} - (R_i + R_{i-k+1})$ is divisible by m and R_{i+1} and $(R_i + R_{i-k+1})$
leave identical remainders when divided by $|m|$. On a binary computer
if we let $m = 2^b$, where b is the number of bits carried by the computer,
the period of the generated pseudo-random numbers equals $p_k \cdot 2^{b-1}$,
where p_k is a constant that depends on k and b (for example, if $k = 16$,
$b = 35$, then $p_{16} = 255$, the sequence of the pseudo-random numbers
will have $255 \cdot 2^{34}$ different values before the sequence repeats itself).

Multiplicative Method

The method starts with a chosen initial number and a constant
multiplier, and by successive multiplication it computes a sequence of
nonnegative integers, which are the pseudo-random numbers.

$$R_{i+1} \equiv aR_i \,(\text{modulo } m) \qquad (5\text{-}2)$$

where a is the constant multiplier. It is suggested that $a = 200t \pm r$ where t is an integer and r is any of the values 3, 11, 13, 19, 21, 27, 29, 37, 53, 59, 61, 67, 69, 77, 83, 91. The initial number of the sequence should be an integer not divisible by 2 or 5. The procedure will produce $5 \times 10^{d-2}$ numbers before repeating for d greater than 3, where d is the number of digits of the random numbers.

The pseudo-random numbers generated by this method have been proven to be uncorrelated and uniformly distributed.

5-2. STATISTICAL TESTING METHODS

There are also cases when experimenters use mixed additive and multiplicative method. The choice of an appropriate method depends on the computational speed, the length of periodicity, and how well the generated numbers behave statistically. There are several statistical methods for testing the randomness of the generated sequence. A few of these are listed below.

Frequency Test

The frequency test is used to test whether the pseudo-random numbers are uniformly distributed. First we consider that all the numbers fall in a unit interval $(0, 1)$ by placing the decimal point in front of each number. We then divided the unit interval into x equal subintervals. If we have generated N pseudo-random numbers, then the expected number of pseudo-random numbers in each subinterval is N/x. A chi-square test may be applied to check the reasonableness of the results:

$$\chi^2 = \frac{x}{N} \sum_{i=1}^{x} \left(f_i - \frac{N}{x} \right)^2 \qquad (5\text{-}3)$$

where f_i denotes the actual number of pseudo-random numbers in the ith subinterval. The chi-square distribution has $x - 1$ degrees of freedom.

Serial Tests

Serial tests are used to test the randomness between successive pseudo-random numbers; that is, to examine whether there is significant correlation between R_i and R_{i+k}, where k is a positive integer and $i = 1$, $2, \ldots, (N - k)$. An autocorrelation coefficient C_k is used for this measure.

$$C_k = \frac{1}{N} \sum_{i=1}^{N-k} R_i R_{i+k} \qquad (5\text{-}4)$$

Statistical theory indicates that when $k \geq 1$, C_k are approximately normally distributed variates with mean equal to $1/4$ and standard deviation equal to $.22/\sqrt{N}$, for truly random samples. Thus the classical test of hypothesis procedure may be used to determine whether we should accept the hypothesis that there is no significant autocorrelation between R_i and R_{i+k}, $[i = 1, 2, \ldots, (N - k)]$.

Tests of Runs

Tests of runs are for testing the random oscillatory nature of the pseudo-random numbers. We either compare the successive numbers in a sequence or compare each number with the mean; for instance, if we make all the numbers fall in a unit $(0, 1)$ interval, the mean is $1/2$. Using the first method, we may denote $R_{i+1} > R_i$ as 0, and $R_{i+1} < R_i$ as 1. A subsequence of K ones, bracketed by zeros at each end, forms a run of ones of length K. A subsequence of K zeros, bracketed by ones at each end forms a run of zeros of length K. The expected values for a truly random sample should be $(2N - 1)/3$ for total number of runs, $2\{(K^2 + 3K + 1)N - (K^3 + 3K^2 - K - 4)\}/(K + 3)!$ for runs of length $1 \leq K \leq N - 1$, and $2/N!$ for runs of length $(N - 1)$. Using the second method, we may denote $R_i < 1/2$ as 0 and $R_i > 1/2$ as 1. The expected total number of runs for a truly random sample should be $(N + 1)/2$ and the expected number of runs of length K is $(N - K + 3)2^{-K-1}$.

5-3. GENERATION OF SAMPLE VALUES FROM GIVEN PROBABILITY DISTRIBUTIONS

Empirical Discrete Distributions

Suppose from the historical data of a firm we have gathered the following information:

Possible Unit Demand in a Day	Frequency in a Year	Probability	Cumulative Probability
0	15	.0411	.0411
1	90	.2466	.2877
2	150	.4110	.6987
3	100	.2739	.9726
4	10	.0274	1.0000
	365 days	1.0000	

And we assume that the demand situation will remain the same, we may generate samples by the following procedure.

(a) Generate pseudo-random numbers with four significant digits.

(b) Demand for the day is obtained by the following rule:

Numbers 0000 through 0410 represent a demand for 0 unit

"	0411	"	2876	"	"	1 "
"	2877	"	6986	"	"	2 units
"	6987	"	9725	"	"	3 "
"	9726	"	9999	"	"	4 "

If the empirical data can be fitted to a theoretical distribution, it is more efficient to use theoretical distribution, since its property will be well known and simulation methods are in many cases already developed and tested. Following are some common theoretical distributions. The decision whether it is an acceptable "good fit" will be based on statistical tests such as the chi-square test.

Theoretical Continuous Distributions

Rectangular Distribution

$$f(X) = \frac{1}{B - A}$$

The range of the distribution is from A to B, and we may generate the variates by the following formula:

$$X = A + (B - A) \cdot R \tag{5-5}$$

where R is a pseudo-random number in unit interval $(0, 1)$.

Exponential Distribution

$$f(X) = Ae^{-AX}$$

If the parameter of the distribution is A, we may generate the variate by the formula

$$X = -\frac{1}{A} \log R \tag{5-6}$$

where R is a pseudo-random number in unit interval $(0, 1)$.

This is an example of the inverse-transformation method.

The cumulation distribution function of the exponential distribution is

$$F(X) = \int_0^X Ae^{-AX} dX = 1 - e^{-AX}$$

When $X = 0$, $F(X) = 0$, and when X approaches infinity, $F(X) = 1$.

Let

$$R = 1 - F(X) = e^{-AX}$$

(The range of R is from 1 to 0, as X varies from 0 to ∞.) Then

$$\log R = -AX$$

and thus

$$X = -\frac{1}{A} \log R$$

In Chapter 1 we have shown that the mean and standard deviation of an exponential distribution equal $1/A$; this fact may be used to test whether the sample values generated by a computer program are exponentially distributed.

Normal Distribution

$$f(X) = \frac{1}{\sigma\sqrt{2\pi}} \; e^{-(X-\mu)^2/2\sigma^2}$$

Normally distributed variates may be generated by summing short sequences of uniformly distributed variates. For the sake of simplifying calculation, a rectangular distribution with its variable y ranging from 0 to 12 is chosen, with mean μ_y equal to 6 and variance σ_y^2 equal to 12. Samples of 12 values each are taken from the rectangular distribution.

The standardized normal variate of the sample means is therefore

$$z = \frac{\bar{y} - \mu_y}{\sigma_y/\sqrt{n}} = \frac{\sum\limits_{i=1}^{12} y_i}{12} - 6$$

Let R_i be a pseudo-random number in unit interval (0, 1), then

$$z = \sum_{i=1}^{12} R_i - 6$$

Given μ and σ as the mean and standard deviation of a normal distribution, the variates of the distribution may be generated by the formula

$$X = \mu + \sigma \cdot z = \mu + \sigma\left(\sum_{i=1}^{12} R_i - 6\right) \tag{5-7}$$

Normal distribution has the property that the interval $(\mu \pm \sigma)$ includes 68 percent of the total occurrences and the $(\mu \pm 2\sigma)$ interval includes 95 percent. This fact may be used to check the validity of a computer program which will supposedly generate normal variates.

Theoretical Discrete Distributions

Binomial Distribution

$$f(X) = \binom{N}{X} p^X (1 - p)^{N-X}$$

The parameters of a binomial distribution are N and p, with $0 \le p \le 1$. We may generate the variates by the rejection method.

1. Generate n pseudo-random numbers, each of them in a unit interval $(0,1)$.
2. Compare each of the pseudo-random number $R_i(i = 1, 2, \ldots, N)$ with p.

   If $R_i \leq p$, it is a success
   If $R_i > p$, it is a failure or rejected

3. Count the number of successes in n comparisons; call it X. X is a variate of the binomial distribution.

Poisson Distribution

$$f(X) = e^{-\lambda} \frac{\lambda^X}{X!}$$

Poisson distribution describes a sequence of independent Bernoulli trials, when the probability of an event p occurring is very small and the sample size N is very large, $\mu = Np$.

To generate Poisson variates, we may take advantage of its relationship with the exponential distribution. The number of times the exponential variates, with mean equals to $1/\lambda$, occurred in a unit time interval constitutes a Poisson variate with mean equals to λ. Figure 5-1 indicates such a relationship.

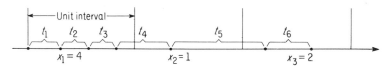

Fig. 5-1. $g(t) = \lambda e^{-\lambda t}$
where t is an exponential variate,
$$f(X) = e^{-\lambda} \frac{\lambda^X}{X!}$$
where X is a Poisson variate.

5-4. SIMULATION OF ECONOMIC SYSTEMS

To quantify economic relationships and to search for guidance in making rational decisions, the economists first introduced marginal analysis; the well-known rule of maximizing the profit of a firm at the price and output where marginal revenue equals marginal cost or where marginal revenue product equals marginal resource cost. This assumes a continuous production function, cost function, and demand function. Later on in application, however, it was found that a large number of products and factors of production are not infinitely divisible, and substitution among products and factors is quite restricted. The management of a firm had only a finite number of choices of production activities. Thus linear programming was introduced. The decision structure becomes that within the constraints of limited quantities of resources; the management's role is to choose a set of production activities that will optimize the firm's objective function. Again, in reality, the objectives of a firm are diversified and the products and factors markets are quite complicated and in many instances cannot be approximated by linear relationships. When we employ nonlinear relationships with complicated feedback interactions among the economic variables, the known analytical methods are unable to analyze the system so as to yield solutions to problems. The computer-simulation method provides a way to overcome these difficulties. The method may not always yield exact solutions, but it will at least give us a more detailed description of the system in question and make comparisons of alternatives in the light of the system's objectives.

The general procedure of simulating an economic system is as follows.

1. Construct a model of the system, which specifies the relationships among relevant economic variables by a set of equations. The equations may describe the operating characteristics of the variables or may only express identities among variables. Some of the variables are *exogenous*, which means their values are determined outside of the model (including policy variables). And some of the variables are *endogenous*, which means their values are generated within the model and are affected by the exogenous variables and other endogenous variables.
2. Assign specific numerical values to the parameters of the model (in empirical studies, these values are estimated from samples taken from the real world) and also to specify arbitrary values for the exogenous variables. (For policy variables, their values are assigned by the policy decision makers.)
3. Make assumptions about the probability distributions of the stochastic disturbance terms of the model.
4. Combine the exogenous variables with the disturbance values to generate values for the endogenous variables by the computer-simulation method.

Following are some examples taken from the general text of economic theories and transformed into computer-simulation models.

Cobweb Model

The model assumes that the quantity demanded of a particular product in a specified time period is inversely related to the price of the product and other factors. The effect of the other factors can be described by a known probability distribution with zero mean and constant variance. The quantity supplied is assumed to depend on the price in the preceding time period and other factors. The effect of the other factors can be described by another known probability distribution with zero mean and constant variance. The product is perishable and the market is assumed to be cleared at the end of each period, subject to a random disturbance. The equations of the model are given as follows.

Exogenous Variables

u_t = a random variate with a known probability distribution, whose mean equals zero, and variance σ_u^2

v_t = a random variate with a known probability distribution, whose mean equals zero, and variance σ_v^2

w_t = a random variate with a known probability distribution, whose mean equals zero, and variance σ_w^2

Endogenous Variables

P_t = price in period t

D_t = quantity demanded in period t

S_t = quantity supplied in period t

Parameters (estimated by econometric methods)

A = level of demand at zero price

B = level of supply when the price in the preceding period is zero

M = marginal demand–price ratio

N = marginal supply–price ratio (where price is the price of preceding period)

Operating Characteristics

$$D_t = A - MP_t + u_t \qquad (5\text{-}8)$$

$$S_t = B + NP_{t-1} + v_t \qquad (5\text{-}9)$$

Market-Clearing Condition (Equilibrium)

$$D_t = S_t + w_t \qquad (5\text{-}10)$$

Solving the equations to find the price relationship, we get

$$P_t = \frac{1}{M}(A - B - NP_{t-1} + u_t - v_t - w_t)$$

or

$$P_t = \frac{1}{M}(A - D_t + u_t) \qquad (5\text{-}11)$$

In conducting computer simulation, we first estimate the values of the parameters A, B, M, N. Then for a given initial price of the product and known probability distributions for u_t, v_t, and w_t we can generate time paths for P_t, S_t, and D_t. When these values are compared with actual time-series data, we can verify whether the model is a good approximation of the real world and whether our estimation of the parameters is accurate. The flow chart of this model is given in Fig. 5-2.

Savings-Investment Model

The model assumes that the government has control of the supply of money through its monetary policy. Further, it assumes stable ratios of savings–income, capital–output, capital–labor, cash–income, etc. With a given initial value of income, the model will generate time paths of income, employment, capital stock, price level, and wage rate.

Exogenous Variables
M_t = supply of money in period t (controlled by government: a policy variable)
u_t = a random variate with a known probability distribution, whose mean equals to zero and variance σ_u^2

Endogenous Variables
Y_t = income or output in period t
K_t = capital stock in period t
N_t = employment in period t
P_t = price level in period t
W_t = wage rate in period t

Parameters (estimated by econometric methods)
A = propensity to save (reciprocal of multiplier)
B = capital–output ratio (accelerator)
C = cash–income ratio (reciprocal of velocity of circulation)
D = capital–labor ratio
E = labor share of output

Financial Market-Clearing Condition (Equilibrium)
$$\text{Savings} = \text{investment} + \text{random variable}$$
$$A Y_t = (K_t - K_{t-1}) + u_t$$
$$= B(Y_t - Y_{t-1}) + u_t \tag{5-12}$$

Operating Characteristics
$$Y_t = \left(\frac{B}{B - A}\right) Y_{t-1} + \frac{u_t}{A - B} \tag{5-13}$$

$$P_t = \frac{M_t}{C Y_t} \tag{5-14}$$

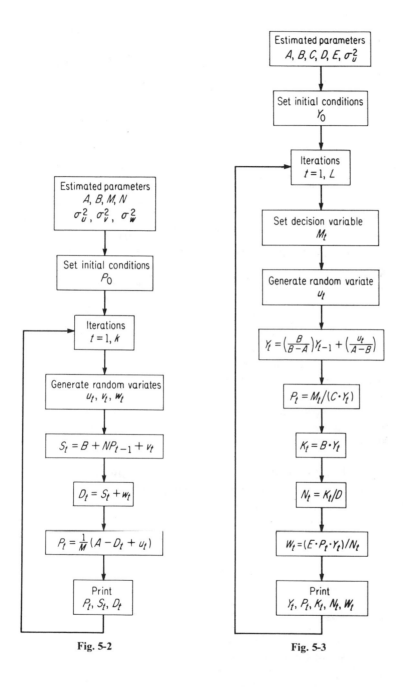

Fig. 5-2   Fig. 5-3

$$K_t = BY_t \tag{5-15}$$

$$N_t = \frac{K_t}{D} \tag{5-16}$$

$$W_t = \frac{EP_tY_t}{N_t} \tag{5-17}$$

In conducting computer simulation, we first estimate the values of the parameters A, B, C, D, E. Then, for a given initial value of income and a known probability distribution of u_t, plus the assigned values of M_t for each period, we can generate time paths for Y_t, P_t, K_t, and W_t. The flow chart of this model is given in Fig. 5-3.

The two models we have illustrated above are extremely simplified in order to demonstrate the technique of simulating economic systems. More complicated models of economic systems may be constructed and the same method used to study their operating characteristics.

In some of the empirical researches the models are not well structured—that is, the concept is not taken directly from certain well-developed economic theories and neatly transformed into an equation or a set of equations. A model may be mostly based on empirical observations. The system is viewed as consisting of groups or elements or entities; they may be job orders, raw materials, machines, tools, personnel; or they may be sales, finished products, trucks. Each element has its special attributes or characteristics; for example, a machine has its production capacities, an employee has job specifications. During the simulation process these attributes are changed by some events which occur according to some preassigned rules or probabilities; for example, the number of elements in each group may increase or decrease, sales may increase from zero to some positive number, a machine may be in operation or it may be idle, an employee may be working on different jobs or may be out to lunch. The simulation will give a dynamic description of the system in operation, so that we may see how things are changing—and if they are not changing in the direction or magnitude as we want them to change, how we can correct or control them.

In the following, we describe two models of the not-well-structured kind. One is a general microeconomic model; the other, a general macroeconomic model. A researcher who has a specific economic model in mind may build a similar model and do experiments with it.

Model of a Firm

The operation of a firm is divided into three major areas. One area is the factors markets, from which the firm draws the factors of production (intermediate products may be included) essential to its production. The prices and available quantities of the factors are given in functional forms similar to the supply curves discussed in economic theories. The

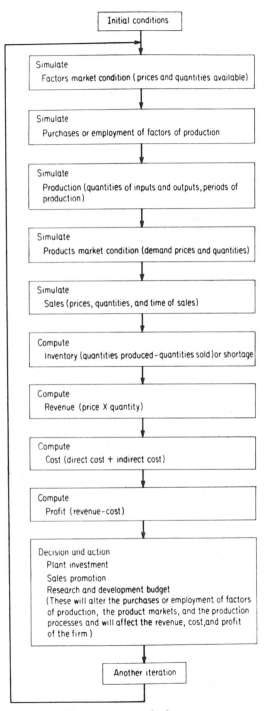

Fig. 5-4. Model of a firm.

firm examines the quantities it requires, the prices it has to pay, and the amount it can obtain and then makes purchase or employment decisions according to some predetermined rules. (The business games are different from the simulating models introduced here in that they involve human decisions in the simulation process and have different teams representing different firms competing with each other in an oligopolistic environment.)

The second area is the production activities inside the firm. The model simulates the transformation of the factors of production (intermediate products may be included) into final products. The quantities of the factors of production used to produce a given amount of finished product and the time elapsed during the production process usually are stochastic measurements. Thus queuing theories and probability distributions may be applied in this part of the simulation.

The third area is the products markets. The demand for the firm's products is simulated according to some given functions similar to the demand curves discussed in economic theories and the pricing rules adopted by the firm. The comparison of the demand and production rates will give inventory quantities and shortage frequencies of the products of the firm.

Finally, at some fixed time interval the total revenue and cost are computed and the total profit of the firm is evaluated.

At the end of each simulation run the user of the model may review the results and revise the decision rules and start another run.

The flow chart of this model is given in Fig. 5-4.

Model of a National Economy

The model implements ideas of Orcutt's *Micro-Analysis of Socio-Economic Systems* and Leontief's *Input-Output Analysis*. It starts with the initial conditions of a national economy, which includes: (a) the existing industrial and final-use sectors. An input-output coefficient matrix [A] may be used to describe the interindustry relationship, and probability functions may be used to describe the effective demand of each final-use sector. The final-use sectors may include both domestic and foreign users of the goods and services; (b) the primary inputs, such as labor, capital, and natural resources. Since the labor force is drawn from the population, a description is given of the population indicating the age and sex composition, the demand for goods and services, and capability and willingness to work under given conditions.

The first step in the simulation process is to simulate the population growth. To the initial population, preestimated birth and death rates of the different age and sex groups are applied to generate the subsequent population. The demand of this new population for different kinds of goods and services is simulated according to some given probability distributions. Foreign demand is estimated according to another given set of probability distributions.

The second step is to estimate the required total output of each industry to satisfy the simulated domestic and foreign demand. The estimation method may be similar to the one we introduced in Sec. 3-7, by multiplying the inverse matrix by the simulated final demand. If 0 is the required total output, $[I - A]^{-1}$ is the inverse matrix and D the simulated final demand, then

$$0 = [I - A]^{-1} D$$

However, here we may add random disturbance terms into the computation.

The third step is to estimate the required primary inputs—labor, capital, and natural resources—to support this output activity. The computation may be the multiplication of the total required output by the labor–output ratio, capital–output ratio, and resource–output ratios plus some random disturbance terms.

The fourth step is to simulate the available primary inputs. The available labor force generated from the new population, the accumulation of capital, and the utilization of natural resources are simulated according to some given probability distributions. Comparing the available primary inputs with the required primary inputs, the deficient or surplus amounts of each primary inputs are shown.

Finally, at the end of each simulation run the user of this model may examine the results and make decisions aiming to change the situation, such as to increase the capital supply by making foreign loans, import raw materials to reduce the shortage of natural resources, or relax immigration laws so that foreign labor may move in. With the changed conditions of the economy, another simulation run may be performed.

The flow chart of this model is given in Fig. 5-5.

The usefulness and validity of a computer simulation experiment, however, depend on a number of factors. We list here the more important ones.

1. *Structure of the econometric model.* Some of the econometric models containing nonlinearities in the endogenous variables may yield perverse simulation results when computer simulation experiments are applied to them. That is, the results will not be consistent with the properties of the reduced form of the model. Therefore the mathematical properties of the model should be carefully examined before computer simulation experiments are conducted.
2. *Estimation techniques.* In the following chapter we will introduce different estimation methods of the parameters of both single equation and simultaneous equations. The current econometric theory does not

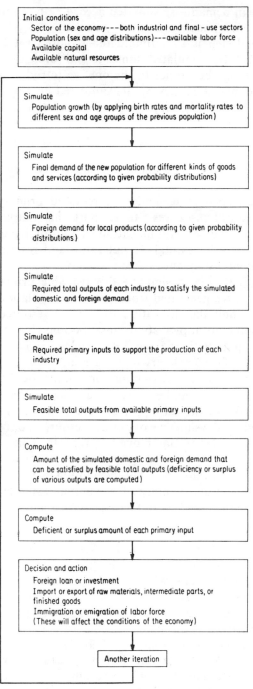

Fig. 5-5. Model of a national economy.

provide any assurance as to which method will give estimators that will yield valid, dynamic, closed-loop simulations. It is possible that that one of the estimation methods may yield parameter values which make the subsequent simulation in no sense resemble the behavior of the system we are trying to emulate. Consequently, comparing the properties of different estimators and choosing the one more suitable for simulation is an important step in the experiment. Sometimes if we find the value of a parameter is unstable with respect to time we may have to treat it as random variable of a given probability distribution in simulation experiments.

3. *Experiment design.* In designing computer simulation experiments, care must be taken in (a) factor selection—that is selecting values for some of the exogenous variables (usually referred to as the policy variables); (b) randomization—that is, we may include or not include the stochastic disturbance terms in the simulation experiments, and if they are included we have to estimate the function form of their distributions; (c) number of replications—that is, we have to decide the adequate sample size of the experiment so that the results will be sufficient for our intended analysis; and (d) length of simulation runs—that is, when the simulation run can be stopped without violating the classical statistical theories.

4. *Data analysis.* After the simulation is done, the result must be analyzed according to sound statistical methods. Regression analysis and analysis of variance are two of the often-used methods. Other methods such as multiple ranking, multiple comparision, and spectral analysis are also often applied, depending on the form of the output data and the purpose of the research.

SELECTED BIBLIOGRAPHY

1. C. P. Bonini, Simulation of Information and Decision Systems in the Firm. Englewood Cliffs, N.J.: Prentice-Hall, 1963.

2. G. P. E. Clarkson and H. A. Simon, "Simulation of Individual and Group Behavior," *American Economic Review*, vol. L, no. 5 (December 1960).

3. K. Cohen, Computer Models of the Shoe, Leather, Hide Sequence. Englewood Cliffs, N.J.: Prentice-Hall, 1960.

4. K. Chu, "Computer Simulation of Certain Stochastic Relationships in Micro-Economic Systems." Unpublished dissertation, Tulane University, 1964.

5. J. W. Forrester, *Industrial Dynamics.* Cambridge, Mass., and New York: M.I.T.–Wiley, 1961.

6. J. Harling, "Simulation Techniques in Operations Research," *Operations Research*, vol. 6 (May–June, 1958).

7. A. C. Hoggatt and F. E. Balderston (eds.), *Symposium on Simulation Models: Methodology and Applications to the Behavioral Sciences.* Cincinnati: South-Western, 1963.

8. E. P. Holland and R. W. Gillespie, *Experiments on a simulated Underdeveloped Economy: Development Plans and Balance of Payments Policies.* Cambridge: M.I.T. Press, 1963.

9. C. McMillan and R. F. Gonzales, *Systems Analysis, A Computer Approach to Decision Models.* Homewood, Ill.: Irwin, 1965.

10. T. H. Naylor, J. L. Balintfy, D. S. Burdick and K. Chu, *Computer Simulation Techniques.* New York: Wiley, 1966.

11. G. H. Orcutt, "Simulation of Economic System," *American Economic Review,* vol 50, no. 5 (December, 1960).

12. G. H. Orcutt, M. Greenberger, J. Korbel, and A. H. Rivlin, *Micro-Analysis of Socio-Economic Systems.* New York: Harper, 1961.

13. M. Shubik, "Simulation of the Industry and the Firm," *American Economic Review,* vol. 50, no. 5 (December, 1960).

14. D. Teichrow and J. F. Lubin, "Computer Simulation, Discussion of the Technique and Comparison of Languages," Working Paper No. 20, Graduate School of Business, Stanford University, Stanford, Calif. (Aug. 26, 1964).

15. K. D. Tocher, *The Art of Simulation.* Princeton, N.J.: Van Nostrand, 1963.

EXERCISES

5-1. For the cobweb model,

$$D_t = 6,000 - 4.5P_t + u_t$$
$$S_t = 1,000 + 0.2P_{t-1} + v_t$$
$$D_t = S_t + W_t$$

Given the initial price P_0 (when $t = 1$) of the commodity equals to $1,000 and u, v, w, are normally distributed variables with means equal to zero and variances equal to 2, 1, and 0.1 respectively, simulate the time paths of P, D, S of the commodity for 100 iterations. Observe the equilibrium positions of the supply and demand situation of the commodity. If the variance of u is doubled, how will it affect the result?

5-2. For the savings-investment model,

$$Y_t = 5\{(K_t - K_{t-1}) + u_t\}$$

$$P_t = 0.3 \frac{M_t}{Y_t}$$

$$K_t = 3 Y_t$$

$$N_t = 0.2K_t$$

$$W_t = 0.6 \frac{P_t Y_t}{N_t}$$

Given initial income $Y_0 = 10,000$ when $t = 1$ and u is a normally distributed variable with mean equals to zero and variance equal to 10. If the time function for M is $M_t = 1.02M_{t-1} + V_t$, with initial money supply $M_0 = 3,000$ (when $t = 1$) and V_t a normally distributed variable with mean equals to zero and variance equals to 1, simulate the time paths of Y, P, K, N, W for 100 iterations. Suggest how the money-supply function should be changed in order to stabilize the income and price.

5-3. Construct a multiplier accelerator model based on Keynesian economic theories. Design several simulation experiments and simulate the model on a computer. Discuss the results.

5-4. Simulate the operation of a service station which operates 12 hours every day with the customers arriving in a Poisson process with the mean equals to 4 customers per hour, and the service time in exponential distribution with the mean equals to 10 minutes. If the facility cost $100 per day and each customer brings $5 revenue to the station, what will be the expected gross profit per day for the station operating for a month? Discuss the validity of the prediction.

5-5. Construct a simulation model of a firm similar to the one described in Fig. 5-4. Program it, design three experiments, and make simulation runs on a computer. Discuss the results.

5-6. Construct a simulation model of a development economy similar to the one described in Fig. 5-5. Program it, design three experiments, and make simulation runs on a computer. Discuss the results.

chapter **6**

Problems of Specification, Estimation, Prediction, and Verification

In the previous chapters we have discussed linear models, nonlinear models and computer simulation models. Each of these models has been adopted in the empirical studies of economic systems.

However, in order to assure that the model will give a good description and will yield accurate predictions of the system under study, the validity of the applied techniques has to be carefully examined. In this chapter we first define the general term "economic model" and the relationships which the model attempts to describe. Then we discuss the problems in specifying the economic relationships, in estimating the values of the parameters, in making predictions, and in verifying the results. Of course not all problems can be solved at this stage, but we will attempt to make the reader aware of these problems and point out some of the available remedies.

6-1. ECONOMIC MODELS

Models are abstracts of reality. In the very complicated economic world we live in, we try to seek out relationships among only a few important variables ("few" in a sense of being manageable: "important" refers to our economic welfare). Of necessity we have to be abstract. Naturally an economic model is not the exact duplication of the real world, but it does facilitate understanding of the more important relationships that constitute our economic environment. Only when we understand these relationships can we expect to make forecasts and policy

130

recommendations with a high degree of confidence. Economic models may contain either microrelationships or macrorelationships, static relationships, or dynamic relationships.

Micro and Macro Relationships

The economic relationship that we want to investigate may be either "micro" or "macro." Microrelationships describe the behavior of a firm; for example, the relationship between the products and the factors of production may be described by a production function and a cost function, the marketing behavior by the demand curve facing the firm. Macrorelationships, on the other hand, refer to the relationships among aggregative economic variables such as national income, investment, consumption, export and import.

Static and Dynamic Relationships

"Static" implies that time is not under consideration. It gives only a cross-sectional view of the relationship among economic variables. While in a "dynamic" situation, time becomes an essential factor, and we are interested in the change of the magnitude of the variables over time.

6-2. PROBLEMS OF SPECIFICATION

When we try to specify the economic relationships by mathematical formulation we encounter problems such as which variables should be included in the equation,[†] what form they should assume (linear or nonlinear), and whether a single equation may be analyzed independently or a complete model of simultaneous equations should be considered all at once. If we fail to include some of the significant explanatory variables

[†] By including irrelevant variable (x_3)

$$y = \hat{b}_2 x_2 + \hat{b}_3 x_3 + e$$

$$\hat{b}_2 = \frac{\Sigma x_3^2 \Sigma x_2 y - \Sigma x_2 x_3 \Sigma x_3 y}{\Sigma x_2^2 \Sigma x_3^2 - (\Sigma x_2 x_3)^2}$$

But in fact,

$$y = b_2 x_2 + u \qquad (E(u^2) = \sigma u^2)$$

$$\hat{b}_2 = b_2 + \frac{\Sigma x_3^2 \Sigma x_2 u - \Sigma x_2 x_3 \Sigma x_3 u}{\Sigma x_2^2 \Sigma x_3^2 - (\Sigma x_2 x_3)^2}$$

$$\text{var}(\hat{b}_2) = E(\hat{b}_2 - b_2)^2$$

$$= \sigma_u^2 \Sigma x_3^2 / [\Sigma x_2^2 \Sigma x_3^2 - (\Sigma x_2 x_3)^2]$$

$$= \frac{\sigma_u^2}{\Sigma x_2^2 (1 - r_{23}^2)} > \frac{\sigma_u^2}{\Sigma x_2^2} \qquad \text{(larger variance)}$$

in the equation, the error term u will not be random, and if we assume the form of an explanatory variable to be linear when in fact it is related to the explained variable in a nonlinear fashion, then we will not get a correct indication from the linear-correlation coefficient. And if the explained variable in one relationship becomes the explanatory variable in another, the single relationship cannot be analyzed independently and a study of the complete simultaneous relationship is required. All these factors may affect the accuracy of the estimation and prediction.

We begin this chapter by giving an example illustrating the danger of omitting an important variable from an equation, which will give us a wrong notion of the relationship.

EXAMPLE:

Assume that the sales of a product are dependent on both the price of the product and the advertisement expenditure. With the following information

Sales	(S)	390	585	780
Price	(P)	1	1.5	2
Advertisement	(A)	10	20	30

we obtain the functional relationship

$$S = 200 - 10P + 20A$$

However, if we omit advertisement expenditure from the relationship and consider only the data of sales and price, the relationship becomes

$$S = 390P$$

which is obviously incorrect.

Factor Analysis—Principal-Axis Method

In specifying a relationship, it is necessary to know first what variables should be included in the relationship as explanatory variables. One method which will tell us the significance of each explanatory variable in explaining the variation of the explained variable is *factor analysis.* A factor is the grouping of one or more similarly behaved variables. In the following, we state the basic procedure of finding the factors by the principal axis method.

First we list all the variables that we think are in some way related. Suppose we have n such variables. We then collect sample data on these variables and compute a symmetric matrix R in such a way that on the diagonal of the matrix, we enter the square of the multiple correlation coefficient of one of the n variables in relation to the other variables. And off the diagonal of the matrix we enter the simple correlation coefficients between each pair of the n variables.

The matrix will be like the following:

$$
R = \begin{bmatrix}
R^2_{1.234\cdots n} & r_{12} & \cdots & r_{1n} \\
r_{12} & R^2_{2.134\cdots n} & \cdots & r_{2n} \\
\vdots & & & \\
r_{1n} & r_{2n} & \cdots & R^2_{n.123\cdots(n-1)}
\end{bmatrix}
$$

Then, we perform row and column operations on matrix R to transform it into a diagonal matrix. (See Chapter 2, transformation procedure.)

$$B^T R B = D$$

and

$$BB^T R B = BD$$

Since B is an orthogonal matrix, the transpose of B is the same as the inverse of B.

$$BB^T = I$$

Thus

$$RB = BD$$

where

$$
BD = \begin{bmatrix}
b_{11} & b_{12} & \cdots & b_{1n} \\
b_{21} & b_{22} & \cdots & b_{2n} \\
\vdots & & & \\
b_{n1} & b_{n2} & \cdots & b_{nn}
\end{bmatrix}
\begin{bmatrix}
\lambda_1 & 0 & \cdots & 0 \\
0 & \lambda_2 & \cdots & 0 \\
\vdots & & & \\
0 & 0 & \cdots & \lambda_n
\end{bmatrix}
$$

Matrix D is a diagonal matrix, on the diagonal are the characteristic roots $\lambda_i (i = 1, 2, \ldots, n)$ and off the diagonal are all zeros. B matrix is called the *matrix of characteristic vectors.* Choose only positive λ and arrange them in descending order. Multiplying $\sqrt{\lambda_i}$ by its respective column (characteristic) vector $b_{ji} (j = 1, 2, \ldots, n)$, we get vectors of coefficients. These coefficients represent the contributions of each variable to each factor.

	Factor 1	Factor 2	$\cdots$	Factor m
Variable 1	Coefficient	Coefficient		Coefficient
Variable 2	$\vdots$	$\vdots$		$\vdots$
$\vdots$	$\vdots$	$\vdots$	$\vdots$	$\vdots$
Variable n	$\vdots$	$\vdots$		$\vdots$

The coefficients in each vector whose values are very close may be grouped together and factors are defined by the grouped variables.

Identification

When more than one relationship has to be considered simultaneously—in other words, when an equation cannot be solved independently but has to be solved together with other equations in a simultaneous-equations model—it may happen that two or more equations consisting of the same variables cannot be distinguished from each other. This kind of problem is called a *problem of identification*. In the following, we use an example to illustrate the problem.

EXAMPLE:

Suppose we have a demand relationship and a supply relationship such as

$$X_d = a + bp \tag{6-1}$$

$$X_s = c + dp \tag{6-2}$$

where X_d is the quantity demanded of a commodity by the consumers at price p. X_s is the quantity of the commodity supplied by the suppliers at price p, while a, b, and c, d, are the parameters of the demand and supply equations respectively.

In the real world we can only observe the intersection points such as shown in Fig. 6-1, which represents the actual transactions made.

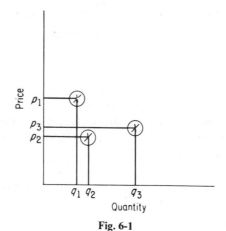

Fig. 6-1

When we join these points together there is no way of telling whether the curve is the demand function or the supply function, or neither.

This is quite evident if we look at Figs. 6-2, 6-3, and 6-4. Figure 6-2 shows that the demand situation is stable, but the supply curve shifted quite often. Thus by joining the observed points we obtain the demand curve. Figure 6-3 shows that the supply condition is quite stable, but the demand curve shifted often through time. Thus by joining the points of

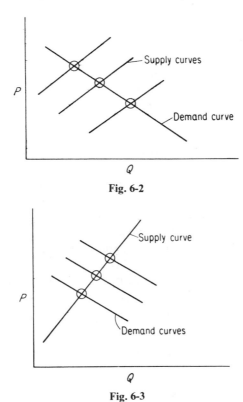

Fig. 6-2

Fig. 6-3

observation we obtain the supply curve. Figure 6-4 indicates that neither demand nor supply condition is stable. Thus we will not be able to obtain either of the curves by joining the observed points.

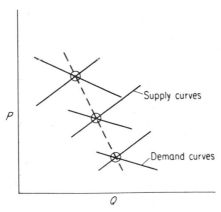

Fig. 6-4

The above illustration shows that sometimes it is impossible to unscramble two equations with the same variables from the statistics. Thus it becomes a specification problem. If such is the case, it is advisable to add different variables in the equations. In other words, if the equations are properly specified, the problem of identification may be avoided.

Detection

A necessary condition for identifying any one of the equations in a simultaneous-equation model is that every other equation in the system must contain at least one variable which is missing from the equation.

A more rigorous expression of the above statement is as follows. Let G be the total number of endogenous variables in the simultaneous-equation system, K the total number of predetermined (exogenous and lagged endogenous) variables in the simultaneous-equation system, g_1 the number of endogenous variables, and k_1 the number of predetermined variables in one of the equations. Also, let g_2 be the number of endogenous variables and k_2 the number of predetermined variables not included in that equation. Thus

$$g_2 = G - g_1, \qquad k_2 = K - k_1$$

The equation is exactly identified if

$$g_2 + k_2 = G - 1$$

which means that the total number of variables excluded from the equation must be equal to the total number of endogenous variables in the simultaneous-equation system less one.

If $g_2 + k_2 < G - 1$, the equation is underidentified, which indicates that the relationship cannot be distinguished statistically from other relationships of the model.

If $g_2 + k_2 > G - 1$, the equation is overidentified. Overidentification will make the estimation of parameters more complicated, since the simple least-squares method cannot be applied directly, and we have to use two-stage least squares or three-stage least squares or the full-information, maximum-likelihood method.

Rank Condition for Identifiability

The identifiability of an equation in a simultaneous linear structural equation model may also be determined by the rank of a submatrix of the reduced-form coefficients. To obtain the submatrix, the entire model has to be cast into reduced form first. And the submatrix for examination is the one which consists of the reduced-form coefficients of the endogenous variables included in the equation and the reduced-form coefficients of the exogenous variables excluded from the equation. If the rank of the submatrix is equal to the number of the endogenous variables in the equation less one ($g_1 - 1$), the equation is identifiable; otherwise it is not.

Correction

When one equation of a simultaneous-equation system is under-identified, a way to correct it is to find another predetermined variable which may serve as an explanatory variable for the other equations.

For example, the supply relation in the simultaneous-equation system (6-1), (6-2), is unidentifiable; however, we find that the quantity demanded is also related to income, and change the model to the following:

$$X_d = a + bp + eY \tag{6-3}$$

$$X_s = c + dp \tag{6-4}$$

Now the equation $X_s = c + dp$ is identifiable, because when income varies, the demand curve will shift, while the supply curve will remain unaffected; thus the situation will be similar to that of Fig. 6-4. The demand function, however, is still unidentifiable.

A numerical example of an unidentifiable relationship is as follows. Given the information

Q	P	q	p	p^2	qp
320	1.5	86	$-.1$	.01	-8.6
200	1	-34	$-.6$	.36	20.4
120	2	-114	.4	.16	-45.6
150	1.5	-84	$-.1$	.01	8.4
315	2	81	.4	.16	32.4
325	1.5	91	$-.1$	.01	-9.1
100	2	-134	.4	.16	-53.6
350	1	116	$-.6$	.36	-69.6
300	2	66	.4	.16	26.4
160	1.5	-74	$-.1$	.01	7.1
2,340	16			1.40	-91.8

where Q is the volume of market transactions and P is the price. The least-squares estimators are

$$\hat{b} = -\frac{91.8}{1.4} = -65.6$$

$$\hat{a} = 234 + 65.6 \times 1.6 = 339$$

the linear-regression line is

$$\hat{Q} = 339 - 65.6P$$

We have no way of telling whether this is the demand function or the supply function, or neither. (See Fig. 6-5.)

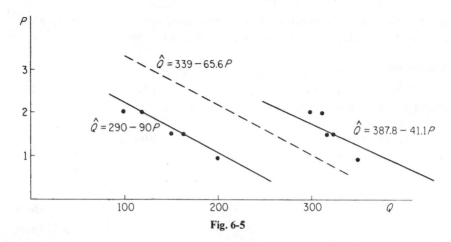

Fig. 6-5

Now, if we further observe that income is one of the explanatory variables of the demand of the product and the information we have is as follows, where Y is the income, t the time periods:

t	Q	P	Y
1	320	1.5	100
2	200	1	50
3	120	2	60
4	150	1.5	45
5	315	2	110
6	325	1.5	120
7	100	2	55
8	350	1	115
9	300	2	105
10	160	1.5	50

We observe that the incomes are similar at time periods 1, 5, 6, 8 and 9; also, they are similar at time periods 2, 3, 4, 7, and 10. If we separate the two groups and apply least-squares method, respectively, we will obtain the demand functions at two different income levels:

t	Q	P	q	p	p^2	pq
1	320	1.5	-2	$-.1$	.01	.2
5	315	2	-7	.4	.16	-2.8
6	325	1.5	3	$-.1$	.01	$-.3$
8	350	1	28	$-.6$	.36	-16.8
9	300	2	-22	.4	.16	-8.8
	1,610	8.0			.70	-28.5

The least-squares estimators are

$$\hat{b} = \frac{-28.5}{.7} = -41.1$$

$$\hat{a} = 322 + 41.1 \times 1.6 = 387.8$$

The estimated demand function at the higher income level becomes

$$\hat{Q} = 387.8 - 41.1P$$

t	Q	P	q	p	p^2	pq
2	200	1	54	−.6	.36	−32.4
3	120	2	−26	.4	.16	−10.4
4	150	1.5	4	−.1	.01	−.4
7	100	2	−46	.4	.16	−18.4
10	160	1.5	14	−.1	.01	−1.4
	730	8.0			.70	−63.0

The least-squares estimators are

$$\hat{b} = \frac{-63}{.7} = -90$$

$$\hat{a} = 146 + 1.6 \times 90 = 290$$

The estimated demand function at the lower income level becomes

$$\hat{Q} = 290 - 90P$$

The shift of demand at different income levels indicates that ordinary least-squares should not be applied to the data to estimate the demand function. In this model only the supply function is identifiable.

6-3. PROBLEMS OF ESTIMATION

In all the models, we have discussed above, the values of the parameters have to be estimated, because even if the model is properly specified it still will not give the real system a quantitative description without correctly estimated parameters.

A good estimator should have the following characteristics:

1. It is unbiased. Using the same estimation process an infinite number of times (each time the sample size remains constant), the average value of the estimators obtained would equal the true value of the parameter being estimated $E(\hat{b}) = b$.
2. It is consistent. As the size of the sample used for the estimation increases to infinity, the estimator would approach the true value of the parameter. $\lim_{n \to \infty} P\{(\hat{b} - b) \leq \epsilon\} = 1$, where ϵ is a very small value. This is referred to as the asymptotic property of an estimator.
3. It is efficient. The estimators obtained by applying the process to different samples differ from one another by a smaller amount than the estimates produced by other methods. $E(\hat{b} - b)^2 = $ minimum.
4. It is sufficient. The estimation method should exhaust all available information provided by the data.

The least-squares estimators we have introduced in Chapter 3 are based on the assumptions that the samples we take from the real world are representative of the true population (no observation errors, no autocorrelation, etc.), the explanatory variables and the error term are independent of each other and the following assumptions hold for the distribution of the error term u.

$$E(u_i) \quad = 0 \qquad \text{for all } i = 1, 2, \ldots, n$$
$$E(u_i u_j) = 0 \qquad \text{for } i \neq j$$
$$\qquad = \sigma_u^2 \quad \text{for } i = j \quad i, j = 1, 2, \ldots, n$$

If these assumptions are violated, the least-squares estimators may be biased and/or inefficient. This can be seen in the following illustrations.

From Chapter 3, the least-squares estimator $\hat{b}$ of a linear relationship $Y = a + bX + u$ is

$$\hat{b} = \frac{\Sigma xy}{\Sigma x^2} = \frac{\Sigma x(bx + u)}{\Sigma x^2}$$

$$= b \frac{\Sigma x^2}{\Sigma x^2} + \frac{\Sigma xu}{\Sigma x^2} = b + \frac{\Sigma xu}{\Sigma x^2}$$

$$E(\hat{b}) = b + E\left(\frac{\Sigma xu}{\Sigma x^2}\right)$$

If the explanatory variable X and the error term u are not independent of each other, Σxu will not vanish; thus $\hat{b}$ is a biased estimator of $b (E(\hat{b}) \neq b)$.[†]

[†]In the demand and supply equations

$$x_d = bp + u \qquad\qquad x_s = dp + v$$

Market clearing,

$$bp + u = dp + v$$

$$p = \frac{u - v}{d - b}$$

The direct least-square estimator

$$\hat{b} = b + \frac{\Sigma pu}{\Sigma p^2}$$

$$\Sigma pu = (\Sigma u^2 - \Sigma uv)/(d - b)$$
$$\Sigma p^2 = \Sigma (u - v)^2/(d - b)^2$$

$$\hat{b} = b + (d - b) \frac{\Sigma u^2 - \Sigma uv}{\Sigma u^2 + \Sigma v^2 - 2\Sigma uv}$$

If u, v are independent, with constant variances

$$\hat{b} = b + (d - b) \frac{\sigma_u^2}{\sigma_u^2 + \sigma_v^2}$$

$$E(\hat{b}) \neq b \qquad (\text{unless } \sigma_u^2 = 0)$$

Also,

$$\text{var}\,(\hat{b}) = E(\hat{b} - b)^2 = E\left(\frac{\Sigma xu}{\Sigma x^2}\right)^2$$

$$= \frac{1}{(\Sigma x^2)^2} E(x_1^2 u_1^2 + x_2^2 u_2^2 + \cdots + x_n^2 u_n^2$$

$$+ 2x_1 x_2 u_1 u_2 + \cdots + 2x_{n-1} x_n u_{n-1} u_n)$$

if $E(u_1^2) \neq E(u_2^2) \cdots \neq E(u_n^2)$. In other words, the variance of u is not a constant. And if u_i, u_j are not independent when $i \neq j$, then there will not be a simple formula to compute var $(\hat{b})$ and the confidence interval for the estimation of b will be large, since the cross-products $E(u_i u_j)$ will not vanish, and thus the least-squares estimator will be inefficient.

In the following section we discuss some of the estimation problems and some known correction methods.

Error of Observation

Let us assume

$$X' = X + u \tag{6-5}$$
$$Y' = Y + v \tag{6-6}$$
$$Y = a + bX \tag{6-7}$$

where X, Y are the true values and X', Y' are the observed values and u, v are the errors of observation. We also assume that u and v are serially and mutually independent.

Difficulty. It follows that

$$Y' = a + bX + v$$
$$= a + b(X' - u) + v$$
$$= a + bX' + (v - bu) \tag{6-8}$$

The covariance of X' and $(v - bu)$ is

$$E[(X' - X)(v - bu)] = E[u(v - bu)]$$
$$= E(uv) - bE(u^2)$$
$$= -b\,\text{var}\,(u) \tag{6-9}$$

Since the covariance does not equal zero, a dependence exists between the error term $(v - bu)$ and the explanatory variable X'. Thus it violates the assumption made when we apply least-squares method in estimating the parameters. $\left(\hat{b} = b + \dfrac{\Sigma x'(v - bu)}{\Sigma x'^2},\ E(\hat{b}) \neq b.\ \text{Biased estimate.}\right)$

Method of Correction

Grouping of Observations. Wald's method—assuming the errors u and v are serially and mutually independent and an even number of observations are taken from the real world. X_i' are ordered in ascending magnitude and Y_i' are the corresponding values of X_i'.

$$X_1', X_2', \ldots, X_m', X_{m+1}', \ldots, X_n'$$
$$Y_1', Y_2', \ldots, Y_m', Y_{m+1}', \ldots, Y_n'$$

where $n = 2m$. Defining the subgroup means as

$$\bar{X}_L' = \frac{1}{m}\sum_{i=1}^{m} X_i' \qquad \bar{X}_H' = \frac{1}{m}\sum_{i=m+1}^{n} X_i'$$

$$\bar{Y}_L' = \frac{1}{m}\sum_{i=1}^{m} Y_i' \qquad \bar{Y}_H' = \frac{1}{m}\sum_{i=m+1}^{n} Y_i'$$

the estimates of a and b are

$$\hat{b} = \frac{\bar{Y}_H' - \bar{Y}_L'}{\bar{X}_H' - \bar{X}_L'} \tag{6-10}$$

$$\hat{a} = \bar{Y}' - \hat{b}\bar{X}' \tag{6-11}$$

where $\bar{X}'$ and $\bar{Y}'$ are the total means.

The estimators can be shown to be consistent provided that the variables are not normally distributed.

Bartlett modifies Wald's method and uses the subgroup means of the K observations ($K < m$) at both ends.

Variance-Ratio Method. Assuming u, v are normally and independently distributed variables with zero means and variances σ_u^2, σ_v^2. Also, assuming that the ratio of the variances can be estimated,

$$\lambda = \frac{\hat{\sigma}_u^2}{\hat{\sigma}_v^2} \tag{6-12}$$

Then the likelihood function is

$$L = f(u_1)f(u_2)\cdots f(u_n)f(v_1)f(v_2)\cdots f(v_n)$$

$$= \frac{1}{(2\pi)^{n/2}}\left[\frac{1}{\sigma_u^n}e^{-\sum_{i=1}^{n}(X_i'-X_i)^2/2\sigma_u^2}\right]$$

$$\cdot\frac{1}{(2\pi)^{n/2}}\left[\frac{1}{\sigma_v^n}e^{-\sum_{i=1}^{n}(Y_i'-a-bX_i)^2/2\sigma_v^2}\right]$$

$$\log L = \text{const.} - \frac{n}{2}\log\sigma_u^2 - \frac{n}{2}\log\sigma_v^2 - \frac{1}{2\sigma_u^2}\sum_{i=1}^{n}(X_i'-X_i)^2$$

$$- \frac{1}{2\sigma_v^2}\sum_{i=1}^{n}(Y_i'-a-bX_i)^2 \tag{6-13}$$

Taking partial derivatives of log L gives

$$\frac{\partial \log L}{\partial X_i} = \frac{1}{\sigma_u^2}(X_i' - X_i) + \frac{b}{\sigma_v^2}(Y_i' - a - bX_i) \qquad i = 1,2,\ldots,n$$

$$\frac{\partial \log L}{\partial a} = \frac{1}{\sigma_v^2}\sum_{i=1}^{n}(Y_i' - a - bX_i)$$

$$\frac{\partial \log L}{\partial b} = \frac{1}{\sigma_v^2}\sum_{i=1}^{n}X_i(Y_i' - a - bX_i)$$

$$\frac{\partial \log L}{\partial \sigma_u^2} = -\frac{n}{2\sigma_u^2} + \frac{1}{2\sigma_u^4}\sum_{i=1}^{n}(X_i' - X_i)^2$$

$$\frac{\partial \log L}{\partial \sigma_v^2} = -\frac{n}{2\sigma_v^2} + \frac{1}{2\sigma_v^4}\sum_{i=1}^{n}(Y_i' - a - bX_i)^2$$

Setting $\dfrac{\partial \log L}{\partial X_i}$ equal to zero gives

$$Y_i' - \hat{a} - \hat{b}\hat{X}_i = -\frac{\hat{\sigma}_v^2}{\hat{b}\hat{\sigma}_u^2}(X_i' - \hat{X}_i)$$

$$(X_i' - X_i) + \lambda\hat{b}(Y_i' - \hat{a} - \hat{b}\hat{X}_i) = 0$$

$$X_i = \frac{X_i' + \lambda\hat{b}Y_i' - \lambda\hat{a}\hat{b}}{1 + \lambda\hat{b}^2} \qquad (6\text{-}14)$$

Setting $\dfrac{\partial \log L}{\partial a}$ equal to zero gives

$$\Sigma(Y_i' - \hat{a} - \hat{b}\hat{X}_i) = 0, \qquad \hat{a} = \bar{Y}' - \hat{b}\hat{\bar{X}}$$

Setting $\dfrac{\partial \log L}{\partial b}$ equal to zero gives

$$\Sigma\hat{X}_i(Y_i' - \hat{a} - \hat{b}\hat{X}_i) = 0$$

Thus also

$$\Sigma(X_i - \hat{\bar{X}})(Y_i' - \hat{a} - \hat{b}\hat{X}_i) = 0$$

Substituting $\hat{a}$ by $(\bar{Y}' - \hat{b}\hat{\bar{X}})$ gives

$$\Sigma(\hat{X}_i - \hat{\bar{X}})[(Y_i' - \bar{Y}') - \hat{b}(\hat{X}_i - \hat{\bar{X}})] = 0$$

$$\Sigma(\hat{X}_i - \bar{X})(Y_i' - \bar{Y}') - \hat{b}\Sigma(\hat{X}_i - \hat{\bar{X}})^2 = 0$$

$$\hat{b} = \frac{\Sigma(\hat{X}_i - \hat{\bar{X}})(Y_i' - \bar{Y}')}{\Sigma(X_i - \hat{\bar{X}})^2} \qquad (6\text{-}15)$$

From Eq. 6-14,

$$X_i = \frac{X_i' - \lambda\hat{b}Y_i' - \lambda\hat{a}\hat{b}}{1 + \lambda b^2},$$

$$\hat{\bar{X}} = \frac{\bar{X}' + \lambda\hat{b}(\bar{Y}' - \hat{a})}{1 + \lambda\hat{b}^2}$$

$$\hat{X}_i - \hat{\bar{X}} = \frac{1}{1 + \lambda\hat{b}^2}[(X_i' - \bar{X}') + \lambda\hat{b}(Y_i' - \bar{Y}')]$$

$$\Sigma(\hat{X}_i - \hat{\bar{X}})(Y_i' - \bar{Y}') = \frac{1}{1 + \lambda\hat{b}^2}$$
$$\cdot[\Sigma(X_i' - \bar{X}')(Y_i' - \bar{Y}') + \lambda\hat{b}\Sigma(Y_i' - \bar{Y}')^2]$$

$$\Sigma(\hat{X}_i - \hat{\bar{X}})^2 = \frac{1}{(1 + \lambda\hat{b}^2)^2}[\Sigma(X_i' - \bar{X}')^2$$
$$+ 2\lambda\hat{b}\Sigma(X_i' - \bar{X}')(Y_i' - \bar{Y}') + \lambda^2\hat{b}^2\Sigma(Y_i' - \bar{Y}')^2]$$

Let

$$m_{x'y'} = \frac{1}{n}\sum_{i=1}^{n}(X_i' - \bar{X}')(Y_i' - \bar{Y}')$$

$$m_{x'x'} = \frac{1}{n}\sum_{i=1}^{n}(X_i' - \bar{X}')^2$$

$$m_{y'y'} = \frac{1}{n}\sum_{i=1}^{n}(Y_i' - \bar{Y}')^2$$

We then have

$$\hat{b} = \frac{(1 + \lambda\hat{b}^2)(m_{x'y'} + \lambda\hat{b}m_{y'y'})}{m_{x'x'} + 2\lambda\hat{b}m_{x'y'} + \lambda^2\hat{b}^2m_{y'y'}}$$
$$\lambda\hat{b}^2 m_{x'y'} - \hat{b}(\lambda m_{y'y'} - m_{x'x'}) - m_{x'y'} = 0$$

Solving the quadratic equation gives

$$\hat{b}_1 = \theta + \sqrt{\theta^2 + \frac{1}{\lambda}} \qquad \hat{b}_2 = \theta - \sqrt{\theta^2 + \frac{1}{\lambda}} \qquad (6\text{-}16)$$

where

$$\theta = \frac{m_{y'y'} - \dfrac{m_{x'x'}}{\lambda}}{2m_{x'y'}}$$

Since $\hat{b}_1$ is always positive and $\hat{b}_2$ is always negative, if the slope of the relationship between X and Y is positive we will use $\hat{b}_1$, otherwise we will use $\hat{b}_2$. And

$$\hat{a} = \bar{Y}' - \hat{b}\bar{X}' \qquad (6\text{-}17)$$

Use of Instrumental Variables. If another variable Z which is independent of both errors u and v can be found, we may use Z as an instrumental variable to avoid observation errors. Originally, we have

$$X' = X + u$$
$$Y' = Y + v$$
$$Y = a + bX$$

We now add

$$X = c + dZ \tag{6-18}$$

Thus

$$X' = c + dZ + u$$

Since Z is independent of u, the least-squares estimate of d is unbiased.

$$\hat{d} = \frac{\Sigma x'z}{\Sigma z^2}$$

and

$$Y = a + b(c + dZ) = (a + bc) + bdZ$$
$$Y' = (a + bc) + bdZ + v$$

Since Z is also independent of v, the least-square estimate of (bd) is unbiased.

$$\widehat{bd} = \frac{\Sigma y'z}{\Sigma z^2}$$

Thus the adjusted least-squares estimator of b is

$$\hat{b} = \frac{\widehat{bd}}{\hat{d}} = \frac{\Sigma y'z}{\Sigma x'z} \tag{6-19}$$

Assuming $\Sigma u = 0$ and $\Sigma v = 0$, the adjusted least-squares estimator of a is

$$\hat{a} = \bar{Y}' - \hat{b}\bar{X}' \tag{6-20}$$

This estimate is good, however, only when there is a high correlation between X and Z.

EXAMPLES:

1. A numerical example of correcting errors in observation is as follows. Let X, Y be the true values, X', Y' be the observed values and u, v the errors in observations, respectively, and assume the following information:

Y	X	v	u	Y'	X'	y'	x'	$x'y'$	y'^2	x^2
7	1	2	1	9	2	-6	-3	18	36	9
9	2	-2	-1	7	1	-8	-4	32	64	16
11	3	2	1	13	4	-2	-1	2	4	1
13	4	-2	-1	11	3	-4	-2	8	16	4
15	5	2	0	17	5	2	0	0	4	0
17	6	-2	-1	15	5	0	0	0	0	0
19	7	0	1	19	8	4	3	12	16	9
21	8	-2	-1	19	7	4	2	8	16	4
23	9	2	1	25	10	10	5	50	100	25
135	45	0	0	135	45			130	256	68

where

$$X' = X + u, \quad Y' = Y + v, \quad E(u) = 0, \quad E(v) = 0$$

and

$$\lambda = \frac{\hat{\sigma}_u^2}{\hat{\sigma}_v^2} = \frac{1}{2}$$

Since

$$n = 9, \quad \bar{X}' = 5, \quad \bar{Y}' = 15, \quad \Sigma x'y' = 130, \Sigma x'^2 = 68$$

the least-squares estimators computed from the observed values are

$$\hat{b} = \frac{\Sigma x'y'}{\Sigma x'^2} = \frac{130}{68} = 1.91$$

$$\hat{a} = \bar{Y}' - \hat{b}\bar{X}' = 15 - 1.91 \times 5 = 5.45$$

The linear-regression equation of the observed values is then

$$\hat{Y}' = 5.45 + 1.91X'$$

For adjustment, since $\Sigma x'y' > 0$,

$$\theta = \frac{\Sigma y'^2 - \dfrac{1}{\lambda}\Sigma x'^2}{2\Sigma x'y'} = \frac{256 - \dfrac{1}{2} \cdot 68}{2 \times 130} = 0.85$$

$$\hat{b} = \theta + \sqrt{\theta^2 + \frac{1}{\lambda}} = 0.85 + \sqrt{.75 + .5} = 1.96$$

Since $\bar{X} = \bar{X}', \bar{Y} = \bar{Y}'$

$$\hat{a} = 15 - 1.96 \times 5 = 5.2$$

The adjusted linear-regression line is then

$$\hat{Y} = 5.2 + 1.96X$$

Using Wald's method, we arrange the observed X' values in ascending order;

X'	Y'
1	7
2	9
3	11
4	13
5	15
5	17
7	19
8	19
10	25

and the subgroup means are

$$X'_L = \frac{1 + 2 + 3 + 4}{4} = 2.5$$

$$X'_H = \frac{5 + 7 + 8 + 10}{4} = 7.5$$

$$Y'_L = \frac{7 + 9 + 11 + 13}{4} = 10$$

$$Y'_H = \frac{17 + 19 + 19 + 25}{4} = 20$$

Thus

$$\text{est} (b) = \frac{Y'_H - Y'_L}{X'_H - X'_L} = \frac{20 - 10}{7.5 - 2.5} = 2$$

2. A demand-supply model,

$$X = a + bP + eY \qquad \text{(demand function)}$$
$$X = c + dP \qquad \text{(supply function)}$$

The total number of endogenous variables in this model is 2 (X and P), $G - 1 = 1$, and the total number of predetermined variables not included in the equation are both zero. Thus $g_2 + k_2 = 0 < G - 1$. The demand function is under identified. In the supply function, the number of endogenous variables excluded from the equation is zero, while the number of predetermined variables not included in the equation is 1. Thus

$$g_2 + k_2 = 1 = G - 1$$

and the supply function is exactly identified. Using Y as the instrumental variable and applying ordinary least squares to the following equation to revise the values of P,

$$P' = \hat{m} + \hat{n}Y$$

Then, regressing the quantity X on P', we may estimate the parameters of the supply function by least squares:

$$X = \hat{c} + \hat{d}P' \qquad \text{where } \hat{d} = \frac{\Sigma xp'}{\Sigma p'^2}.$$

(This procedure will be generalized in the next section as the two stages least squares method.)

Numerical Illustration

Assume that in the market we observe the transactions of a product as shown in the table (quantities purchased and sold at various prices). We do not know whether the relationship represents a demand function or supply function. However, we are told that the quantity demanded is also a function of income Y whereas the quantity supplied is not.

X	P	Y	x	p	y	py	y^2
80	4.0	10	−17	−2.5	−5	12.5	25
90	4.5	12	−7	−2.0	−3	6.0	9
95	6.0	15	−2	.5	0	0	0
91	5.5	10	−6	−1.0	−5	5.0	25
96	7.0	14	−1	.5	−1	−.5	1
98	6.5	18	1	0	3	0	9
95	6.0	15	−2	−.5	0	0	0
100	8.0	17	3	1.5	2	3.0	4
110	8.5	19	13	2.0	4	8.0	16
115	9.0	20	18	2.5	5	12.5	25
						46.5	114

$$\bar{X} = 97, \bar{P} = 6.5, \bar{Y} = 15$$

Since the data show high correlation between income and price ($r = .8$), we may use income as an instrumental variable to replace the original P by estimated P (P'), which is based on the least-squares regressions of P on Y. Then apply least squares again to X and P' to estimate the regression coefficients of the supply function:

$$\hat{n} = \frac{\Sigma py}{\Sigma y^2} = \frac{46.5}{114} = .408$$

$$\hat{m} = \bar{P} - \hat{n}\bar{Y} = 6.5 - .408(15) = .38$$

$$P' = .38 + .408Y$$

Y	P'	p'	x	$p'x$	p'^2
10	4.460	−2.040	−17	34.680	4.161600
12	5.276	−1.224	−7	8.568	1.498176
15	6.500	0	−2	0	0
10	4.460	−2.040	−6	12.240	4.161600
14	6.092	−0.408	−1	0.408	.166464
18	7.724	1.224	1	1.224	1.498176
15	6.500	0	−2	0	0
17	7.316	0.814	3	2.448	0.665856
19	8.132	1.632	13	21.216	2.663424
20	8.540	2.040	18	36.720	4.161600
				117.504	18.976896

$$\bar{P}' = 6.5$$

$$\hat{d} = \frac{\Sigma p'x}{\Sigma p'^2} = \frac{117.504}{18.976896} = 6.2$$

$$\hat{c} = \bar{X} - \hat{d}\bar{P}' = 97 - 6.2\,(6.5) = 56.7$$

The supply function is estimated to be $\hat{X}_s = 56.7 + 6.2P$

(If we apply least squares to the original data (P), the estimate,

$$\hat{d} = \frac{\Sigma px}{\Sigma p^2} = \frac{139.5}{24.5} = 5.69$$

will be a biased and inconsistent estimate.)

Correlation Between Explanatory Variables and Error Term

As we indicated at the beginning of this chapter, if the explanatory variable and the error term are correlated the direct least-squares estimator will be biased and inefficient. One method of avoiding this kind of problem is applying the two-stage least-squares method.

Two-Stage Least-Squares Method

Similar to the method outlined in the section on the use of instrumental variables, we may also use the relationship of the explanatory variable with an exogenous variable (can be more than one) to erase the explanatory variable of the stochastic component associated with the disturbance term. The method is known as the *two-stage least-squares method*.

Suppose

$$Y = a + bX + u \qquad (6\text{-}21)$$

where X is correlated with u, and

$$X = c + dZ + e \qquad (6\text{-}22)$$

where Z is not correlated with e. In the first stage, we use least squares to estimate d and c:

$$\hat{d} = \frac{\Sigma xz}{\Sigma z^2} \qquad (6\text{-}23)$$

$$\hat{c} = \bar{X} - \hat{d}\bar{Z} \qquad (6\text{-}24)$$

where x, z are the deviations. Thus

$$\hat{X}' = \hat{c} + \hat{d}Z \qquad (6\text{-}25)$$

where $\hat{X}'$ is not correlated with e or u.

In the second stage

$$Y = a + b(\hat{X}' + e) + u$$
$$= a + b\hat{X}' + (be + u)$$

Since $\hat{X}'$ is not correlated with $(be + u)$, so least squares may be used to estimate a and b:

$$\hat{b} = \frac{\Sigma y\hat{x}'}{\Sigma \hat{x}'^2} \tag{6-26}$$

$$\hat{a} = \bar{Y} - \hat{b}\hat{\bar{X}} \tag{6-27}$$

A numerical example:

Y	X	Z	y	x	z	xy	xz	-yz	x^2	z^2	$\hat{X}$	$\hat{x}$	$\hat{x}^2$	$\hat{x}y$
10	5	2	-30	-7	-7	210	49	210	49	49	4.38	-7.62	57.99	228.5
19	8	4	-21	-4	-5	84	20	105	16	25	6.56	-5.44	29.58	114.2
16	6	3	-24	-6	-6	144	36	144	36	36	5.47	-6.53	42.60	156.6
22	7	5	-18	-5	-4	90	20	72	25	16	7.65	-4.35	18.93	78.3
33	10	8	-7	-2	-1	14	2	7	4	1	10.91	-1.09	1.18	7.6
45	12	11	5	0	2	0	0	10	0	4	14.18	2.18	4.74	10.9
48	13	12	8	1	3	8	3	24	1	9	15.26	3.27	10.66	26.1
61	15	15	21	3	6	63	18	126	9	36	18.53	6.53	42.63	137.1
70	20	14	30	8	5	240	40	150	64	25	17.44	5.44	29.57	163.4
76	24	16	36	12	7	432	84	252	144	49	19.62	7.62	58.02	274.2
400	120	90				1,285	272	1,100	348	250			295.9	1,196.7

1. Ordinary least-quarter estimator:

$$\hat{Y} = \hat{a} + \hat{b}X$$

$$\hat{b} = \frac{\Sigma xy}{\Sigma x^2} = \frac{1.285}{348} = 3.693 \quad (\hat{a} = -4.316)$$

2. Z as an instrumental variable:

$$\hat{X} = \hat{c} + \hat{d}Z$$

$$\hat{d} = \frac{\Sigma xz}{\Sigma z^2} = \frac{272}{250} = 1.088$$

$$\hat{Y} = (\hat{a} + \widehat{bc}) + \widehat{bd}Z$$

$$\widehat{bd} = \frac{\Sigma yz}{\Sigma z^2} = \frac{1,100}{250} = 4.4$$

$$\text{est } (b) = \frac{4.4}{1.088} = 4.0441$$

3. Two-stage least-squares:
   First Stage

$$\hat{d} = \frac{\Sigma xz}{\Sigma z^2} = 1.088$$

$$\hat{c} = \bar{X} - \hat{d}\bar{Z} = 12 - 1.088(9) = 2.208$$

Compute

$$\hat{X}' = \hat{c} + \hat{d}Z$$

$$= 2.208 + 1.088Z$$

   Second Stage

$$\hat{Y} = \hat{a} + \hat{b}\hat{X}'$$

$$\text{est } (b) = \frac{\Sigma \hat{x}'y}{\Sigma \hat{x}^2} = \frac{1,196.7}{295.9} = 4.0441$$

The instrument-variable method and the two-stage least-squares method are the same in this example since only one exogenous variable (Z) is involved.

Heteroscedasticity

In using least-squares method to estimate parameters, we assume that the error terms u_i $(i = 1, 2, \ldots, n)$ have constant variance, $E(u_i^2) = \sigma_u^2$. If this condition is not satisfied ($E(u_i^2) \neq$ constant), we have the problem of *heteroscedasticity*, and the least-squares estimator will be inefficient. One example is the relationship between consumption and income. When income is high, the variance of the consumption expenditure along the mean value expressed by the income-consumption regression line may be larger than that at low income.

A numerical example illustrating the effect of heteroscedasticity on the efficiency of the least square estimation of parameters is given below.

Assume $Y = 10 + 2X + u$

(1)   The error term is taken from distributions with constant variance

X	u	Y	x	y	xy	x^2	u^2
1	1	13	−3.5	−6	21.0	12.25	1
2	0	14	−2.5	−5	12.5	6.25	0
3	−1	15	−1.5	−4	6.0	2.25	1
4	0	18	−.5	−1	.5	.25	0
5	1	21	.5	2	1.0	.25	1
6	0	22	1.5	3	4.5	2.25	0
7	−1	23	2.5	4	10.0	6.25	1
8	0	26	3.5	7	24.5	12.25	0
36		152			80.0	42.00	4

$$\bar{X} = 4.5, \ \bar{Y} = 19, \ \hat{\sigma}_u^2 = \frac{\Sigma u^2}{n-2} = .667, \ \hat{b} = \frac{\Sigma xy}{\Sigma x^2} = \frac{80}{42} = 1.9$$

$$\text{var}(\hat{b}) = \frac{\hat{\sigma}_u^2}{\Sigma x^2} = \frac{.667}{42} = .0159$$

(2)   The error term is taken from distributions with unequal variances. (The variance of u increases as the value of X increases.)

X	u	Y	x	y	xy	x^2	u^2
1	.5	12.5	−3.5	−6.5	22.75	12.25	.25
2	−.5	13.5	−2.5	−5.5	13.75	6.25	.25
3	.8	16.8	−1.5	−2.2	3.30	2.25	.64
4	−.8	17.2	−.5	−1.8	.90	.25	.64
5	1.1	21.1	.5	2.1	1.05	.25	1.21
6	−1.1	20.9	1.5	1.9	2.85	2.25	1.21
7	1.5	25.5	2.5	6.5	16.25	6.25	2.25
8	−1.5	24.5	3.5	5.5	19.25	12.25	2.25
36		152.0			80.10	42.00	8.70

$$\bar{X} = 4.5, \bar{Y} = 19, \quad \hat{\sigma}_u^2 = \frac{8.7}{6} = 1.45, \quad \hat{b} = \frac{80.1}{42} = 1.907$$

$$\text{var}(\hat{b}) = \frac{1.45}{42} = .0345$$

Compare the above two cases. Case (1) we assume homoscedastic, while case (2) is heteroscedastic. When least-squares method is applied to them, both yield $\hat{b}$ approximately equal to 1.9 (compare to true value of $b = 2$). However, the variance of $\hat{b}$ in case (2) is more than twice as great as that in case (1). In the following example we will show by definite proof that in the case of heteroscedasticity, least-squares is not an efficient estimator if applied to the original data.

EXAMPLE:

$$Y_i = a + bX_i + u_i \ (i = 1, 2, \ldots, n) \tag{6-28}$$

Assume the X_i values are fixed constant and

$$E(u_i) = 0 \tag{6-29}$$
$$E(u_i u_j) = 0 \text{ when } i \neq j \tag{6-30}$$
$$E(u_i^2) = X_i^2 \sigma_u^2 \tag{6-31}$$

which indicates that for different i the variance of the error term u_i will be different. If we apply the least-squares method directly to Eq. 6-28, we obtain

$$\hat{b} = \frac{\Sigma xy}{\Sigma x^2}$$

Since $\hat{b} = b + \dfrac{\Sigma xu}{\Sigma x^2}$ (see Chapter 3),

$$E(\hat{b}) = b + \frac{1}{\Sigma x^2}\{x_1 E(u_1) + \cdots + x_n E(u_n)\}$$

the estimator is unbiased. However, the variance of b becomes

$$\text{var}(\hat{b}) = E(\hat{b} - b)^2$$

$$= E\frac{(\Sigma xu)^2}{(\Sigma x^2)^2}$$

$$= \frac{1}{(\Sigma x^2)^2} E(x_1^2 u_1^2 + \cdots + x_n^2 u_n^2 + 2x_1 x_2 u_1 u_2$$

$$+ \cdots + 2x_{n-1} x_n u_{n-1} u_n)$$

$$= \frac{1}{(\Sigma x^2)^2} [x_1^2 E(u_1^2) + \cdots + x_n^2 E(u_n^2)]$$

$$= \frac{\sigma_u^2}{(\Sigma x^2)^2} [x_1^4 + \cdots + x_n^4] = \sigma_u^2 \frac{\Sigma x^4}{(\Sigma x^2)^2}$$

However, if we multiply Eq. 6-28 by $\frac{1}{X_i}$,

$$\frac{Y_i}{X_i} = \frac{a}{X_i} + b + \frac{u_i}{X_i} \qquad (6\text{-}32)$$

The variance of the transformed error term then will be

$$E\left(\frac{u_i}{X_i}\right)^2 = \frac{1}{X_i^2}(X_i^2 \sigma_u^2) = \sigma_u^2$$

which indicates that Eq. 6-32 is homoscedastic and the least-squares method is directly applicable. The least-squares estimate of b, after the original data X_i and Y_i have been multiplied by $\frac{1}{X_i}$, is as follows:

$$\hat{b} = \frac{\sum \left(\frac{x_i}{x_i}\right)\left(\frac{y_i}{x_i}\right)}{\sum \left(\frac{x_i}{x_i}\right)^2} = \frac{1}{n}\sum \frac{y_i}{x_i}$$

And

$$\text{var}(\hat{b}) = E\left[\frac{\sum \left(\frac{x_i}{x_i}\right)\left(\frac{u_i}{x_i}\right)}{\sum \left(\frac{x_i}{x_i}\right)^2}\right]^2$$

$$= \frac{1}{n^2}\left(E\left(\frac{u_1}{x_1}\right)^2 + \cdots + E\left(\frac{u_n}{x_n}\right)^2 + 2E\left(\frac{u_1 u_2}{x_1 x_2}\right)\cdots\right)$$

$$= \frac{n\sigma_u^2}{n^2} = \frac{\sigma_u^2}{n}$$

Since

$$\frac{\sum x^4}{(\sum x^2)^2} > \frac{1}{n} \dagger$$

$$\text{var}(\hat{b}) > \text{var}(\hat{b})$$

$$\dagger \frac{\sum x^4}{(\sum x^2)^2} = \frac{(x_i^4 + x_2^4 + \cdots + x_n^4)}{(x_i^4 + x_2^4 + \cdots + x_n^4) + 2(x_1^2 x_2^2 + x_1^2 x_3^2 \cdots)}$$

But

$$(x_i^2 - x_j^2)^2 > 0, \quad x_i^4 + x_j^4 > 2x_i x_j, \quad (n-1)\sum x^4 > 2(x_1^2 x_2^2 + x_1^2 x_3^2 \cdots)$$

Thus

$$\frac{\sum x^4}{(\sum x^2)^2} = \frac{\sum x^4}{\sum x^4 + [(n-1)\cdot x^4 - A]}$$

where A is a positive number.

$$\frac{\sum x^4}{(\sum x^2)^2} = \frac{\sum x^4}{n\sum x^4 - A}$$

we conclude $\hat{b}$ is not an efficient estimate in the case of heteroscedasticity, and the least-squares method may not be applied directly to the original data.

Also, heteroscedasticity may be caused by omitting some variables from the equation, whose values change systematically with the sample observations of the other variables in the equation. If such is the case, we have to respecify the relationship or add more explanatory variables in the equation to make the residual-error term random.

Autocorrelation

When we apply the least-squares method in estimating parameters we assume

$$E(u_t u_{t+k}) = 0 \quad \text{for all} \quad k \neq 0$$

where u is the error term.

However, if we have omitted some variables in the equation which move in phase, or if we make consistent measurement errors, there may appear a serial interdependence of the error term—that is, $E(u_t u_{t+k}) \neq 0$, when $k \neq 0$. This we call *autocorrelation*, or serial correlation.

Difficulty. Let us postulate autocorrelation of the error term u with one period lag as follows:

$$Y_t = a + bX_t + u_t \tag{6-35}$$

and

$$u_t = ru_{t-1} + e_t \tag{6-36}$$

where $|r| < 1$, and

$$E(e_t) = 0$$
$$E(e_t e_{t+k}) = \sigma_e^2 \qquad k = 0$$
$$= 0 \qquad k \neq 0 \text{ for all } t$$

Then

$$u_t = ru_{t-1} + e_t$$
$$= r(ru_{t-2} + e_{t-1}) + e_t$$
$$= e_t + re_{t-1} + r^2 e_{t-2} + \cdots$$
$$= \sum_{k=0}^{\infty} r^k e_{t-k}$$

---

which is greater than $\dfrac{\Sigma x^4}{n\Sigma x^4}$. Therefore

$$\frac{\Sigma x^4}{(\Sigma x^2)^2} > \frac{1}{n}$$

The variance of u_t is

$$E(u_t^2) = E(e_t + re_{t-1} + \cdots)^2$$
$$= E(e_t^2) + r^2 E(e_{t-1})^2 + \cdots + rE(e_t e_{t-1}) + \cdots$$
$$= \sigma_e^2(1 + r^2 + r^4 + \cdots)$$

Since $|r| < 1$,

$$\sigma_u^2 = \frac{\sigma_e^2}{1 - r^2} \tag{6-37}$$

(when $|r|$ is a large fraction approaching 1, σ_u^2 will be very large). The covariance of u_t and u_{t-1} is

$$E(u_t u_{t-1}) = E[(e_t + re_{t-1} \cdots)(e_{t-1} + re_{t-2} + \cdots)]$$
$$= E[\{e_t + r(e_{t-1} \cdots)\}(e_{t-1} + re_{t-2} + \cdots)]$$
$$= rE(e_{t-1} + re_{t-2} \cdots)^2$$
$$= r[E(e_{t-1})^2 + r^2 E(e_{t-2})^2 \cdots] = r\sigma_e^2[1 + r^2 + \cdots]$$
$$= r\frac{\sigma_e^2}{1 - r^2}$$
$$= r\sigma_u^2 \tag{6-38}$$

which will not vanish. In general terms,

$$E(u_t u_{t-k}) = r^k \sigma_u^2 \qquad \text{for } k \neq 0$$

or

$$\frac{E(u_t u_{t-k})}{\sigma_u^2} = r^k \qquad \text{for } k \neq 0 \tag{6-39}$$

where r^k is defined as the kth autocorrelation coefficient of the u series. If we use least-squares formulas to estimate a and b, we may get unbiased estimates; however, the sample variance will be unduly large and makes it an inefficient method of estimation.

Method of Detection

The Durbin-Watson d statistic is given by

$$d = \frac{\sum_{t=2}^{n} (\hat{u}_t - \hat{u}_{t-1})^2}{\sum_{t=1}^{n} \hat{u}_t^2} \tag{6-40}$$

where n is the number of observations at equal time intervals. Durbin and Watson have tabulated the lower and upper bounds d_L and d_U for various values of the number of explanatory variables and sample size. If $d < d_L$, we reject the hypothesis that the disturbance is random and accept the hypothesis of positive autocorrelation. If $d > d_U$, we do not

ILLUSTRATIVE CRITICAL POINTS OF THE DURBIN-WATSON TEST FOR AUTOCORRELATION

Sample Size, n	Error Probability, α	Number of Explanatory Variables							
		1		2		3		4	
		d_L	d_U	d_L	d_U	d_L	d_U	d_L	d_U
15	.01	.81	1.07	.70	1.25	.59	1.46	.49	1.70
	.05	1.08	1.36	.95	1.54	.82	1.75	.69	1.97
20	.01	.95	1.15	.86	1.27	.77	1.41	.68	1.57
	.05	1.20	1.41	1.10	1.54	1.00	1.68	.90	1.83
25	.01	1.05	1.21	.98	1.30	.90	1.41	.83	1.52
	.05	1.29	1.45	1.21	1.55	1.12	1.66	1.04	1.77
30	.01	1.13	1.26	1.07	1.34	1.01	1.42	.94	1.51
	.05	1.35	1.49	1.28	1.57	1.21	1.65	1.14	1.74
40	.01	1.25	1.34	1.20	1.40	1.15	1.46	1.10	1.52
	.05	1.44	1.54	1.39	1.60	1.34	1.66	1.29	1.72
50	.01	1.32	1.40	1.28	1.45	1.24	1.49	1.20	1.54
	.05	1.50	1.59	1.46	1.63	1.42	1.67	1.38	1.72
60	.01	1.38	1.45	1.35	1.48	1.32	1.52	1.28	1.56
	.05	1.55	1.62	1.51	1.65	1.48	1.69	1.44	1.73
80	.01	1.47	1.51	1.44	1.54	1.42	1.57	1.39	1.60
	.05	1.61	1.66	1.59	1.69	1.56	1.72	1.53	1.74
100	.01	1.51	1.56	1.50	1.58	1.48	1.60	1.46	1.63
	.05	1.65	1.69	1.63	1.72	1.61	1.74	1.59	1.76

reject the hypothesis of random disturbance. If $d_L < d < d_U$, the test is inconclusive, and we will have to make more observations.

Method of Correction

Suppose we apply the straightforward least-squares method to two sets of observed data X'_t, $Y'_t(t = 1, 2, \ldots, n)$ and find the regression line

$$\hat{Y}' = \hat{a} + \hat{b}X' \tag{6-41}$$

We also compute the residuals for every observation:

$$\hat{u} = Y' - \hat{Y}'$$

And using the Durbin-Watson statistic, we have found that there exists a first-order autocorrelation in the residuals $\hat{u}$:

$$\hat{u}_t = r\hat{u}_{t-1} + e_t \tag{6-42}$$

We estimate the coefficient r by the formula

$$\hat{r} = \frac{\sum\limits_{t=2}^{n} \hat{u}_t \hat{u}_{t-1}}{\sum\limits_{t=2}^{n} \hat{u}_{t-1}^2} \tag{6-43}$$

and transform the observed values of x and y to the following:

$$Y_t = Y'_t - \hat{r}Y'_{t-1} \qquad (6\text{-}44)$$

$$X_t = X'_t - \hat{r}X'_{t-1} \qquad (6\text{-}45)$$

Then apply least squares to the transformed variables and obtain another regression line:

$$\hat{Y}_t = \hat{a} + \hat{b}X_t \qquad (6\text{-}46)$$

But

$$
\begin{aligned}
\hat{Y}_t &= \hat{Y}'_t - \hat{r}\hat{Y}'_{t-1} \\
&= (\hat{a} + \hat{b}X'_t) - \hat{r}(\hat{a} + \hat{b}X'_{t-1}) \\
&= \hat{a}(1 - \hat{r}) + \hat{b}(X'_t - \hat{r}X'_{t-1}) \\
&= \hat{a}(1 - \hat{r}) + \hat{b}X_t \qquad (6\text{-}47)
\end{aligned}
$$

Thus we should use $\hat{b}$ as an estimate of b. And since the constant term in this new regression line is an estimate of $a(1 - \hat{r})$, we should use $\hat{a}/(1 - \hat{r})$ as an estimate of a. The original regression line of the observed values is then revised to

$$\hat{Y}' = \frac{\hat{a}}{1 - \hat{r}} + \hat{b}X' \qquad (6\text{-}48)$$

A numerical example of a case of autocorrelation is given as follows. Assume the information as shown in the table.

Y'	X'	y'	x'	x'^2	$x'y'$	Y'	$\hat{u}$	$\Delta\hat{u}$	$\hat{u}^2$	$(\Delta\hat{u})^2$
1	13	−33	−38	1,444	1,254	−.3	1.3		1.69	
6	17	−28	−34	1,156	952	3.3	2.7	1.4	7.29	1.96
18	32	−16	−19	361	304	16.8	1.2	−1.5	1.44	2.25
19	38	−15	−13	169	195	22.2	−3.2	−4.4	10.24	19.36
25	45	−9	−6	36	54	28.5	−3.5	−.3	12.25	.09
36	56	2	5	25	10	38.4	−2.4	1.1	5.76	1.21
40	58	6	7	49	42	40.2	−.2	2.2	.04	4.84
58	75	24	24	576	576	55.5	2.5	2.7	6.25	7.29
66	85	32	34	1,156	1,088	64.5	1.5	−1.0	2.25	1.00
71	91	37	40	1,600	1,480	69.9	1.1	−.4	1.21	.16
340	510			6,572	5,955				48.42	38.16

The least-squares estimators are

$$\hat{b} = \frac{5,955}{6,572} = 0.9$$

$$\hat{a} = 34 - 51 \times 0.9 = -12$$

$$Y' = -12 + 0.9X'$$

and

$$\hat{u} = Y' - \hat{Y}'$$

$$\Delta\hat{u}_t = \hat{u}_t - \hat{u}_{t-1}$$

The Durbin-Watson statistic is

$$d = \frac{\Sigma(\Delta\hat{u})^2}{\Sigma\hat{u}^2} = \frac{38.16}{48.42} = .79$$

which is very low and indicates first-order positive autocorrelation. For adjustment we first compute the first-order autoregressive coefficient as follows:

$\hat{u}_t$	$\hat{u}_{t-1}$	$\hat{u}_t\hat{u}_{t-1}$
1.3		
2.7	1.3	3.51
1.2	2.7	3.24
−3.2	1.2	−3.84
−3.5	−3.2	11.20
−2.4	−3.5	8.40
−.2	−2.4	.48
2.5	−.2	−.50
1.5	2.5	3.75
1.1	1.5	1.65
		27.89

$$\hat{u}_t = r\hat{u}_{t-1} + e_t$$

$$\hat{r} = \frac{\sum\limits_{t=2}^{n} \hat{u}_t\hat{u}_{t-1}}{\sum\limits_{t=2}^{n} \hat{u}_{t-1}^2} = \frac{27.89}{47.21} = .59$$

The Y' and X' values are adjusted by the formulas

$$Y_t = Y'_t - 0.59\,Y'_{t-1}$$
$$X_t = X'_t - 0.59\,X'_{t-1}$$

Y_t	X_t	y_t	x_t	x_t'	$x_t y_t$
5.4	9.5	−15.0	−18.9	357.21	283.50
14.5	22.2	−5.9	−6.2	38.44	36.58
8.6	19.6	−11.8	−8.8	77.44	103.84
14.0	23.1	−10.4	−5.3	28.09	55.12
21.6	30.1	1.2	1.7	2.89	2.04
19.2	25.7	−1.2	−2.7	7.29	3.24
34.9	41.6	14.5	13.2	174.24	191.40
32.5	41.8	12.1	13.4	179.56	162.14
32.9	42.0	12.9	13.6	184.96	175.44
183.6	255.6			1,050.12	1,013.30

$$\hat{b} = \frac{1,013.30}{1,050.12} = .965$$

$$\hat{a} = 20.4 - 28.4 \times .965 = -7.01$$
$$\hat{Y} = \hat{a} + \hat{b}\hat{X} = -7.01 + .965X$$

Since

$$Y_t = Y_t' - r(Y_{t-1}')$$
$$= (\hat{a} + \hat{b}X_t') - \hat{r}(\hat{a} + \hat{b}X_{t-1}')$$
$$= \hat{a}(1 - \hat{r}) + \hat{b}(X_t' - \hat{r}X_{t-1}')$$
$$= \hat{a}(1 - \hat{r}) + \hat{b}X_t$$

Thus $\hat{\hat{a}}$ is an estimate of $a(1 - r)$, and b is an estimate of $\hat{\hat{b}}$. The relationship between the original observations of Y and X is expressed as follows:

$$\hat{Y}' = \left(\frac{\hat{\hat{a}}}{1 - r}\right) + \hat{\hat{b}}X'$$

$$= \frac{-7.01}{1 - .59} + .965X'$$

$$= -17.1 + .965X'$$

Multicollinearity

When some of the explanatory variables in a relation are so highly correlated that it becomes difficult to measure their separate influences on the explained variable, we have problem of *multicollinearity*.

Difficulty. Suppose

$$Y = b_1 + b_2 X_2 + b_3 X_3 + e \qquad (6\text{-}49)$$

and

$$X_2 = cX_3 \qquad (6\text{-}50)$$

The least-squares estimates of b_2 and b_3 according to Eqs. 3-24 and 3-25 are

$$b_{12.3} = \frac{(\Sigma yx_2)(\Sigma x_3^2) - (\Sigma yx_3)(\Sigma x_2 x_3)}{(\Sigma x_2^2)(\Sigma x_3^2) - (\Sigma x_2 x_3)^2} \qquad (6\text{-}51)$$

$$b_{13.2} = \frac{(\Sigma yx_3)(\Sigma x_2^2) - (\Sigma yx_2)(\Sigma x_2 x_3)}{(\Sigma x_2^2)(\Sigma x_3^2) - (\Sigma x_2 x_3)^2} \qquad (6\text{-}52)$$

However, $b_{12.3}$ and $b_{13.2}$ have a common denominator:

$$(\Sigma x_2^2)(\Sigma x_3^2) - (\Sigma x_2 x_3)^2 = (\Sigma c^2 x_3^2)(\Sigma x_3^2) - (\Sigma cx_3 x_3)^2$$
$$= c^2(\Sigma x_3^2)^2 - c^2(\Sigma x_3^2)^2$$
$$= 0$$

Therefore the least-squares method breaks down here. For cases where the explanatory variables are highly but not perfectly correlated, the variance of the estimator will be large, thus losing the significance or efficiency of the estimation. (Examples of such are given below.)

Method of Correlation

When we find multicollinearity exists between two explanatory variables, we should either omit one variable from the relation or replace them by another variable which is a combination of both. Factor analysis may be used to determine the grouping variables.

Examples of multicollinearity: $\hat{X}_1 = a_{1.23} + b_{1.23}X_2 + b_{13.2}X_3$.
CASE 1 (perfect correlation between the explanatory variables):

X_1	X_2	X_3	x_1	x_2	x_3	x_1^2	x_2^2	x_3^2	x_1x_2	x_1x_3	x_2x_3
2	2	1	-9	-4	-4	81	16	16	36	36	16
8	4	3	-3	-2	-2	9	4	4	6	6	4
11	6	5	0	0	0	0	0	0	0	0	0
14	8	7	3	2	2	9	4	4	6	6	4
20	10	9	9	4	4	81	16	16	36	36	16
55	30	25				180	40	40	84	84	40

$$s_1 = \sqrt{\frac{\Sigma x_1^2}{n}} = 6 \qquad s_2 = \sqrt{\frac{\Sigma x_2^2}{n}} = 2.828$$

$$s_3 = \sqrt{\frac{\Sigma x_3^2}{n}} = 2.828 \qquad r_{23} = \frac{\Sigma x_2 x_3}{n s_2 s_3} = 1$$

which indicates perfect correlation between X_2 and X_3.

$$r_{12} = \frac{\Sigma x_1 x_2}{n s_1 s_2} = .99 \qquad r_{13} = \frac{\Sigma x_1 x_3}{n s_1 s_3} = .99$$

Thus

$$r_{12} = r_{13}$$

$$b_{12.3} = \frac{r_{12} - r_{13}r_{23}}{1 - r_{23}^2} \frac{s_1}{s_2} = \frac{0}{0} \qquad \text{(undefined)}$$

$$b_{13.2} = \frac{r_{13} - r_{12}r_{23}}{1 - r_{23}^2} \frac{s_1}{s_3} = \frac{0}{0} \qquad \text{(undefined)}$$

Therefore the coefficients cannot be estimated by the least-squares method. (There are infinite number of regression planes can fit the data).
CASE 2 $(r_{23} = .9)$:

X_1	X_2	X_3	x_1	x_2	x_3	x_1^2	x_2^2	x_3^2	x_1x_2	x_1x_3	x_2x_3
2	2	1	-9	-4	-4	81	16	16	36	36	16
8	4	3	-3	-2	-2	9	4	4	6	6	4
11	6	5	0	0	0	0	0	0	0	0	0
16	8	9	5	2	4	25	4	16	10	20	8
18	10	7	7	4	2	49	16	4	28	14	8
						164	40	40	80	76	36

$$s_1 = 5.727 \qquad s_2 = 2.828 \qquad s_3 = 2.828$$
$$r_{23} = .9 \qquad r_{12} = .9878 \qquad r_{13} = .9384$$
$$b_{12.3} = 1.5276 \qquad b_{13.2} = .5245$$
$$b_{23} = r_{23}\frac{s_2}{s_3} = .9 \qquad b_{32} = r_{23}\frac{s_3}{s_2} = .9$$

Applying the formulas

$$x_{1.23} = x_1 - b_{12.3}x_2 - b_{13.2}x_3$$
$$x_{2.3} = x_2 - b_{23}x_3$$
$$x_{3.2} = x_3 - b_{32}x_2$$

we obtain

$x_{1.23}$	$x_{2.3}$	$x_{3.2}$	$x^2_{1.23}$	$x^2_{2.3}$	$x^2_{3.2}$
−.790	−.4	−.4	.6273	.16	.16
1.102	−.2	−.2	1.2189	.04	.04
0	0	0	0	0	0
.1526	−1.6	2.2	.0233	2.56	4.84
.1593	2.2	−1.6	.0254	4.84	2.56
			1.8957	7.6	7.6

Thus

$$\text{var}(b_{12.3}) = \frac{\sigma^2}{\Sigma x^2_{2.3}} = \frac{\Sigma x^2_{1.23}}{(n-3)\Sigma x^2_{2.3}} = .125$$

$$\text{var}(b_{13.2}) = \frac{\sigma^2}{\Sigma x^2_{3.2}} = \frac{\Sigma x^2_{1.23}}{(n-3)\Sigma x^2_{3.2}} = .125$$

CASE 3 $(r_{23} = .6)$:

X_1	X_2	X_3	x_1	x_2	x_3	x^2_1	x^2_2	x^2_3	x_1x_2	x_1x_3	x_2x_3
4	2	3	−7	−4	−2	49	16	4	28	14	8
6	4	1	−5	−2	4	25	4	16	10	20	8
15	6	9	4	0	4	16	0	16	0	16	0
14	8	5	3	2	0	9	4	0	6	0	0
16	10	7	5	4	2	25	16	4	20	10	8
						124	40	40	64	60	24

$$s_1 = 4.98 \qquad s_2 = 2.828 \qquad s_3 = 2.828$$
$$r_{23} = .6 \qquad r_{12} = .9089 \qquad r_{13} = .8526$$
$$b_{12.3} = 1.0933 \qquad b_{13.2} = .8454$$
$$b_{23} = .6 \qquad b_{32} = .6$$

Computing $x_{1.23}$, $x_{2.3}$, and $x_{3.2}$,

$x_{1.23}$	$x_{2.3}$	$x_{3.2}$	$x_{1.23}^2$	$x_{2.3}^2$	$x_{3.2}^2$
.9360	−2.8	.4	.8761	7.84	.16
.5682	.4	−2.8	.3229	.16	7.84
.6184	−2.4	4.0	.3824	5.76	16.00
.8134	2.0	−1.2	.6616	4.00	1.44
−1.0640	2.8	−.4	1.1321	7.84	.16
			3.3751	25.6	25.6

$$\text{var}(b_{12.3}) = .0659 \qquad \text{var}(b_{13.2}) = .0659$$

These examples show that when the correlation between the explanatory variable decreases, the variance of the estimator decreases, which makes the estimation more efficient.

Simultaneous Relationships Among Variables

Reduced-Form Equations and the Indirect Least-Squares Method. In a simultaneous-equation model, if the explanatory variable in one equation also appears as an explained variable in another or vice versa, we may not apply the direct least-squares method to estimate the parameters of each equation since it violates the assumption that the explanatory variable and the error term should be independent of each other. The following is an example illustrating the problem and a way to avoid it.

EXAMPLE:
Suppose we have two relationships among these variables,

$$Y_t = a + bX_t + u_t \qquad (6\text{-}53)$$
$$X_t = Y_t + Z_t \qquad (6\text{-}54)$$

where the values of Y and X are determined in the model. They are the endogenous variables. While the value of Z is determined outside the system, Z affects the values of the endogenous variables, but is not affected by them. Z is an exogenous variable.

Now, we want to estimate the values of a and b. If we apply the direct least-squares method to Eq. 6-53, we will get a biased result because X and u are correlated through the relationship of Eq. 6-54. A modified way to estimate a and b which will avoid this trouble is first to transform the equations to the reduced form, that is, let each of the endogenous variables be expressed as functions of the exogenous variable.

Thus from Eqs. 6-53 and 6-54 we obtain

$$Y_t = a + b(Y_t + Z_t) + u_t$$

Therefore

$$Y_t = \frac{b}{1-b}Z_t + \frac{a}{1-b} + \frac{u_t}{1-b} \tag{6-55}$$

$$X_t = \left(\frac{b}{1-b}Z_t + \frac{a}{1-b} + \frac{u_t}{1-b}\right) + Z_t$$

and

$$X_t = \frac{1}{1-b}Z_t + \frac{a}{1-b} + \frac{u_t}{1-b} \tag{6-56}$$

We then apply the least-squares method to the reduced-form equations, we get the following estimates of the parameters:

$$\left(\frac{\hat{b}}{1-\hat{b}}\right) = \frac{\Sigma zy}{\Sigma z^2} \tag{6-57}$$

$$\left(\frac{1}{1-\hat{b}}\right) = \frac{\Sigma zx}{\Sigma z^2} \tag{6-58}$$

where $z = Z - \bar{Z}$, $y = Y - \bar{Y}$ and $x = X - \bar{X}$.

(Assuming that u_t is normally distributed with constant variance and zero mean)

$$\left(\frac{\hat{a}}{1-\hat{b}}\right) = \bar{Y} - \left(\frac{\hat{b}}{1-b}\right)\bar{Z} = \bar{Y} - \frac{\Sigma zy}{\Sigma z^2}\bar{Z} = \frac{\bar{Y}\Sigma z^2 - \bar{Z}\Sigma zy}{\Sigma z^2} \tag{6-59}$$

or

$$\left(\frac{\hat{a}}{1-\hat{b}}\right) = \bar{X} - \left(\frac{1}{1-\hat{b}}\right)\bar{Z} = \bar{X} - \frac{\Sigma zx}{\Sigma z^2}\bar{Z} = \frac{\bar{X}\Sigma z^2 - \bar{Z}\Sigma zx}{\Sigma z^2} \tag{6-60}$$

Since $X_t = Y_t + Z_t$, $\Sigma zx = \Sigma zy + \Sigma z^2$. From Eq. 6-57 and Eq. 6-58, solving for $\hat{b}$,

$$\hat{b} = \frac{\Sigma zy}{\Sigma zx} \tag{6-61}$$

From Eq. 6-59 or Eq. 6-60, solving for $\hat{a}$,

$$\hat{a} = \frac{\bar{Y}\Sigma z^2 - \bar{Z}\Sigma zy}{\Sigma zx} \tag{6-62}$$

Notice that $\hat{a}$ and $\hat{b}$ are the unbiased estimators of the reduced-form equations, but may not be unbiased estimators of a and b in the original equations, yet they will be consistent estimators. This method is known as the *indirect least-squares method*.

A numerical example is as follows. Assume that the relationships between consumption C, income Y, and investment I are

(1) $C_t = \hat{a} + \hat{b}Y_t + e_t$

(2) $Y_t = C_t + I_t$

and assume the following sample observations:

t	C	t	Y	c	i	y	cy	y^2	ci	i^2	yi
1	80	4	84	−45	−10	−55	2,475	3,025	450	100	550
2	90	6	96	−35	−8	−43	1,505	1,849	280	64	344
3	105	10	115	−20	−4	−24	480	576	80	16	96
4	110	10	120	−15	−4	−19	285	361	60	16	76
5	120	12	132	−5	−2	−7	35	49	10	4	14
6	130	14	144	5	0	5	25	25	0	0	0
7	135	15	150	10	1	11	110	121	10	1	11
8	150	19	169	25	5	30	750	900	125	25	150
9	155	20	175	30	6	36	1,080	1,296	180	36	216
10	175	30	205	50	16	66	3,300	4,356	800	256	1,056
	1,250	140	1,390				10,045	12,558	1,995	518	2,513

If we use the direct least-squares method to estimate the marginal propensity to consume, b, we will get an inconsistent estimate

$$\hat{b} = \frac{m_{cv}}{m_{yy}} = \frac{10,045}{12,558} = 0.7999$$

If we transform the original equations into the reduced form and treat investment as exogenous to the system, we get

$$(1) \quad C_t = \frac{\hat{a}}{1 - \hat{b}} + \frac{\hat{b}}{1 - \hat{b}} I_t + \frac{1}{1 - \hat{b}} e_t$$

$$(2) \quad Y_t = \frac{\hat{a}}{1 - \hat{b}} + \frac{1}{1 - \hat{b}} I_t + \frac{1}{1 - \hat{b}} e_t$$

Applying the direct least-squares method to the reduced-form equations, the estimated marginal propensity to consume becomes

$$\frac{\hat{b}}{1 - \hat{b}} = \frac{m_{ci}}{m_{ii}} = \frac{1,995}{518} = 3.85$$

Thus

$$\hat{b} = \frac{3.85}{1 + 3.85} = 0.7938$$

or

$$\frac{1}{1 - \hat{b}} = \frac{m_{yi}}{m_{ii}} = \frac{2,513}{518} = 4.85$$

and

$$\hat{b} = \frac{4.85 - 1}{4.85} = 0.7938$$

or if we treat investment I as the instrumental variable and use the indirect least-squares method to estimate the marginal propensity to consume, we also get

$$\hat{b} = \frac{m_{ci}}{m_{yi}} = \frac{1,995}{2,513} = 0.7938$$

The example illustrates that when the value of b is between 0 and 1, the direct least-squares estimator will have an upward biasedness. For unidentifiable relationships, however, we cannot obtain the estimation of the structural coefficients from the reduced-form coefficients.

Illustration:

$$y_1 + a_{12}y_2 - b_{11}x_1 = u_1$$
$$a_{21}y_1 + y_2 - b_{22}x_1 = u_2$$

where y_1, y_2 are endogenous variables, x_1 is an exogenous variable, u_1, u_2 are stochastic terms, and $a_{12}, a_{21}, b_{11}, b_{22}$ are structural coefficients. Since each equation has the same variables, they are unidentifiable. Now, the reduced-form equations will be as follows.

$$\begin{bmatrix} 1 & a_{12} \\ a_{21} & 1 \end{bmatrix} \begin{bmatrix} y_1 \\ y_2 \end{bmatrix} = \begin{bmatrix} b_{11} \\ b_{22} \end{bmatrix} x_1 + \begin{bmatrix} u_1 \\ u_2 \end{bmatrix}$$

or

$$\begin{bmatrix} y_1 \\ y_2 \end{bmatrix} = \begin{bmatrix} 1 & a_{12} \\ a_{21} & 1 \end{bmatrix}^{-1} \begin{bmatrix} b_{11} \\ b_{22} \end{bmatrix} x_1 + \begin{bmatrix} 1 & a_{12} \\ a_{21} & 1 \end{bmatrix}^{-1} \begin{bmatrix} u_1 \\ u_2 \end{bmatrix}$$

since

$$\begin{bmatrix} 1 & a_{12} \\ a_{21} & 1 \end{bmatrix}^{-1} = \begin{bmatrix} \dfrac{1}{1 - a_{12}a_{21}} & \dfrac{-a_{12}}{1 - a_{12}a_{21}} \\ \dfrac{-a_{21}}{1 - a_{12}a_{21}} & \dfrac{1}{1 - a_{12}a_{21}} \end{bmatrix}$$

then

$$y_1 = \left(\frac{b_{11} - a_{12}b_{22}}{1 - a_{12}a_{21}} \right) x_1 + \frac{u_1 - a_{12}u_2}{1 - a_{12}a_{21}}$$

$$y_2 = \left(\frac{b_{22} - a_{21}b_{11}}{1 - a_{12}a_{21}} \right) x_1 + \frac{u_2 - a_{21}u_1}{1 - a_{12}a_{21}}$$

Apply least squares on the reduced-form equations, we can estimate the values of the reduced-form coefficients $\left(\dfrac{b_{11} - a_{12}b_{22}}{1 - a_{12}a_{21}} \right)$ and $\left(\dfrac{b_{22} - a_{21}b_{11}}{1 - a_{12}a_{21}} \right)$. However, we cannot transform them to the values of the structural coefficients a_{12}, a_{21}, b_{11}, and b_{22}, because there are four unknowns with only two equations.

Least-Variance Ratio. Another method of estimating the parameters when the explained variable in one relationship becomes the explanatory variable in another relationship is called the *least-variance ratio method.* Suppose we have an economic relationship between Y and X expressed in deviation terms as follows:

$$y = bx + u$$

and that there is another variable Z related to X, as $x = y + z$, but Z is not directly related to Y. If we specify the relationship as

$$y = bx + cx + v$$

we know that c should be zero. However, in a finite sample, c will be a nonzero coefficient, while the variance of v will be slightly smaller than that of u. The least-variance-ratio method is designed to find an estimator of b that minimizes the ratio of the variance of u and v.

$$u = y - bx$$
$$v = y - bx - cz$$
$$= u - cz$$

Thus $u = v + cz$. The least-squares estimator of c is

$$\hat{c} = \frac{\Sigma uz}{\Sigma z^2}$$

$$\min\left(\frac{\Sigma u^2}{\Sigma v^2}\right) = \min\left(\frac{\Sigma u^2}{\Sigma(u - cz)^2}\right)$$

$$= \min\left(\frac{\Sigma u^2}{\Sigma u^2 - 2\frac{\Sigma uz}{\Sigma z^2}(\Sigma uz) + \left(\frac{\Sigma uz}{\Sigma z^2}\right)^2 \Sigma z^2}\right)$$

$$= \min\left(\frac{\Sigma u^2}{\Sigma u^2 - \left(\frac{\Sigma uz}{\Sigma z^2}\right)^2}\right)$$

which should equal 1, since Σu^2 and $(\Sigma uz/\Sigma z^2)^2$ are all positive values and the condition for minimizing the ratio is

$$\Sigma uz = 0$$

or

$$\Sigma(y - \hat{b}x)z = 0$$
$$\Sigma yz - \hat{b}\Sigma xz = 0$$

The least-variance ratio estimator of b in this case is then

$$\hat{b} = \frac{\Sigma yz}{\Sigma xz}$$

which in this simple model is the same as the indirect least-squares estimator.

Minimizing the variance ratio between the error terms is similar to the maximization of the likelihood function in the estimation of the parameters of a single equation, when all exogenous or predetermined variables are arbitrarily included in the equation. The latter method is called the *limited-information method.*

Full-Information, Maximum-Likelihood Method. Another method of estimating the parameters of a simultaneous-equation model is called the *full-information, maximum-likelihood method.* The method estimates all the parameters simultaneously instead of estimating the parameters of each equation individually. In a simultaneous-equation model,

$$a_{11}y_1 + a_{12}y_2 + \cdots + a_{1k}y_k + b_{11}x_1 + \cdots + b_{1m}x_m = u_1$$
$$a_{21}y_1 + a_{12}y_2 + \cdots + a_{2k}y_k + b_{21}x_1 + \cdots + b_{2m}x_m = u_2$$
$$\vdots$$
$$a_{n1}y_1 + a_{n2}y_2 + \cdots + a_{nk}y_k + b_{n1}x_1 + \cdots + b_{nm}x_m = u_n$$

where $y_1, y_2, \ldots, y_k$ are the endogenous variables, $x_1, x_2, \ldots, x_m$ are the exogenous variables and $u_1, u_2, \ldots, u_n$ are the error terms, the conditional probability of y given x may be expressed in a likelihood function:

$$L = P(y_i \mid x_i)$$
$$= P(u_i \mid x_i)\left|\frac{\partial u_i}{\partial y_i}\right|$$

Assuming u_i is serially and mutually independent and is independent of x_i,

$$L = P(u_i)\left|\frac{\partial u_i}{\partial y_i}\right|$$
$$= P(u_i)\,|a_{ij}|$$

where a_{ij} are the coefficients of the endogenous variables. Theoretically speaking, taking partial derivatives of the likelihood function (or the logarithm of it) with respect to the coefficients and setting the derivatives equal to zero will yield the maximum-likelihood estimators of the parameters or coefficients. However, the method results in very complicated nonlinear equations, and solutions are difficult to obtain. We use the following simple model to illustrate this.

$$a_{11}y_1 + a_{12}y_2 - b_{11}x_1 = u_1$$
$$a_{21}y_1 + a_{22}y_2 - b_{22}x_2 = u_2$$

Given that the variances of the probability distributions of u_1 and u_2 are σ_{11} and σ_{22}, respectively, and that their covariance is σ_{12}.

Then the logarithm of the likelihood function of this model is

$$\log L = \text{const.} + 2 \log \begin{vmatrix} a_{11} & a_{12} \\ a_{21} & a_{22} \end{vmatrix} - \frac{1}{2} \Sigma \left([u_1 \quad u_2] \begin{bmatrix} \sigma_{11} & \sigma_{12} \\ \sigma_{12} & \sigma_{22} \end{bmatrix}^{-1} \begin{bmatrix} u_1 \\ u_2 \end{bmatrix} \right)$$

Taking partial derivatives of log L with respect to a_{11} and b_{11} and setting the expressions equal to zero, we get the equations

$$\frac{\partial \log L}{\partial a_{11}} = \frac{2a_{22}}{(a_{11}a_{22} - a_{12}a_{21})} - \frac{1}{2} \frac{\left(\partial \Sigma \, [u_1 \quad u_2] \begin{bmatrix} \sigma_{11} & \sigma_{12} \\ \sigma_{12} & \sigma_{22} \end{bmatrix}^{-1} \begin{bmatrix} u_1 \\ u_2 \end{bmatrix} \right)}{\partial a_{11}} = 0$$

$$\frac{\partial \log L}{\partial b_{11}} = -\frac{1}{2} \frac{\partial \Sigma \left([u_1 \quad u_2] \begin{bmatrix} \sigma_{11} & \sigma_{12} \\ \sigma_{12} & \sigma_{22} \end{bmatrix}^{-1} \begin{bmatrix} u_1 \\ u_2 \end{bmatrix} \right)}{\partial b_{11}} = 0$$

(For other coefficients, the derivatives may be obtained in the same manner.)

They are complicated nonlinear equations and it will be difficult to solve them to find the maximum-likelihood estimators of the coefficients.

A special case of the model, which does not involve solving non-linear equations, has the following characteristics: (a) the a_{ij} matrix is a triangular matrix with all the elements on the principal diagonal equal to one, and (b) the covariances of the error terms equal to zero.

In our model

(a) $a_{11} = a_{22} = 1$ and $a_{12} = 0$

$$y_1 - b_{11}x_1 = u_1$$
$$a_{21}y_1 + y_2 - b_{22}x_2 = u_2$$

Therefore the following determinant holds:

$$\begin{vmatrix} a_{11} & a_{12} \\ a_{21} & a_{22} \end{vmatrix} = \begin{vmatrix} 1 & 0 \\ a_{21} & 1 \end{vmatrix} = 1$$

(b) The covariance $\sigma_{12} = 0$

The logarithm of the likelihood functions becomes

$$\log L = \text{const.} + 0 - \frac{1}{2} \Sigma \left([u_1 \quad u_2] \begin{bmatrix} \frac{1}{\sigma_{11}} & 0 \\ 0 & \frac{1}{\sigma_{22}} \end{bmatrix} \begin{bmatrix} u_1 \\ u_2 \end{bmatrix} \right)$$

$$= \text{const.} - \frac{1}{2} \Sigma \frac{u_1^2}{\sigma_{11}} - \frac{1}{2} \Sigma \frac{u_2^2}{\sigma_{22}}$$

$$= \text{const.} = \frac{1}{2\sigma_{11}} \Sigma (y_1 - b_{11}x_1)^2$$

$$- \frac{1}{2\sigma_{22}} \Sigma (a_{21}y_1 + y_2 - b_{22}x_2)^2$$

Taking partial derivatives of log L,

$$\frac{\partial \log L}{\partial b_{11}} = \frac{1}{\sigma_{11}} \Sigma (y_1 - b_{11} x_1) x_1$$

$$= \frac{1}{\sigma_{11}} (\Sigma x_i y_1 - b_{11} \Sigma x_1^2)$$

$$\frac{\partial \log L}{\partial b_{22}} = \frac{1}{\sigma_{22}} \Sigma (a_{21} y_1 + y_2 - b_{22} x_2) x_2$$

$$= \frac{1}{\sigma_{22}} (a_{21} \Sigma x_2 y_1 + \Sigma x_2 y_2 - b_{22} \Sigma x_2^2)$$

$$\frac{\partial \log L}{\partial a_{21}} = -\frac{1}{\sigma_{22}} \Sigma (a_{21} y_1 + y_2 - b_{22} x_2) y_1$$

$$= -\frac{1}{\sigma_{22}} (a_{21} \Sigma y_1^2 + \Sigma y_1 y_2 - b_{22} \Sigma x_2 y_1)$$

Setting the derivatives equal to zero, and solving for parameter estimates,

$$\hat{b}_{11} = \frac{\Sigma x_1 y_1}{\Sigma x_1^2}$$

$$\hat{b}_{22} = \frac{(\Sigma x_2 y_2)(\Sigma y_1^2) - (\Sigma x_2 y_1)(\Sigma y_1 y_2)}{(\Sigma x_2^2)(\Sigma y_1^2) - (\Sigma x_2 y_1)^2}$$

$$\hat{a}_{21} = \frac{(\Sigma x_2 y_2)(\Sigma x_2 y_1) - (\Sigma x_2^2)(\Sigma y_1 y_2)}{(\Sigma x_2^2)(\Sigma y_1^2) - (\Sigma x_2 y_1)^2}$$

When $a_{21} = 0$,

$$\hat{b}_{22} = \frac{\Sigma x_2 y_2}{\Sigma x_2^2}$$

Thus in this particular case, where the determinant $|a_{ij}|$ is unity and the error terms are not correlated, using the full-information, maximum-likelihood method is the same as applying ordinary least squares to each equation in turn.

Three-Stage Least-Squares Method

The two-stage least-squares method may be used in estimating the parameters of each equation in a simultaneous-equations system individually after the error component of the explanatory variables is purged. Zellner and Theil, however, furtherly suggest that by using the variance-covariance matrix of the error terms derived from the two-stage estimates and premultiplying each equation of a simultaneous-equation model by all predetermined variables, generalized least squares may then be applied to the whole set of equations to estimate all the parameters simultaneously. The method is called *three-stage least squares*, since it requires one stage more than two-stage least squares. The estimates are supposed to be more efficient.

EXAMPLE:

A simultaneous-equation system†

$$C_t = a_1 + a_2 Y_t + a_3 Y_{t-1} + v_t \qquad \text{(consumption behavior)}$$
$$I_t = b_1 + b_2 Y_t + b_3 I_{t-1} + w_t \qquad \text{(investment behavior)}$$
$$Y_t = C_t + I_t + Z_t \qquad \text{(identity)}$$

where Z_t is an exogenous variable, Y_{t-1} and I_{t-1} are lagged variables C_t, I_t, Y_t the current endogenous variables, and v_t, w_t disturbance terms. Since in both the consumption and investment functions, the current endogenous variable on the left-hand side of the equation is not explained by predetermined (exogenous and lagged) variables alone, ordinary least squares cannot be applied directly to the equation, otherwise the estimate will be biased and inconsistent.

Now if we apply two-stage least squares to the consumption and investment functions, we may avoid this difficulty. In the first stage, we apply least squares to

$$Y_t = c_1 + c_2 Y_{t-1} + c_3 I_{t-1} + c_4 Z_t + u_t \qquad \text{(where } Y_t \text{ is explained}$$
$$\text{by all the predetermined variables)}$$

and obtain the revised Y values (reduced form of Y)

$$Y'_t = \hat{c}_1 + \hat{c}_2 Y_{t-1} + \hat{c}_3 I_{t-1} + \hat{c}_4 Z_t$$

The idea is to purge Y of the stochastic component associated with disturbance terms v and w. (Note Y is the only endogenous variable which appears on the right-hand side of the consumption and investment equations.)

$$\hat{C}_t = a_1 + a_2 Y'_t + a_3 Y_{t-1} + v'_t \qquad \text{(where } Y'_t \text{ now is independent of}$$
$$v'_t \text{ and } w'_t)$$

$$\hat{I}_t = b_1 + b_2 Y'_t + b_3 I_{t-1} + w'_t$$

---

†The total number of the endogenous variables (C_t, Y_t, I_t) are $G = 3$ and the predetermined variables (Y_{t-1}, I_{t-1}, Z_t) are $K = 3$. For the consumption function, the endogenous variables included in the equation are $(C_t, Y_t) g_1 = 2$ and the predetermined variable included in the equation is $(Y_{t-1}) k_1 = 1$, thus

$$g_2 = G - g_1 = 1, \qquad k_2 = K - k_1 = 2$$
$$g_2 + k_2 = 3, \qquad G - 1 = 2$$

Since

$$g_2 + k_2 > G - 1$$

the equation is overidentified. For the investment function, the endogeneous variables in the equation are $(I_t, Y_t), g_1 = 2$ and the predetermined variable included in equation is $(Y_{t-1}), k_1 = 1$.

$$g_2 + k_2 > G - 1$$

The equation is also overidentified.

and obtain the two-stage least-squares estimates $\hat{a}_1, \hat{a}_2, \hat{a}_3$ and $\hat{b}_1, \hat{b}_2, \hat{b}_3$, respectively.

Three-stage least squares is based on generalized least squares using the variance-covariance matrix obtained from the two-stage estimates to reduce the variance of the estimate. Following the previous example,

$$\hat{C}_t = \hat{a}_1 + \hat{a}_2 Y'_t + \hat{a}_3 Y_{t-1}$$
$$\hat{I}_t = \hat{b}_1 + \hat{b}_2 Y'_t + \hat{b}_3 I_{t-1}$$

Define

$$\Sigma e_c^2 = \sum_{t=1}^{n} (C_t - \hat{C}_t)^2 \quad \text{and} \quad \Sigma e_i^2 = \sum_{t=1}^{n} (I_t - \hat{I}_t)^2 \quad (n \text{ is sample size})$$

and

$$\begin{bmatrix} \dfrac{\Sigma e_c^2}{n-3} & \dfrac{\Sigma e_c e_i}{n-3} \\[2mm] \dfrac{\Sigma e_i e_c}{n-3} & \dfrac{\Sigma e_i^2}{n-3} \end{bmatrix}^{-1} = \begin{bmatrix} S_{cc} & S_{ci} \\ S_{ic} & S_{ii} \end{bmatrix} = V^{-1}$$

The general formula for the third-stage estimate is

$$\begin{bmatrix} a_1^* \\ \vdots \\ a_k^* \end{bmatrix} = \begin{bmatrix} s_{11} Z_1^T X (X^T X)^{-1} X^T Z_1 \cdots s_{1m} Z_1^T X (X^T X)^{-1} X^T Z_m \\ \vdots \qquad\qquad \vdots \\ s_{m1} Z_m^T X (X^T X)^{-1} X^T Z_1 \cdots s_{mm} Z_m^t X (X^T X)^{-1} X T Z_m \end{bmatrix}^{-1}$$

$$\times \begin{bmatrix} s_{11} Z_1^T X (X^T X)^{-1} X^T y_1 + \cdots + s_{1m} Z_1^T X (X^T X)^{-1} X^T y_m \\ \vdots \qquad\qquad \vdots \\ s_{m1} Z_m^T X (X^T X)^{-1} X^T y_1 + \cdots + s_{mm} Z_m^t X (X^T X)^{-1} X^T y_m \end{bmatrix}$$

where X represents all predetermined variables in the system, Z_i represents all the variables in equation i except y_i which is the endogenous variable on the left side of the equal sign in equation i.

Now in this example

$$s_{11} = S_{cc}, \quad s_{12} = s_{21} = S_{ci}, \quad s_{22} = S_{ii}$$

and the matrices are

$$(\mathrm{I}) = Z_1^T X = \begin{bmatrix} \Sigma y_t y_{t-1} & \Sigma y_t i_{t-1} & \Sigma y_t z_t \\ \Sigma y_{t-1}^2 & \Sigma y_{t-1} i_{t-1} & \Sigma y_{t-1} z_t \end{bmatrix}$$

$$(\mathrm{II}) = Z_2^T X = \begin{bmatrix} \Sigma y_t y_{t-1} & \Sigma y_t i_{t-1} & \Sigma y_t z_t \\ \Sigma i_{t-1} y_{t-1} & \Sigma i_{t-1}^2 & \Sigma i_{t-1} z_t \end{bmatrix}$$

$$(\text{III}) = (X^T X)^{-1} = \begin{bmatrix} \Sigma y_{t-1}^2 & \Sigma y_{t-1} i_{t-1} & \Sigma y_{t-1} z_t \\ \Sigma i_{t-1} y_{t-1} & \Sigma i_{t-1}^2 & \Sigma i_{t-1} z_t \\ \Sigma z_t y_{t-1} & \Sigma z_t i_{t-1} & \Sigma z_t^2 \end{bmatrix}^{-1}$$

$$(\text{IV}) = X^T Z_1 = \begin{bmatrix} \Sigma y_{t-1} y_t & \Sigma y_{t-1}^2 \\ \Sigma i_{t-1} y_t & \Sigma i_{t-1} y_{t-1} \\ \Sigma z_t y_t & \Sigma i_{t-1} y_{t-1} \end{bmatrix}$$

$$(\text{V}) = X^T Z_2 = \begin{bmatrix} \Sigma y_{t-1} y_t & \Sigma y_{t-1} i_{t-1} \\ \Sigma i_{t-1} y_t & \Sigma i_{t-1}^2 \\ \Sigma z_t y_t & \Sigma z_t i_{t-1} \end{bmatrix}$$

$$(\text{VI}) = X^T y_1 = \begin{bmatrix} \Sigma y_{t-1} c_t \\ \Sigma i_{t-1} c_t \\ \Sigma z_t c_t \end{bmatrix}$$

$$(\text{VII}) = X^T y_2 = \begin{bmatrix} \Sigma y_{t-1} i_t \\ \Sigma i_{t-1} i_t \\ \Sigma z_t i_t \end{bmatrix}$$

Thus the three-stage least squares estimates are

$$\begin{bmatrix} a_2^* \\ a_3^* \\ b_2^* \\ b_3^* \end{bmatrix} = \begin{bmatrix} s_{cc}(\text{I})(\text{III})(\text{IV}), & s_{ci}(\text{I})(\text{III})(\text{V}) \\ s_{ci}(\text{II})(\text{III})(\text{IV}), & s_{ii}(\text{II})(\text{III})(\text{V}) \end{bmatrix}^{-1}$$

$$\times \begin{bmatrix} s_{cc}(\text{I})(\text{III})(\text{VI}) + s_{ci}(\text{I})(\text{III})(\text{VII}) \\ s_{ci}(\text{II})(\text{III})(\text{VI}) + s_{ii}(\text{II})(\text{III})(\text{VII}) \end{bmatrix}$$

$$a_1^* = \bar{C}_t - {}'a_2^* \bar{Y}_t - a_3^* \bar{Y}_{t-1}$$
$$b_1^* = \bar{I}_t - b_2^* \bar{Y}_t - b_3^* \bar{I}_{t-1}$$

where $\bar{C}_t$, $\bar{Y}_t$, $\bar{I}_t$, $\bar{Y}_{t-1}$, and $\bar{I}_{t-1}$ are the mean values from $t = 1$ to n. The advantage of the three-stage least-squares estimation method is that it is supposed to be more efficient.

For forecasting the time paths of the endogenous variables, the reduced form may be used. The simultaneous-equations model may be written as follows:

$$Y_{t+1} = C_{t+1} + I_{t+1} + Z_{t+1}$$
$$C_{t+1} = \hat{a}_1 + \hat{a}_2 Y_{t+1} + \hat{a}_3 Y_t$$
$$I_{t+1} = \hat{b}_1 + \hat{b}_2 Y_{t+1} + \hat{b}_3 I_t$$

or

$$
\begin{bmatrix} 1 & -1 & -1 \\ -\hat{a}_2 & 1 & 0 \\ -\hat{b}_2 & 0 & 1 \end{bmatrix}
\begin{bmatrix} Y_{t+1} \\ C_{t+1} \\ I_{t+1} \end{bmatrix}
=
\begin{bmatrix} 0 & 1 & 0 & 0 \\ \hat{a}_1 & 0 & \hat{a}_3 & 0 \\ \hat{b}_1 & 0 & 0 & \hat{b}_3 \end{bmatrix}
\begin{bmatrix} 1 \\ Z_{t+1} \\ Y_t \\ I_t \end{bmatrix}
$$

$$
\begin{bmatrix} Y_{t+1} \\ C_{t+1} \\ I_{t+1} \end{bmatrix}
=
\begin{bmatrix} 1 & -1 & -1 \\ -\hat{a}_2 & 1 & 0 \\ -\hat{b}_2 & 0 & 1 \end{bmatrix}^{-1}
\begin{bmatrix} 0 & 1 & 0 & 0 \\ \hat{a}_1 & 0 & \hat{a}_3 & 0 \\ \hat{b}_1 & 0 & 0 & \hat{b}_3 \end{bmatrix}
\begin{bmatrix} 1 \\ Z_{t+1} \\ Y_t \\ I_t \end{bmatrix}
$$

Given the value of Z in period $(t + 1)$ and Y, I in period t, we may forecast the values of Y, C, I in period $(t + 1)$. [The parameters $\hat{a}_1$, $\hat{a}_2$, b_3 may be either the two-stage or three-stage least-squares estimates.]

Numerical Example

Assume the sample data of the model

$$C_t = a_1 + a_2 Y_t + a_3 Y_{t-1} + v_t$$
$$I_t = b_1 + b_2 Y_t + b_3 I_{t-1} + w_t$$
$$Y_t = C_t + I_t + Z_t$$

are as follows:

t	Y	C	I	Z
0	90	79	10	7
1	97	80	11	8
2	98	82	11.5	8.5
3	101	85	12	9
4	109	90	12	9
5	110	90	14	8
6	130	99	18	10
7	119	98	20	9
8	127	95	15	9
9	141	100	16	10

1. The two-stage least-squares estimates:

$$\sum_{t=1}^{9} Y_t = 1{,}032$$

$\Sigma Y_{t-1} = 981$	$\Sigma C_t = 819$	$\Sigma Z_t = 80.5$
$\Sigma Y_{t-1}^2 = 108{,}485$	$\Sigma C_{t-1} = 798$	$\Sigma Z_{t-1} = 77.5$
$\Sigma Y_t Y_{t-1} = 113{,}923$	$\Sigma I_t = 129.5$	$\Sigma Z_t^2 = 724.25$
$\Sigma Y_t I_{t-1} = 14{,}454.5$	$\Sigma I_{t-1} = 123.5$	
$\Sigma Y_t Z_t = 9{,}303$	$\Sigma I_{t-1}^2 = 1{,}786.25$	
$\Sigma Y_{t-1} C_t = 90{,}019$	$\Sigma I_{t-1} Z_t = 1{,}113$	
$\Sigma Y_{t-1} I_{t-1} = 13{,}779$	$\Sigma I_t I_{t-1} = 1{,}838.5$	
$\Sigma Y_{t-1} Z_t = 8{,}818.5$		

The normal equations are

$$
\begin{bmatrix} n \\ \Sigma Y_{t-1} \\ \Sigma I_{t-1} \\ \Sigma Z_t \end{bmatrix} \hat{c}_1 +
\begin{bmatrix} \Sigma Y_{t-1} \\ \Sigma Y_{t-1}^2 \\ \Sigma Y_{t-1} I_{t-1} \\ \Sigma Y_{t-1} Z_t \end{bmatrix} \hat{c}_2 +
\begin{bmatrix} \Sigma I_{t-1} \\ \Sigma I_{t-1} Y_{t-1} \\ \Sigma I_{t-1}^2 \\ \Sigma I_{t-1} Z_t \end{bmatrix} \hat{c}_3 +
\begin{bmatrix} \Sigma Z_t \\ \Sigma Z_t Y_{t-1} \\ \Sigma Z_t I_{t-1} \\ \Sigma Z_t^2 \end{bmatrix} \hat{c}_4
$$

$$
=
\begin{bmatrix} \Sigma Y_t \\ \Sigma Y_t Y_{t-1} \\ \Sigma Y_t I_{t-1} \\ \Sigma Y_t Z_t \end{bmatrix}
$$

solving the equations,

$$\hat{c}_1 = -46.464763, \quad \hat{c}_2 = 0.566060, \quad \hat{c}_3 = 0.260344, \quad \hat{c}_4 = 10.717093$$

First Stage:

$$Y_t' = -46.464763 + 0.56606 Y_{t-1} + 0.260344 I_{t-1} + 10.717093 Z_t$$

t	Y'	$\sum_{t=1}^{9} Y_t' = 1032.001$
1	92.821	$\Sigma Y_t'^2 = 120{,}000.051$
2	102.402	$\Sigma Y_t' Y_{t-1} = 113{,}923.108$
3	108.457	$\Sigma Y_t' C_t = 94{,}733.84$
4	110.285	$\Sigma Y_t' I_{t-1} = 14{,}454.513$
5	104.097	$\Sigma Y_t' I_t = 15{,}147.671$
6	126.618	
7	128.263	
8	122.557	
9	136.501	

$$
\begin{bmatrix} n \\ \Sigma Y'_t \\ \Sigma Y_{t-1} \end{bmatrix} \hat{a}_1 + \begin{bmatrix} \Sigma Y'_t \\ \Sigma Y_t'^2 \\ \Sigma Y'_t Y_{t-1} \end{bmatrix} \hat{a}_2 + \begin{bmatrix} \Sigma Y_{t-1} \\ \Sigma Y_{t-1} Y'_t \\ \Sigma Y^2_{t-1} \end{bmatrix} \hat{a}_3 = \begin{bmatrix} \Sigma C_t \\ \Sigma C_t Y'_t \\ \Sigma C_t Y_{t-1} \end{bmatrix}
$$

solving the equations,

$$\hat{a}_1 = 33.121, \quad \hat{a}_2 = 0.388, \quad \hat{a}_3 = 0.123$$

Second Stage:

$$\hat{\hat{C}}_t = 33.121 + 0.388 Y'_t + 0.123 Y_{t-1}$$

and

$$
\begin{bmatrix} n \\ \Sigma Y'_t \\ \Sigma I_{t-1} \end{bmatrix} \hat{b}_1 + \begin{bmatrix} \Sigma Y'_t \\ \Sigma Y_t'^2 \\ \Sigma Y'_t I_{t-1} \end{bmatrix} \hat{b}_2 + \begin{bmatrix} \Sigma I_{t-1} \\ \Sigma I_{t-1} Y'_t \\ \Sigma I^2_{t-1} \end{bmatrix} \hat{b}_3 = \begin{bmatrix} \Sigma I_t \\ \Sigma I_t Y'_t \\ \Sigma I_t I_{t-1} \end{bmatrix}
$$

solving the equations,

$$\hat{b}_1 = 4.724, \quad \hat{b}_2 = 0.140, \quad \hat{b}_3 = 0.223$$
$$\hat{\hat{I}}_t = 4.724 + 0.14 Y'_t + 0.223 I_{t-1}$$

2. The three-stage least squares estimates:

t	$\hat{C}$	$\hat{I}$	e_c	e_i	y	c	i	z
0	—	—	—	—	−22.2	−10.8	−3.95	−1.75
1	80.19	10.50	−.19	.50	−15.2	−9.8	−2.95	−0.75
2	84.78	12.07	−2.75	−.57	−14.2	−7.8	−2.45	−0.25
3	87.27	13.03	−2.27	−1.03	−11.2	−4.8	−1.95	0.25
4	88.34	13.39	1.66	−1.39	−3.2	0.2	−1.95	0.25
5	86.92	12.53	3.08	1.47	−2.2	0.2	0.05	−0.75
6	95.77	16.12	3.23	1.88	17.8	9.2	4.05	1.25
7	98.89	17.25	−.89	2.75	6.8	8.2	6.05	0.25
8	95.33	16.90	−.33	−1.90	14.8	5.2	1.05	0.25
9	101.70	17.73	−1.70	−1.73	28.8	10.2	2.05	1.25

$$
V^{-1} = \begin{bmatrix} s_{cc} & s_{ci} \\ s_{ci} & s_{ii} \end{bmatrix} = \begin{bmatrix} \dfrac{\Sigma e_c^2}{n-3} & \dfrac{\Sigma e_c e_i}{n-3} \\ \dfrac{\Sigma e_c e_i}{n-3} & \dfrac{\Sigma e_i^2}{n-3} \end{bmatrix}^{-1}
$$

$$
= \begin{bmatrix} 6.56 & 2.23 \\ 2.23 & 3.91 \end{bmatrix}^{-1} = \begin{bmatrix} .19 & -.11 \\ -.11 & .32 \end{bmatrix}
$$

(I)

$$
\begin{bmatrix} \Sigma y_t y_{t-1} & \Sigma y_t i_{t-1} & \Sigma y_t z_t \\ \Sigma y_{t-1}^2 & \Sigma y_{t-1} i_{t-1} & \Sigma y_{t-1} z_t \end{bmatrix} = \begin{bmatrix} 1363.96 & 288.11 & 76.65 \\ 1648.16 & 324.06 & 38.40 \end{bmatrix}
$$

(II)

$$
\begin{bmatrix} \Sigma y_t y_{t-1} & \Sigma y_t i_{t-1} & \Sigma y_t z_t \\ \Sigma i_{t-1} y_{t-1} & \Sigma i_{t-1}^2 & \Sigma i_{t-1} z_t \end{bmatrix} = \begin{bmatrix} 1363.96 & 288.11 & 76.65 \\ 324.06 & 92.02 & 7.96 \end{bmatrix}
$$

(III)

$$
\begin{bmatrix} \Sigma y_{t-1}^2 & \Sigma y_{t-1} i_{t-1} & \Sigma y_{t-1} z_t \\ \Sigma i_{t-1} y_{t-1} & \Sigma i_{t-1}^2 & \Sigma i_{t-1} z_t \\ \Sigma z_t y_{t-1} & \Sigma z_t i_{t-1} & \Sigma z_t^2 \end{bmatrix}^{-1} = \begin{bmatrix} 1648.16 & 288.11 & 38.40 \\ 324.06 & 92.02 & 7.96 \\ 38.40 & 7.96 & 4.56 \end{bmatrix}^{-1}
$$

$$
= \begin{bmatrix} 0.00167 & -0.00474 & -0.00583 \\ -0.00551 & 0.02838 & -0.00317 \\ -0.00448 & -0.00966 & 0.27391 \end{bmatrix}
$$

(IV)

$$
\begin{bmatrix} \Sigma y_{t-1} y_t & \Sigma y_{t-1}^2 \\ \Sigma i_{t-1} y_t & \Sigma i_{t-1} y_{t-1} \\ \Sigma z_t y_t & \Sigma z_t y_{t-1} \end{bmatrix} = \begin{bmatrix} 1363.96 & 1648.16 \\ 288.11 & 324.06 \\ 76.65 & 38.40 \end{bmatrix}
$$

(V)

$$
\begin{bmatrix} \Sigma y_{t-1} & \Sigma y_{t-1} i_{t-1} \\ \Sigma i_{t-1} y_t & \Sigma i_{t-1}^2 \\ \Sigma z_t y_t & \Sigma z_t i_{t-1} \end{bmatrix} = \begin{bmatrix} 1363.96 & 324.06 \\ 288.11 & 92.02 \\ 76.65 & 7.96 \end{bmatrix}
$$

(VI)

$$
\begin{bmatrix} \Sigma y_{t-1} c_t \\ \Sigma i_{t-1} c_t \\ \Sigma z_t c_t \end{bmatrix} = \begin{bmatrix} 713.44 \\ 148.54 \\ 35.60 \end{bmatrix}
$$

(VII)

$$
\begin{bmatrix} \Sigma y_{t-1} i_t \\ \Sigma i_{t-1} i_t \\ \Sigma z_t i_t \end{bmatrix} = \begin{bmatrix} 288.36 \\ 60.57 \\ 11.21 \end{bmatrix}
$$

$$\begin{bmatrix} a_2^* \\ a_3^* \\ b_2^* \\ b_3^* \end{bmatrix} = \begin{bmatrix} s_{cc}(\text{I})(\text{III})(\text{IV}); & s_{ci}(\text{I})(\text{III})(\text{V}) \\ s_{ci}(\text{II})(\text{III})(\text{IV}); & s_{ii}(\text{II})(\text{III})(\text{V}) \end{bmatrix}^{-1}$$

$$\times \begin{bmatrix} s_{cc}(\text{I})(\text{III})(\text{VI}) + s_{ci}(\text{I})(\text{III})(\text{V}) \\ s_{ci}(\text{II})(\text{III})(\text{VI}) + s_{ii}(\text{II})(\text{III})(\text{V}) \end{bmatrix} = \begin{bmatrix} 0.445 \\ 0.055 \\ 0.135 \\ 0.225 \end{bmatrix}$$

$$a_1^* = \overline{C}_t - a_2 \overline{Y}_t - a_3^* \overline{Y}_{t-1} = 33.978$$
$$b_1^* = \overline{I}_t - b_2^* \overline{Y}_t - b_3^* \overline{I}_{t-1} = 4.329$$

The three-stage least-squares-estimated equations are

$$C_t^* = 33.978 + 0.445\, Y_t + 0.055\, Y_{t-1}$$
$$I_t^* = +4.329 + 0.135\, Y_t + 0.225\, I_{t-1}$$

Aggregation

In forming a model for describing or predicting the behavior characteristics of an economy it often happens that we have to aggregate partial information to get the total information—for example, we may only have the demand information on steak, pork, chickens, etc., separately and want to estimate the demand function for meat. Or we may have only the demand functions of subregions A, B, and C, yet have to know the aggregate demand function of the entire area. If the functions are all linear, it will be simpler to aggregate.

EXAMPLE:

$$Y_{it} = a + bX_{it} + u_{it}$$
$$(i = 1, 2, \ldots, n)$$

Aggregating i from 1 to n,

$$\sum_{i=1}^{n} Y_{it} = na + b \sum_{i=1}^{n} X_{it} + \sum_{i=1}^{n} u_{it}$$

Thus

$$\overline{Y}_t = a + b\overline{X}_t + \overline{u}_t$$

And we may assume that parameters a and b are the same for individuals: $i = 1, 2, \ldots, n$. However, if the functions are nonlinear, then the aggregation process becomes more difficult and extreme care must be taken.

EXAMPLE:

$$Y_{it} = a + b_1 X_{it} + b_2 X_{it}^2 + u_{it}$$
$$(i = 1, 2, \ldots, n)$$

Aggregating i from 1 to n,

$$\sum_{i=1}^{n} Y_{it} = na + b_1 \sum_{i=1}^{n} X_{it} + b_2 \sum_{i=1}^{n} X_{it}^2 + \sum_{i=1}^{n} u_{it}$$

Thus

$$\overline{Y}_t = a + b_1 \overline{X}_t + b_2 \frac{\sum_{i=1}^{n} X_{it}^2}{n} + \overline{u}_t$$

$$= a + b_1 \overline{X}_t + b_2 \frac{\sum_{i=1}^{n} (X_{it} - \overline{X}_t)^2}{n} + b_2 \overline{X}_t^2 + \overline{u}_t$$

$$= a + b_1 \overline{X}_t + b_2 \overline{X}_t^2 + b_2 \operatorname{var}(X_{it}) + \overline{u}_t$$

which indicates that in order to estimate the expected Y in time period t, we need to know not only the average value but also the dispersion of X.

Pooling Cross-Section and Time-Series Data

Time-series data are difficult to obtain. If we make observations in short intervals, say in months or weeks, we may encounter problems of autocorrelation. But if we make observations less frequently, say in years, then our sample size will be very small and also the structure of the economy may have changed very significantly during the observation period. Thus in order to avoid the aforementioned difficulties we may sometimes have to pool cross-section and time-series data to obtain enough samples for evaluation.

EXAMPLE:

$$Q_{it} = a + bY_{it} + cP_t + u_{it}$$
$$i = 1, 2, \ldots, N \quad \text{(cross-section sample size)}$$
$$t = 1, 2, \ldots, T \quad \text{(time-series sample size)}$$

The equation indicates that the demand for a product Q is linearly related to real income Y (cross-section relationship) and price of the product P (time-series relationship). (P is assumed to be constant in all market areas i for time t.)

We also assume Q_t and the error term u_t are independent

$$Q_t = \sum_{i=1}^{N} Q_{it}, \quad u_t = \sum_{i=1}^{N} u_{it}$$

In pooling the cross-section observations of the effect of Y on Q and the time-series observations of the effect of P on Q, we change the equation to

$$\sum_{i=1}^{N} Q_{it} - \hat{b} \sum_{i=1}^{N} Y_{it} = a + cP_t + u_t$$

($\hat{b}$ is estimated by regressing Q_i on Y_i)

On the left-hand side of the equation is the demand for the product with the effect of income variations removed. If we call this combined term X, then

$$X_t = a + cP_t + u_t$$

and

$$\overline{X}_t = a + c\overline{P}_t.$$

Assuming the distribution of u has a zero mean and constant variance, we may apply the least-squares method to estimate a and c. However, if we suspect that X_t may not be independent of u_t since it consists of a component of real income Y_{it}, we may modify the equation as follows,

$$\sum_{i=1}^{T} X_t Q_t = a \sum_{t=1}^{T} Q_t + c \sum_{t=1}^{T} P_t Q_t$$

where $Q_t = \sum_{i=1}^{N} Q_{it}$. Then, finally, estimate the parameters by regression method. $\left(\text{Note that } \sum_{i=1}^{T} u_t \cdot Q_t = 0, \text{ because we assume } Q_t \text{ and } u_t \text{ are independent.} \right)$

6-4. PROBLEMS OF PREDICTION

After we have built a model, collected sample data, and estimated the parameters—in other words, when we have a description of the real system—we might further attempt to predict the unobserved or future values of the endogenous variables of the model.

For the unobserved values which occur in the same period when we take the sample data, the predictive power of the model will be high. However, for predicting future values, the further away they are from the original sampling period the larger the variation will be; proper adjustments have to be made in order to give the predicted value a reasonable degree of accuracy. In the following, we list some of the commonly used prediction techniques.

Interpolation and Extrapolation

In Chapter 3 we indicated a case that is a two-variable linear-regression model $\hat{Y}_0 = \hat{a} + \hat{b}X_0$. Given an X value, the predicted value of Y will be

$$(\hat{a} + \hat{b}X_0) \pm t_{\alpha/2} \hat{\sigma}_u \sqrt{1 + \frac{1}{n} + \frac{(X_0 - \overline{X})^2}{\Sigma x^2}}$$

The given value of X_0 may or may not lie within the range of the original sample observations. If X_0 lies within the range, the technique of predicting the respective Y value is called *interpolation*; otherwise it is called *extrapolation*. The prediction equation indicates that the larger the value of $(X_0 - \overline{X})$ the larger will be the confidence interval. In other words, the further away the given X value is from the original sample mean, the less confidence we will have in the predicted Y value.

In case of simultaneous-equations model, such as the following:

$$BY_t = \sum_{j=1}^{k} B_j Y_{t-j} + AX_t + U_t$$

where
$Y_t = n \times 1$ vector of endogenous variables
$Y_{t-j} = n \times 1$ vector of lagged endogenous variables, where $j = 1$, ..., k represents different time lags
$X_t = m \times 1$ vector of exogenous variables
$U_t = n \times 1$ vector of random-error terms
$A, B, B_j =$ coefficient matrices whose parameters have been estimated by econometric methods

If the model is a linear model that is all the relations between variables are in linear form, then we may use matrix algebra to obtain the solution

$$Y_t = B^{-1} \sum_{j=1}^{k} B_j Y_{t-j} + B^{-1} AX_t + B^{-1} U_t$$

where B^{-1} is the inverse of B. If X_t are given at each time period t and the distributions of U_t are known, the time paths of Y_t can be generated by computer simulation techniques.

If the model is nonlinear in variables, we may use Gauss-Seidel method to solve the simultaneous nonlinear equations. We use a two-equation nonlinear model to explain the method:

$$Y_{(1)} = f_1(Y_{(1)}, Y_{2t}, Y_{1,t-1}, Y_{2,t-1}, X_{(1)}, X_{2t})$$
$$Y_{2t} = f_2(Y_{(1)}, Y_{2t}, Y_{1,t-1}, Y_{2,t-1}, X_{(1)}, X_{2t})$$

Where Y_{1t}, Y_{2t} are current endogenous variables, $Y_{1,t-1}$, $Y_{2,t-1}$ are lagged endogenous variables, $X_{(1)}$, X_{2t} are exogenous variables (they may be treated as policy variables, whose values are set by the policy decision makers) and f_1, f_2 are nonlinear functions.

Since the functions are nonlinear, we may not be able to obtain reduced form for each current endogenous variable. However, we already know the values of the lagged endogenous variables and the exogenous variables, and we may choose starting values for $Y_{(1)}$ and Y_{2t} based on informed guesses or on recent observed values. We then substitute these values into the equations

$$Y_{1t}^{(1)} = f_1(Y_{1t}^{(0)}, Y_{2t}^{(0)}, Y_{1,t-1}, Y_{2,t-1}, X_{1t}, X_{2t})$$
$$Y_{2t}^{(1)} = f_2(Y_{1t}^{(0)}, Y_{2t}^{(0)}, Y_{1,t-1}, Y_{2,t-1}, X_{1t}, X_{2t})$$

Where $Y_{1t}^{(0)}$, $Y_{2t}^{(0)}$ are the starting values and $Y_{1t}^{(1)}$ and $Y_{2t}^{(1)}$ are the values of Y_{1t} and Y_{2t} after the first iteration.

By holding the values of $Y_{1,t-1}$, $Y_{2,t-1}$, X_{1t}, X_{2t} constant, we may continue the iterative procedure:

$$Y_{1t}^{(2)} = f_1(Y_{1t}^{(1)}, Y_{2t}^{(1)}, Y_{1,t-1}, Y_{2,t-1}, X_{1t}, X_{2t})$$
$$Y_{2t}^{(2)} = f_2(Y_{1t}^{(1)}, Y_{2t}^{(1)}, Y_{1,t-1}, Y_{2,t-1}, X_{1t}, X_{2t})$$
$$\vdots$$
$$Y_{1t}^{(r+1)} = f_1(Y_{1t}^{(r)}, Y_{2t}^{(r)}, Y_{1,t-1}, Y_{2,t-1}, X_{1t}, X_{2t})$$
$$Y_{2t}^{(r+1)} = f_2(Y_{1t}^{(r)}, Y_{2t}^{(r)}, Y_{1,t-1}, Y_{2,t-1}, X_{1t}, X_{2t})$$

until the following inequality is satisfied,

$$\frac{Y_{1t}^{(r+1)} - Y_{1t}^{(r)}}{Y_{1t}^{(r)}} < \epsilon$$

and

$$\frac{Y_{2t}^{(r+1)} - Y_{2t}^{(r)}}{Y_{2t}^{(r)}} < \epsilon$$

where ϵ is a very small number representing the specified degree of accuracy. Then, $Y_{1t}^{(r+1)}$ and $Y_{2t}^{(r+1)}$ are the predicted values of Y_1 and Y_2 in the tth period, given the lagged values of the endogenous variables and the values of the exogenous variables in the tth period.

Whether the procedure will converge, e.g., the equations have a solution, depends sometimes on the normalization of current endogenous variables and/or the ordering of the equations in the system. However, no simple rule is available for the optimal ordering.

Smoothing Time-Series Data

Using the econometric model to forecast future events is to predict the situation as it would be if the assumptions based on which the model is built were fulfilled. If the assumptions were not fulfilled—in other words, if something unforeseen or unexpected were to occur—then the prediction will be inaccurate. However, besides the unforeseen change in the operating characteristics of the economic system, the time paths of the endogenous variables (we refer to the difference-equation models and the computer-simulation models) may contain random or short-term fluctuations that will blur the picture of our long-term forecasting. In such a case we need to smooth the data. The following methods are commonly used.

Moving Average

$$\hat{X}_t = \frac{X_{t-k} + X_{t-k+1} + X_{t-k+2} + \cdots + X_{t-1}}{k}$$

where $X_{t-k}, X_{t-k+1}, \ldots, X_{t-1}$, are the most recent k observations on variable X, we employ them to forecast the X value for the next period.

Average of Changes

$$X_t = X_{t-1} + \frac{\Delta X_{t-1} + \Delta X_{t-2} + \cdots + \Delta X_{t-k}}{k}$$

where

$$\Delta X_{t-k} = (X_{t-k} - X_{t-k-1})$$

or

$$X_t = \frac{k+1}{k} X_{t-1} - \frac{1}{k} X_{t-k-1}$$

Exponential Smoothing. The basic principle of exponential smoothing is to assign more weight to these more recent observations and less for those more remote past observations while computing the averages. The one-period exponential-smoothing formula is as follows:

$$\hat{X}_t = \hat{X}_{t-1} + \alpha(X_{t-1} - \hat{X}_{t-1})$$

where X is the actual value of X, $\hat{X}$ is the forecast value of X, and α is the coefficient of the correction term, always smaller than one.

The formula also may be written as

$$\hat{X}_t = \alpha X_{t-1} + (1 - \alpha)\hat{X}_{t-1} \quad \text{or} \quad \hat{\bar{X}}_t = \alpha X_{t-1} + (1 - \alpha)\bar{X}_{t-1}$$

Thus for n-period exponential smoothing the general formula is

$$\hat{X}_t = \alpha[X_{t-1} + (1 - \alpha)X_{t-2} + \cdots + (1 - \alpha)^{n-1} X_{t-n+1}] + (1 - \alpha)^n X_{t-n}$$

where $\hat{X}_{t-n}$ is the initial estimate of the mean of the process and $0 \leq \alpha \leq 1$.

When regression coefficients are used to forecast the future value of X, we may either use the last value of X or several time-lagged values of X:

last-value model

$$\hat{X}_t = \hat{a} + \hat{b}X_{t-1} \quad \text{[assume the error terms follow normal distribution } N(0, \sigma^2)]$$

autoregressive model (distributed lags)

$$\hat{X}_t = \hat{a} + \hat{b}_1 X_{t-1} + \hat{b}_2 X_{t-2} + \cdots + \hat{b}_k X_{t-k} \quad \text{[assume as above]}$$

6-5. SPECTRAL AND CROSS-SPECTRAL ANALYSIS OF TIME-SERIES DATA

When the time-series data of an economic variable manifests strong cyclical movement, it is necessary to analyze the time related process for description and prediction purposes. One method of analysis is to break down the data into power spectra and analyze the contribution to the total variance of the process. If a band contributes a large proportion of the total variance, it is considered to be an important component of the process. The method of analysis presented in this section is called the *spectral-analysis method*. It does not require the specification of a model. However, the decomposition of the process is done under the assumption of "covariance stationary"—that is, (1) the time series have no apparent trend in mean, and (2) the time series have no apparent trend in variance $E[X(t) - E\{X(t)\}]^2 = \sigma_x^2$ for all t (homoscedastic). (Methods for analyzing nonstationary time series data are much more complicated and are not covered in this text. However, if the time series only have trend in mean but have constant variance, we may use a linear equation system, the Kalman filter, to remove the trend first, then spectral analysis can be applied to the adjusted data.) For the analysis of a single economic variable, the method is called *spectral analysis*. For the discovery and analysis of the relationships between two or more economic variables, the method is called *cross-spectral analysis*.

Spectral Analysis

The linear regression model concerns only the linear trend of the relationships among economic variables. However, economic theory also deals with cyclical movement of economic variables. The method of spectral analysis used initially in the electrical engineering problems to analyze cyclical movement has recently been introduced into the analysis of economic time series. The basic approach is as follows.

Given a covariance-stationary time series $X(t)$, i.e., (1) $E\{X(t)\}$ and $E[X(t) - E\{X(t)\}]^2$ are independent of time, (2) $E\{x(t), x(t + L)\}$ is a function of L alone, where L is the time lag, we may approximate $X(t)$ by the sum of a number of cosine and sine functions which is called the *Fourier transform* of the autocovariance function of $X(t)$.

$$
\begin{aligned}
f_{x(t)}(\theta) &= \frac{1}{2\pi} \sum_{L=-\infty}^{\infty} C_{xx}(L) e^{-iL\theta\dagger} \qquad (-\pi \leq \theta \leq \pi) \\
&= \frac{1}{2\pi} \{C_{xx}(0) e^0 + C_{xx}(1) e^{-i\theta} + C_{xx}(-1) e^{i\theta} \\
&\qquad\qquad + C_{xx}(2) e^{-2\theta} + C_{xx}(-2) e^{i2\theta} \cdots \} \\
&= \frac{1}{2\pi} \{C_{xx}(0) + C_{xx}(1)[\cos\theta - i\sin\theta]
\end{aligned}
$$

†The inverse of the Fourier transform is

$$
C_{xx}(L) = \int_{-\pi}^{\pi} f_{x(t)}(\theta) e^{iL\theta} d\theta
$$

with

$$
L = 0, \quad C_{xx}(0) = \int_{-\pi}^{\pi} f_{x(t)}(\theta) d\theta
$$

The result may be interpreted as a breakdown of the variance of the time series into portions associated with the components of the series of different frequency.

$$+ C_{xx}(-1)[\cos \theta + i \sin \theta]$$
$$+ C_{xx}(2)[\cos 2\theta - i \sin 2\theta]$$
$$+ C_{xx}(-2)[\cos 2\theta + i \sin 2\theta] \cdots \}$$

$$= \frac{1}{2\pi} \left\{ C_{xx}(0) + 2 \sum_{L=1}^{\infty} C_{xx}(L) \cos L\theta \right\}$$

where $C_{xx}(L)$ is the autovariance of $X(t)$ of L time lag, given a sample of T observations, and $C_{xx}(L) = C_{xx}(-L)$.

Since the final version of the transformation only contains cosine terms, it is also referred to as the *Fourier cosine transform*. Also, because sinusoidal (cosine and sine) functions are continuous functions, the relevant value (power of the spectrum) should be the area under the curve. However, in economic observations, we record only discrete data, therefore we need to make the following adjustment to make use of the method of analysis:

$$f_{xx}(k) = \frac{1}{2\pi} \left\{ C_{xx}(0) + 2 \sum_{L=1}^{M} C_{xx}(L) \cos \frac{\pi kL}{M} W(L/M) \right\}$$

where

1. k is a given time lag and M is the longest time lag possible given T. T is the total number of observations. In practical application, T should be more than 100 observations and M should be less than $T/3$.
2. $W(L/M)$ are the weights put on each covariance term as adjustment factor for viewing the continuous time series at some discrete points. They are called the *Parzen windows*.†

$$W(L/M) = \begin{cases} 1 - \frac{6L^2}{M^2} \left(1 - \frac{L}{M} \right) & 0 \le L \le M/2 \\ 2 \left(1 - \frac{L}{M} \right)^3 & M/2 \le L \le M \end{cases}$$

when the covariance terms are computed by the following formula:

$$C_{xx}(L) = \frac{1}{T} \sum_{t=1}^{T-L} x(t) x(t + L)$$

†Besides the Parzen estimate, there is another estimate called *Tukey-Hanning estimate*, in which

$$C_{xx}(L) = \frac{1}{T - L} \sum_{t=1}^{T-L} x(t) x(t + L)$$

and

$$f_{xx}(k) = \frac{1}{2\pi} \left[C_{xx}(0) + 2 \sum_{L=1}^{M-1} C_{xx}(L) \cos \frac{\pi kL}{M} + C_{xx}(M) \cos \pi k \right]$$

However, since Parzen estimate never gives negative value, in this text we introduce Parzen's method. Also, when the number of observations T is much greater than the largest lag M, the difference of these two estimates is negligible.

The k which yields the largest value of the Fourier transform ($f_{xx}(k)$) is interpreted as the most significant in explaining the variance of $X(t)$. The period of the most significant cycle can then be computed from the k by the following formula:

$$\frac{k\pi}{M} \simeq \frac{2\pi}{\alpha} \qquad \text{(where } \alpha \text{ is the period)}$$

or

$$\alpha = \frac{2M}{k}$$

Cross-Spectral Analysis

When we are examining the relationship of the cycles of two stationary time series (no trend and homoscedastic) we use the method of cross-spectral analysis. The cosine and sine transformations of the even and odd parts of the cross-covariance function is computed in polar form as follows:

$$f_{xy}(k) = P_{xy}(k) - iQ_{xy}(k) \qquad (k = 0, 1, \ldots, M)$$

Here $P_{xy}(k)$ is the real part of the cross-spectrum, called *cospectrum*:

$$P_{xy}(k) = \frac{1}{2\pi}\left\{C_{xy}(0) + \sum_{L=1}^{M} [C_{xy}(L) + C_{yx}(L)] \cos \frac{\pi kL}{M} W(L/M)\right\}$$

and

$$C_{xy}(L) = \frac{1}{T}\sum_{t=1}^{T-L} x(t)\,y(t+L), \qquad C_{yx}(L) = \frac{1}{T}\sum_{t=1}^{T-L} y(t)\,x(t+L)$$

The term $W(L/M)$ is same as in autospectrum.

And $Q_{xy}(k)$ is the imaginary part of the cross-spectrum, called *quadrature spectrum*:

$$Q_{xy}(k) = \frac{1}{2\pi}\sum_{L=1}^{M} [C_{xy}(L) - C_{yx}(L)] \sin \frac{\pi kL}{M} W(L/M)$$

The cross-spectrum is measured by the amplitude and phase of each respective time lag:

$$\text{Amplitude } A(k) = \sqrt{P_{xy}(k)^2 + Q_{xy}(k)^2}$$

$$\text{Phase } \theta(k) = \tan^{-1}\left(\frac{Q_{xy}(k)}{P_{xy}(k)}\right)$$

$$(A(k)\,e^{it(k)} = P_{xy}(k) - iQ_{xy}(k))$$

The squared correlation coefficient of the two time series is called *coherence*, which measures the relationship of the two time series of a given frequency associated with k lags:

$$\text{Coherence} = \frac{P_{xy}(k)^2 + Q_{xy}(k)^2}{f_{xx}(k) \cdot f_{yy}(k)}$$

The regression coefficient of $X(t)$ on $Y(t)$ of each respective time lag is called *gain*:

$$\text{Gain} = \frac{\sqrt{P_{xy}(k)^2 + Q_{xy}(k)^2}}{f_{yy}(k)}$$

The time lag k, which yields high values of coherence and gain, indicates that the two time series are related in that particular frequency (expressed by time lag k), and the period of the related cycles can be computed by the following formula:

$$\alpha \cong \frac{2M}{k}$$

while the difference in phase between the two time series can be computed by a second formula:

$$\frac{2\pi}{\alpha} \cong \frac{\theta(k)}{\beta} \qquad (\text{where } \beta = \text{difference in phase})$$

or

$$\beta \cong \frac{\alpha \cdot \theta(k)}{2\pi}$$

Numerical Example (Spectral Analysis)

t	$X(t)$	$x(t)$	$x^2(t)$
1	10	-1.2	2.25
2	9	-2.5	6.25
3	8	-3.5	12.25
4	11	$-.5$	.25
5	12	.5	.25
6	13	1.5	2.25
7	11	$-.5$	.25
8	10	-1.5	2.25
9	14	2.5	6.25
10	12	.5	.25
11	15	3.5	12.25
12	13	1.5	2.75
	138		47.00

$$\bar{X} = \frac{138}{12} = 11.5 \qquad (T = 12)$$

Let $M = 11$, $k = 1, 2, \ldots, 11$ and $L = 1, 2, \ldots, 11$.†

$$(1) \qquad C_{xx}(L) = \frac{1}{T} \sum_{t=1}^{T-L} x(t) x(t + L)$$

$$C_{xx}(0) = \text{var}(X) = 3.917$$
$$C_{xx}(1) = 1.604$$
$$C_{xx}(2) = .75$$
$$C_{xx}(3) = -.3542$$
$$C_{xx}(4) = -.3333$$
$$C_{xx}(5) = .6458$$
$$C_{xx}(6) = -.0417$$
$$C_{xx}(7) = -.5625$$
$$C_{xx}(8) = -1.5$$
$$C_{xx}(9) = -1.229$$
$$C_{xx}(10) = -.75$$
$$C_{xx}(11) = -.1875$$

$$(2) \qquad W(L/M) = \begin{cases} 1 - \dfrac{6L^2}{M^2}\left(1 - \dfrac{L}{M}\right) & 0 \le L \le M/2 \\[2ex] 2\left(1 - \dfrac{L}{M}\right)^3 & M/2 < L \le M \end{cases}$$

$$W(1/11) = .9549$$
$$W(2/11) = .8377$$
$$W(3/11) = .6754$$
$$W(4/11) = .4951$$
$$W(5/11) = .3233$$
$$W(6/11) = .1878$$
$$W(7/11) = .0962$$
$$W(8/11) = .0406$$
$$W(9/11) = .0120$$
$$W(10/11) = .0015$$
$$W(11/11) = 0$$

†This example only illustrates the computational aspect of the analysis, in real-world investigation, the common guide is

$$\frac{\text{(Number of observations/Number of lags)}}{(M) \qquad\qquad\qquad (T)} \ge 3$$

Since the required number of observations is usually large (over 100 data points), use of computer programs is almost a necessity.

$$(3) \quad f_{xx}(k) = \frac{1}{2\pi} \left\{ C_{xx}(0) + 2 \sum_{L=1}^{M} C_{xx}(L) \cos \frac{\pi k L}{M} W(L/M) \right\}$$

$$f_{xx}(1) = \frac{1}{2\pi} \left\{ 3.917 + 2 \left(1.604 \times \cos \frac{\pi}{11} \times .9549 + .75 \right. \right.$$

$$\times \cos \frac{2\pi}{11} \times .8377 - .3542 \times \cos \frac{3\pi}{11}$$

$$\times .6754 - .3333 \cos \frac{4\pi}{11} \times .4951 + .6458$$

$$\times \cos \frac{5\pi}{11} \times .3238 - .0417 \times \cos \frac{6\pi}{11} \times .1874 - .5625$$

$$\times \cos \frac{7\pi}{11} \times .0962 - 1.5 \times \cos \frac{8\pi}{11} \times .0406 - 1.229$$

$$\left. \left. \times \cos \frac{9\pi}{11} \times .012 - .75 \times \cos \frac{10\pi}{11} \times .0015 \right) \right\} = 1.22$$

$$f_{xx}(2) = 1.11$$
$$f_{xx}(3) = .967$$
$$f_{xx}(4) = .853$$
$$f_{xx}(5) = .535$$
$$f_{xx}(6) = .226$$
$$f_{xx}(7) = .179$$
$$f_{xx}(8) = .290$$
$$f_{xx}(9) = .380$$
$$f_{xx}(10) = .345$$
$$f_{xx}(11) = .292$$

When k is small it represents low frequency. If a time series has a long-term trend, the $f_{xx}(k)$ with small k usually has large value due to the trend. Since we are using spectral analysis to separate the significant cyclical component from the other components of the series we should disregard the $f_{xx}(k)$ with small values of k. The noticeable peak in this example is when $k = 9$. (The other peak $k = 1$ represents a trend in the data, which strictly speaking should be filtered out first before conducting analysis.) The corresponding frequency may be found by the following approximation.†

$$\frac{k\pi}{M} \simeq \frac{2\pi}{\alpha} \qquad$$ (where 2π represents a whole cycle, α is the period of the cycle associated with $k = 9$)

†C. W. J. Granger and M. Hatanaka, *Spectral Analysis of Economic Time Series* (Princeton, N.J.: Princeton University Press, 1964).

$$\frac{9\pi}{11} \cong \frac{2\pi}{\alpha}$$

$$\alpha \cong 2.4 \text{ month cycle}$$

Cross-Spectral Analysis

t	$X(t)$	$Y(t)$	$x(t)$	$y(t)$
1	10	4	-1.5	-1.167
2	9	5	-2.5	$-.167$
3	8	4	-3.5	-1.167
4	11	3	$-.5$	-2.167
5	12	5	$.5$	$-.167$
6	13	6	1.5	$.833$
7	11	7	$-.5$	1.833
8	10	8	-1.5	2.833
9	14	5	2.5	$-.167$
10	12	4	$.5$	-1.167
11	15	5	3.5	$-.167$
($T = 12$) 12	13	6	1.5	$.833$

Let $M = 11$, $k = 1, 2, \ldots, 11$ and $L = 1, 2, \ldots, 11$:

(1) $C_{xx}(L) = \dfrac{1}{T} \sum\limits_{t=1}^{T-L} x(t) x(t + L)$ (values same as the previous example)

(2) $\qquad\qquad\qquad C_{yy}(L) = \dfrac{1}{T} \sum\limits_{t=1}^{T-L} y(t) y(t + L)$

$C_{yy}(0) = \text{var}(Y) = 1.806$

$C_{yy}(1) = .8032$

$C_{yy}(2) = -.1991$

$C_{yy}(3) = -.4792$

$C_{yy}(4) = -.5927$

$C_{yy}(5) = -.22$

$C_{yy}(6) = .0694$

$C_{yy}(7) = -.1411$

$C_{yy}(8) = -.1017$

$C_{yy}(9) = .0348$

$C_{yy}(10) = .0046$

$C_{yy}(11) = .081$

(3) $W(L/M) = \begin{cases} 1 - \dfrac{6L^2}{M^2}\left(1 - \dfrac{L}{M}\right) & 0 \le L \le M/2 \\[2mm] 2\left(1 - \dfrac{L}{M}\right)^3 & M/2 \le L \le M \end{cases}$ (values same as in previous example)

(4) $$f_{yy}(k) = \frac{1}{2\pi}\left\{ C_{yy}(0) - 2\sum_{L=1}^{M} C_{yy}(L)\cos\frac{\pi kL}{M} W(L/M) \right\}$$

$$f_{yy}(1) = .3699$$
$$f_{yy}(2) = .5671$$
$$f_{yy}(3) = .6135$$
$$f_{yy}(4) = .5223$$
$$f_{yy}(5) = .3052$$
$$f_{yy}(6) = .2335$$
$$f_{yy}(7) = .2228$$
$$f_{yy}(8) = .2105$$
$$f_{yy}(9) = .1879$$
$$f_{yy}(10) = .1631$$
$$f_{yy}(11) = .24$$

(5) $$C_{xy}(k) = \frac{1}{T}\sum_{t=1}^{T-L} x(t)\,y(t+L)$$

$$C_{xy}(0) = \text{cov}(XY) = .25$$
$$C_{xy}(1) = 1.188$$
$$C_{xy}(2) = 1.195$$
$$C_{xy}(3) = .327$$
$$C_{xy}(4) = 1.055$$
$$C_{xy}(5) = -1.410$$
$$C_{xy}(6) = -.625$$
$$C_{xy}(7) = .063$$
$$C_{xy}(8) = .278$$
$$C_{xy}(9) = -.062$$
$$C_{xy}(10) = -.153$$
$$C_{xy}(11) = -.104$$

(6) $$C_{yx} = \frac{1}{T}\sum_{t=1}^{T-L} y(t)\,x(t+L)$$

$$C_{yx}(0) = C_{xy}(0) = .25$$
$$C_{yx}(1) = .174$$
$$C_{yx}(2) = .236$$
$$C_{yx}(3) = 1.062$$
$$C_{yx}(4) = 1.139$$

$$C_{yx}(5) = .021$$
$$C_{yx}(6) = -.209$$
$$C_{yx}(7) = -.59$$
$$C_{yx}(8) = -.861$$
$$C_{yx}(9) = -.243$$
$$C_{yx}(10) = -.361$$
$$C_{yx}(11) = -.146$$

$$(7) \quad P_{xy}(k) = \frac{1}{2\pi}\left\{ C_{xy}(0) + \sum_{L=1}^{M} [C_{xy}(L) + C_{yx}(L)] \cos \frac{\pi kL}{M} W(L/M) \right\}$$

$$P_{xy}(1) = .5617$$
$$P_{xy}(2) = .2568$$
$$P_{xy}(3) = -.1344$$
$$P_{xy}(4) = -.2427$$
$$P_{xy}(5) = -.0570$$
$$P_{xy}(6) = .0902$$
$$P_{xy}(7) = -.0111$$
$$P_{xy}(8) = -.1986$$
$$P_{xy}(9) = -.0589$$
$$P_{xy}(10) = -.0122$$
$$P_{xy}(11) = -.0618$$

$$(8) \quad Q_{xy}(k) = \frac{1}{2\pi}\left\{ \sum_{L=1}^{M} [C_{xy}(L) - C_{yx}(L)] \sin \frac{\pi kL}{M} W(L/M) \right\}$$

$$Q_{xy}(1) = -.0238$$
$$Q_{xy}(2) = .0841$$
$$Q_{xy}(3) = .2819$$
$$Q_{xy}(4) = .3102$$
$$Q_{xy}(5) = .1722$$
$$Q_{xy}(6) = .1402$$
$$Q_{xy}(7) = .1136$$
$$Q_{xy}(8) = -.0056$$
$$Q_{xy}(9) = -.1311$$
$$Q_{xy}(10) = -.1365$$
$$Q_{xy}(11) = .1592$$

(9)

$$\text{Coherence} = \frac{P_{xy}^2(k) + Q_{xy}^2(k)}{f_{xx}(k) \, f_{yy}(k)}$$

k	coherence
1	.7080
2	.1159
3	.1599
4	.3478
5	.1974
6	.5215
7	.3262
8	.5704
9	.3721
10	.3348
11	.4158

(10)

$$\text{Gain} = \frac{\sqrt{P_{xy}^2(k) + Q_{xy}^2(k)}}{f_{yy}(k)}$$

k	gain
1	1.5199
2	.4765
3	.5022
4	.7542
5	.5944
6	.7139
7	.5121
8	.9439
9	.7648
10	.8400
11	.7117

(11)

$$\text{Amplitude:} \quad A(k) = \sqrt{P_{xy}^2(k) + Q_{xy}^2(k)}$$

k	amplitude
1	.5622
2	.2702
3	.3081
4	.3939

5	.1814
6	.1667
7	.1141
8	.1987
9	.1437
10	.1370
11	.1708

(12)   Phase: $\theta(k) = \tan^{-1}\left(\dfrac{Q_{xy}(k)}{P_{xy}(k)}\right)$

k	phase
1	2.4 degrees
2	18.1
3	64.5
4	51.9
5	71.7
6	57.2
7	84.4
8	1.6
9	65.8
10	84.9
11	68.8

When $k = 8$, the coherence and gain have high values, which indicates that the two series $X(t)$ and $Y(t)$ are related in that particular frequency. (In order to have a meaningful relationship, the individual cyclical component of the specified frequency for both $X(t)$ and $Y(t)$ must also be significant.)

$$\frac{k\pi}{M} = \frac{8\pi}{11} \cong \frac{2\pi}{\alpha} \qquad \alpha = 2.7\text{-month cycle}$$

The difference in phase between the two time series may be computed by the formula

$$2\pi: \alpha = \theta(k): \beta$$

or

$$\beta = \theta(k)\,\frac{\alpha}{2\pi} = \theta(k)\,\frac{M}{k\pi}$$

$$= 1.6 \cdot \frac{11}{8 \times 180} = \frac{17.6}{1440} = 0.012 \text{ month}$$

(almost no difference in phase)

6-6. PROBLEMS OF VERIFICATION

In building an econometric model, we are concerned about two objectives. First, we must be assured that the model is a good description of the real system. This involves several things.

1. Does the model include all the explanatory variables which are significant in explaining the values or the change of values of the explained variables?
2. Are the variables included in the model properly specified in the correct functional relationships?
3. Are the samples taken representative, and are the methods used to estimate the parameters of the model correct and consistent with all the assumptions?

Second, how good is the model's predictive power? This not only requires the necessary conditions stated above, it also involves the stability of the model and the nature of the economic system. For example, the production technological relationship may be more stable than the market-demand relationship. If the nature or characteristic of a system is unstable, then provision has to be made in the model to anticipate the change. One example is found in the fact that the relationship of consumption and income in wartime may be quite different from the same relationship in peacetime. Thus we may specify the relationship as

$$C = aX_1 + bX_2 + cY$$

where X_1 = 1 in peacetime, 0 in wartime
$\quad\ X_2$ = 0 in peacetime, 1 in wartime
$\quad\ X_1, X_2$ are sometimes called *dummy variables*.

To answer the questions raised above we have only two procedures. One is to check the logic of the model. The relationships or operating characteristics of the model should be consistent with economic theories and hypotheses. In other words, there should be logical explanations about the relationships. Why do the variables behave as they do, and what are the economic motivations behind them? The other is to compare the data generated from the model with the empirical data and examine how good the former fits the latter, applying statistical tests such as the chi-square test or analysis of variance to determine validity acceptance.

A practical suggestion along this line is to use the model to make forecasts for five successive years beyond each regression period. By comparing those forecasts with the empirical data (kind of retrospective predictions) we can have some assurance whether the model is a valid one and fit the real-world situation.

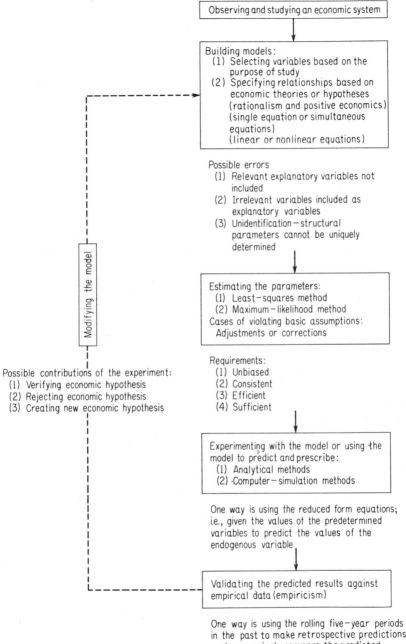

Observing and studying an economic system

Building models:
(1) Selecting variables based on the purpose of study
(2) Specifying relationships based on economic theories or hypotheses (rationalism and positive economics) (single equation or simultaneous equations) (linear or nonlinear equations)

Possible errors
(1) Relevant explanatory variables not included
(2) Irrelevant variables included as explanatory variables
(3) Unidentification—structural parameters cannot be uniquely determined

Estimating the parameters:
(1) Least—squares method
(2) Maximum—likelihood method
Cases of violating basic assumptions:
Adjustments or corrections

Requirements:
(1) Unbiased
(2) Consistent
(3) Efficient
(4) Sufficient

Modifying the model

Possible contributions of the experiment:
(1) Verifying economic hypothesis
(2) Rejecting economic hypothesis
(3) Creating new economic hypothesis

Experimenting with the model or using the model to predict and prescribe:
(1) Analytical methods
(2) ·Computer—simulation methods

One way is using the reduced form equations; i.e., given the values of the predetermined variables to predict the values of the endogenous variable

Validating the predicted results against empirical data (empiricism)

One way is using the rolling five—year periods in the past to make retrospective predictions and successively compare the predicted results against known empirical data for validation purpose

Mean square error

$$\text{MSE}(\hat{\theta}) = E(\hat{\theta} - \theta)^2$$

where θ is the parameter and $\hat{\theta}$ is an estimate of θ.

$$\begin{aligned}
\text{MSE}(\hat{\theta}) &= E[\hat{\theta} - E(\hat{\theta}) + E(\hat{\theta}) - \theta]^2 \\
&= E(\hat{\theta} - E(\hat{\theta}))^2 + (E(\hat{\theta}) - \theta)^2 \\
&= \text{var}(\hat{\theta}) + (\text{biased } \hat{\theta})^2
\end{aligned}$$

An estimator having small mean square error will be a good one.

6-7. CONCLUSION

In order to understand our economic environment better we build models. Their functions are to describe the existing relationship and to predict unobserved events. By studying such models we hope to find ways of improving our economic well-being. However, in extending past and current observations to forecast future occurrences we assume that the overall situation either will remain the same or the rate of change will be constant. Using econometric models to predict future events presupposes that all the assumptions and expectations based on which the model is constructed will be fulfilled. If these conditions are not met the forecast or prediction will be incorrect. However, even in the process of building the model we are forced to make a detailed examination of the real system and thereby learn a great deal about it. And when we compare the predicted values with the empirical values we have a base for discovering which of our assumptions are wrong. As the analytical tools are continuously improved and data-collection and processing techniques become even more advanced, we may one day be able to predict the future with high accuracy. Only then may we hope to control the economic situations according to our desires by implementing some well-chosen economic policies.

The flow chart on page 195 summarizes the material introduced in this text and restates the logical flow of studying an economic system by econometric methods.

SELECTED BIBLIOGRAPHY

1. Irma Adelman and F. L. Adelman, "The Dynamic Properties of the Klein-Goldberger Model," *Econometrica*, vol. XXVII (October 1959), pp. 596–625.

2. W. J. Baumol, *Economic Theory and Operations Analysis*, 2d ed. Englewood Cliffs, N.J.: Prentice-Hall, 1965.

3. C. F. Christ, "Aggregate Econometric Models," *American Economic Review*, vol. XLVI (June 1956), pp. 385–408.

4. A. S. Goldberger, *Econometric Theory*. New York: Wiley, 1964.

5. H. Hotelling, "Problems of Prediction," *American Journal of Sociology*, vol. XLVIII (1942–1943), pp. 61–76.

6. J. Johnston, *Econometric Methods*. New York: McGraw-Hill, 1963.

7. L. R. Klein, *An Introduction to Econometrics*. Englewood Cliffs, N.J.: Prentice-Hall, 1962.

8. Albert Madansky, "The Fitting of Straight Lines when both Variables are Subject to Error," *Journal of American Statistical Association*, vol. LIV (1959), pp. 173–205.

9. J. D. Sargan, "The Estimation of Econometric Relationships Using Instrumental Variables," *Econometrica*, vol. XXVI (1958), pp. 393–415.

10. A. Zellner and H. Theil, "Three-Stage Least Squares: Simultaneous Estimation of Simultaneous Equations," *Econometrica*, vol. XXX (1962), pp. 54–78.

EXERCISES

6-1. Examine the identifiability of the parameters in the following models:

(a)
$$Y_1 + a_{12} Y_2 \qquad\quad = u_1$$
$$a_{21} Y_1 + \quad Y_2 + b_{21} X_1 = u_2$$

where the variances of u_1 and u_2 equal σ_{11}, σ_{22} respectively, and the covariance of u_1, u_2 equals σ_{12}.

(b)
$$Y_1 + a_{12} Y_2 \qquad\quad = u_1$$
$$a_{21} Y_1 + \quad Y_2 + b_{21} X_1 = u_2$$

where the variances of u_1 and u_2 equal σ_{11}, σ_{22} respectively and the covariance of u_1, u_2 equals σ_{12}.

(c)
$$Y_1 + a_{12} Y_2 \qquad\qquad\qquad = u_1$$
$$a_{21} Y_1 + \quad Y_2 + b_{21} X_1 + b_{22} X_1 = u_2$$

where the variances of u_1 and u_2 equal σ_4, σ_{22} respectively and the covariance of u_1, u_2 equals zero.

(d)
$$Y_1 + a_{12} Y_2 \qquad\qquad\qquad = u_1$$
$$a_{21} Y_1 + \quad Y_2 + b_{21} X_1 + b_{22} X_2 = u_2$$

where the variances of u_1 and u_2 equal σ_{11}, σ_{22} respectively but the covariance of u_1, u_2 equals zero.

6-2. Given the observed data of X and Y as follows:

	X'	Y'
1	20	45
2	25	65
3	50	70
4	80	125
5	75	130
6	90	150
7	105	165
8	110	180
9	130	200
10	125	205
11	160	230
12	175	250

Knowing that the ratio of the error variance of the observed data of X and Y is $\lambda = \frac{1}{3}$, estimate the parameters of $\hat{Y} = \hat{a} + \hat{b}x$.

6-3. If the known ratio λ is 3, what will be the estimated values of the parameters?

6-4. Use Wald's method to reestimate the parameters in Exercise 6-2.

6-5. Let the number of observations in each subgroup be 4, and use Bartlett's method to reestimate the parameters in Exercise 6-2.

6-6. Given the following data:

X	Y
10	100
15	105
30	115
40	120
45	125
55	135
60	140
70	160
85	165
90	170

(a) Use the least-squares method to estimate the parameters of $\hat{Y} = \hat{a} + \hat{b}X$.

(b) Use Durbin-Watson statistics to test whether autocorrelation exists in the error term.

(c) If autocorrelation is significant, adjust the observed data so that they will be free of autocorrelation.

6-7. Given the following data:

X	Y
2	6
8	25
12	40
20	65
25	80
28	100
35	120
40	150
55	200
60	350

(a) Use the least-squares method to estimate the parameters of $Y = \hat{a} + \hat{b}x$.

(b) Calculate the error terms between the original Y and the estimated Y.

(c) Examine whether heteroscedasticity might exist in the data.

6-8. Estimate the parameters of the consumption function of the following model by two-stage least-squares method and three-stage least-squares method.

$$Y_t = C_t + I_t + A_t$$
$$C_t = a_1 + a_2 Y_t + u_{1t}$$
$$I_t = b_1 + b_2 Y_t + b_3 I_{t-1} + u_{2t}$$

Where A is exogenous to the system

t	Y_t	C_t	I_t	A_t
1	13.9	10.7	1.02	2.18
2	14.3	10.9	1.08	2.32
3	14.8	11.2	1.12	2.48
4	15.3	11.1	1.05	3.15
5	15.3	11.0	0.98	3.32
6	15.9	11.4	1.07	3.43
7	16.6	12.0	1.28	3.32
8	17.2	12.4	1.47	3.31
9	17.5	12.5	1.59	3.41
10	17.8	12.8	1.67	3.33
11	17.7	13.1	1.71	2.89

6-9. Prepare a spectral analysis on the quarterly data of U.S. gross national product after World War II.

6-10. Prepare a cross-spectral analysis on the quarterly data of money supply and GNP, or on federal government spending and GNP after World War II.

List of Selected Articles on Applied Econometrics

DEMAND AND CONSUMPTION

Balestra, Pietro, and Marc Nerlove. "Pooling Cross Section and Time Series Data in the Estimation of a Dynamic Model: The Demand for Natural Gas," *Econometrica*, July 1966, pp. 585–612.

Barten, A. P. "Estimating Demand Equations," *Econometrica*, April 1968, pp. 213–251.

Court, Robin H. "Utility Maximization and The Demand for New Zealand Meats," *Econometrica*, July–October 1967, pp. 424–446.

McMahon, Walter W. "An Economic Analysis of Major Determinants of Expenditures on Public Education," *Review of Economics and Statistics*, Vol. LII (August 1970), pp. 242–252.

Parks, Richard W. "Systems of Demand Equations: An Empirical Comparison of Alternative Functional Forms," *Econometrica*, October 1969, pp. 629–650.

Paroush, Jacob. "The Order of Acquisition of Consumer Durables," *Econometrica*, January 1965, pp. 225–235.

Pollak, Robert A., and Terence J. Wales. "Estimation of the Linear Expenditure System," *Econometrica*, October 1969, pp. 611–628.

Powell, Alan. "A Complete System of Consumer Demand Equations for the Australian Economy Fitted by A Model of Additive Preferences," *Econometrica*, July 1966, pp. 661–675.

Simon, Julian L. "The Price Elasticity of Liquor in the United States and a Simple Method of Determination," *Econometrica*, January 1966, pp. 193–205.

Theil, H. "The Information Approach to Demand Analysis," *Econometrica*, January 1965, pp. 67–87.

Tolley, G. S., Y. Wang, and R. G. Fletcher. "Re-examination of the Time Series Evidence on Food Demand," *Econometrica*, October 1969, pp. 695–705.

Wu, De-Min. "An Empirical Analysis of Household Durable Goods Expenditure," *Econometrica*, October 1965, pp. 761–780.

Yoshihara, Kunio. "An Application to the Japanese Expenditure Pattern," *Econometrica*, April 1969, pp. 257–274.

Zellner, A., D. S. Huang, and L. C. Chan. "Further Analysis of the Short-Run Consumption Function with Emphasis on the Role of Liquid Assets," *Econometrica*, July 1965, pp. 571–581.

PRODUCTION AND COST

Coen, Robert M., and Bert G. Hickman. "Constrained Joint Estimation of Factor Demand and Production Functions," *Review of Economics and Statistics*, Vol. LII (August 1970), pp. 287–300.

Eads, George, Marc Nerlove, and William Raduchel. "A Long-Run Cost Function for the Local Service Airline Industry: An Experience in Nonlinear Estimation," *Review of Economics and Statistics*, Vol. LI (August 1969), pp. 258–270.

Evans, Michael K. "An Industry Study of Corporate Profits," *Econometrica*, April 1968, pp. 343–364.

Feldstein, Martin S. "The Rising Price of Physicians' Services," *Review of Economics and Statistics*, Vol. LII (May 1970), pp. 121–133.

Fisher, Franklin M., and Peter Temin. "Regional Specialization and the Supply of Wheat in the United States, 1867–1914," *Review of Economics and Statistics*, Vol. LII (May 1970), pp. 134–149.

Fisk, P. R. "The Estimation of Marginal Product from Cobb-Douglas Production Function," *Econometrica*, January 1966, pp. 162–172.

Goldberger, Arthur S. "The Interpretation and Estimation of Cobb-Douglas Functions," *Econometrica*, July–October 1968, pp. 464–472.

Levhari, David L., and Eytan Sheshinski. "A Microeconomic Production Function," *Econometrica*, May 1970, pp. 559–573.

Munlak, Yair, and Irving Hoch. "Consequences of Alternative Specifications in Estimation of Cobb-Douglas Production Functions," *Econometrica*, October 1965, pp. 814–828.

Vined, H. D. "Econometrics of Joint Production," *Econometrica*, April 1968, pp. 322–336.

Wickens, Michael R. "Estimation of the Vintage Cobb-Douglas Production Function for the United States 1900–1960," *Review of Economics and Statistics*, Vol. LII (May 1970), pp. 187–193.

Zarembka, Paul. "On the Empirical Relevance of the CES Production Function," *Review of Economics and Statistics*, Vol. LII (February 1970), pp. 47–53.

INVESTMENT AND FINANCIAL MARKET

Almon, Shirley. "The Distributed Lag Between Capital Appropriation and Expenditures," *Econometrica*, January 1965, pp. 178–196.
    . "Lags Between Investment Decisions and Their Causes," *Review of Economics and Statistics*, Vol. L (May 1968), pp. 193–206.
Bonomo, Vittorio, and Charles Schotta. "A Spectral Analysis of Post-Accord Federal Open Market Operations," *American Economic Review*, March 1969, pp. 50–61.
Bryan, William R., and Willard T. Carleton. "Short-Run Adjustments of an Individual Bank," *Econometrica*, April 1967, pp. 321–347.
Eisner, Robert, and M. I. Nadiri. "Investment Behavior and Neo-Classical Theory," *Review of Economics and Statistics*, Vol. L (August 1968), pp. 369–382.
Feldstein, Martin, and Otto Eckstein. "The Fundamental Determinants of the Interest Rate," *Review of Economics and Statistics*, Vol. LII (November 1970) pp. 363–375.
Forgenson, Dale W., Jerald Hunter, and M. Ishag Nadiri. "A Comparison of Alternative Econometric Models of Quarterly Investment Behavior," *Econometrica*, March 1970, pp. 187–212.
———. "The Predictive Performance of Econometric Models of Quarterly Investment Behavior," *Econometrica*, March 1970, pp. 213–224.
Hamburger, Michael J. "Household Demand for Financial Assets," *Econometrica*, January 1968, pp. 97–118.
Huang, David S. "The Short-Run Flows of Nornfarm Residential Mortgage Credit," *Econometrica*, April 1966, pp. 433–459.
Ierson, Gail. "Effect of Economic Policy on the Term Structure of Interest Rates," *Review of Economics and Statistics*, Vol. LIII (February 1970) pp. 1–11.
Jorgenson, Dale W., and James A. Stephenson. "Investment Behavior in U.S. Manufacturing, 1947–1960," *Econometrica*, April 1967, pp. 169–220.
Kassouf, Sheen T. "An Econometric Model for Option Price with Implications for Investors' Expectations and Audacity," *Econometrica*, October 1969, pp. 685–694.
Kmenta, J., and J. G. Williamson. "Determinants of Investment Behavior: United States Railroads, 1872–1941," *Review of Economics and Statistics*, Vol. XLVIII (May 1966), pp. 172–181.

Maddala, G. S., and Robert C. Vogel. "Estimating Lagged Relationships in Corporate Demand for Liquid Assets," *Review of Economics and Statistics*, Vol. LI (February 1969), pp. 53–61.

Nerlove, Marc. "Factors Affecting Differences Among Rates of Return on Investments in Individual Common Stocks," *Review of Economics and Statistics*, Vol. L (August 1968), pp. 312–331.

Niehans, Jürg, and Heidi Schelbert-Syfri. "Simultaneous Determination of Interest and Prices in Switzerland by a Two-Market Model for Money and Bonds," *Econometrica*, April 1966, pp. 408–423.

Ying, Charles C. "Stock Market Prices and Volumes of Sales," *Econometrica*, July 1966, pp. 676–685.

ECONOMIC DEVELOPMENT AND INTERNATIONAL TRADE

Arndt, Sven W. "International Short-Term Capital Movements: A Distributed Lag Model of Speculation in Foreign Exchange," *Econometrica*, January 1968, pp. 59–70.

Brubaker, Earl R. "Embodied Technology, The Asymptotic Behavior of Capital's Age, and Soviet Growth," *Review of Economics and Statistics*, Vol. L (August 1968), pp. 304–311.

Chenery, Hollis B., and Lance Taylor. "Development Patterns: Among Countries and Over Time," *Review of Economics and Statistics*, Vol. L (November 1968), pp. 391–416.

Desai, Meghnad. "An Econometric Model of the World Tin Economy, 1946–1961," *Econometrica*, January 1966, pp. 105–134.

Dudley, Leonard, and Peter Passell. "The War in Vietnam and the United States Balance of Payments," *Review of Economics and Statistics*, Vol. L (November 1968), pp. 437–442.

Dutta, Manoranjan. "Measuring the Role of Price in International Trade: Some Further Tests," *Econometrica*, July 1965, pp. 600–607.

Eltetö, O., and E. Frigyes. "New Income Inequality Measures as Efficient Tools for Causal Analysis and Planning," *Econometrica*, April 1968, pp. 383–396.

Gisser, Micha. "Schooling and the Farm Problem," *Econometrica*, July 1965, pp. 582–592.

Houthakker, H. S., and Stephen P. Magee. "Income and Price Elasticities in World Trade," *Review of Economics and Statistics*, Vol. LI (May 1969), pp. 111–125.

Kaplan, Norman M. "Retardation in Soviet Growth," *Review of Economics and Statistics*, Vol. L (August 1968), pp. 293–303.

Kloek, T., and H. Theil. "International Comparisons of Prices and Quantities Consumed," *Econometrica*, July 1965, pp. 535–556.

Officer, Lawrence H., and Jules R. Hurtubise. "Price Effects of the Kennedy Round on Canadian Trade," *Review of Economics and Statistics*, Vol. LI (August 1969), pp. 320–333.

Phillips, Llad, Harold L. Votey, Jr., and Darold E. Maxwell. "A Synthesis of the Economic and Demographic Models of Fertility: An Econometric Test," *Review of Economics and Statistics*, Vol. LI (August 1969), pp. 298–308.

Stuvel, G. "A Systematic Approach to Macroeconomic Policy Design," *Econometrica*, January 1965, pp. 114–140.

Yotopoulos, Pan A., and Lawrence J. Lau. "A Test for Balanced and Unbalanced Growth," *Review of Economics and Statistics*, Vol. LII (November 1970), pp. 376–383.

NATIONAL ECONOMY AND ECONOMETRIC MODELS

Adelman, Irma, and Cynthia Taft Morris. "An Econometric Model of Socio-Economic and Political Change in Underdeveloped Countries, *American Economic Review*, December 1968, pp. 1184–1218.

Black, Stanley W., and R. Robert Russell. "An Alternative Estimate of Potential GNP," *Review of Economics and Statistics*, Vol. LI (February 1969), pp. 70–76.

Crouch, R. L. "A Model of the United Kingdom's Monetary Sector," *Econometrica*, July–October 1967, pp. 398–418.

Duesenberry, James E., Otto Eckstein, Gary Fromm. "A Simulation of the United States Economy in Recession," *Econometrica*, October 1960.

Evans, Michael K. "An Econometric Model of the Israeli Economy 1952–1965," *Econometrica*, September 1970, pp. 624–660.

Fromm, Gary, and Lawrence R. Klein. "The Brookings Model Volume: A Review Article: A Comment," *Review of Economics and Statistics*, Vol. L (May 1968), pp. 235–240.

Griliches, Zvi. "The Brookings Model Volume: A Review Article," *Review of Economics and Statistics*, Vol. L (May 1968), pp. 215–234.

Leser, C. E. V. "The Role of Macroeconometric Models in Short-Term Forecasting," *Econometrica*, October 1966, pp. 862–872.

Liu, Ta-Chung. "An Exploratory Quarterly Econometric Model of Effective Demand in the Postwar United States," *Econometrica*, July 1963.

———. "A Monthly Recursive Econometric Model of the United States: A Test of Feasibility," *Review of Economics and Statistics*, Vol. LI (February 1969), pp. 1–13.

Marwah, Kanta. "An Econometric Model of Colombia: A Prototype Devaluation View," *Econometrica*, April 1969, pp. 228–251.

Smith, Paul E. "An Econometric Growth Model of the United States," *American Economic Review*, September 1963.

Stekler, H. O. "Forecasting with Econometric Models: An Evaluation," *Econometrica*, July–October 1968, pp. 437–463.

Tsukui, Jinkichi. "Application of A Turnpike Theorem to Planning for Efficient Accumulation: An Example for Japan," *Econometrica*, January 1968, pp. 172–186.

Index